SELLING
AMERICA
SHORT

SELLING AMERICA SHORT

The SEC and Market Contrarians in the Age of Absurdity

Richard C. Sauer

WILEY

John Wiley & Sons, Inc.

Published by John Wiley & Sons, Inc., Hoboken, New Jersey.
Published simultaneously in Canada.

For general information on our other products and services or for technical support, please contact our Customer Care Department within the United States at (800) 762-2974, outside the United States at (317) 572-3993, or fax (317) 572-4002.

Wiley also publishes its books in a variety of electronic formats. Some content that appears in print may not be available in electronic books. For more information about Wiley products, visit our web site at www.wiley.com.

Library of Congress Cataloging-in-Publication Data:

Sauer, Richard.
   Selling America short : the SEC and market contrarians in the age of absurdity /
Richard C. Sauer.
      p.   cm.
   Includes index.
      ISBN 978-0-470-58211-4 (cloth)
   1. Sauer, Richard.   2. United States. Securities and Exchange Commission.
3. Stock exchanges—United States.   4. Finance—Corrupt practices—United States.
5. Fraud investigation—United States.   I. Title.
   HG4910.S28 2010
   332.6092—dc22   2009049435
[B]

Printed in the United States of America.

10 9 8 7 6 5 4 3 2 1

For Eileen and Neal, two good eggs

The pure products of America
Go crazy
—William Carlos Williams

Contents

Prologue

At the advanced age of 38, I joined the U.S. Securities and Exchange Commission as a lowly staff attorney. The year was 1990. I was coming off a stint suing boiler-room consumer frauds for another federal agency and, before that, my extended and largely misspent youth had included episodes as a screenwriter, semiprofessional student, and reluctant law firm flunky.

I remained at the SEC for 13 years, confounding previous doubts about my employability, and even crawled up a few rungs on the bureaucratic ladder. Most of that time was spent chasing financial frauds, beginning, as one colleague put it, "before that was cool." Before, that is, Enron and WorldCom and other turn-of-the-century financial scandals made people wonder whether our business leaders should be seen as presumptive felons, including those paragons of capitalism who loom like stuffed predators from the covers of *Fortune* and *BusinessWeek*. Including *them* most particularly. And, of course, long before the events of these last turbulent years led many to question whether the stock market is at bottom a huge confidence game that can collapse as abruptly as a carnival tent in a windstorm.

The SEC did more than pay the mortgage. It took me to odd parts of the world. It allowed me to work with some tenaciously admirable people in an environment not calculated to bring out the best in any of us. It gave me the satisfaction of helping to recover many millions of dollars for investors and banish some bad people from the financial world. It also gave me insomnia and migraines and a reluctance to believe any opinion on American business and its regulation that has taken on the color of consensus.

I left in 2003 to become a partner in a law firm and defend public companies against my former colleagues, no longer seen as dedicated public servants but now as the jack-booted thugs of The Man. The work was easier than it sounds, it being generally more difficult to acquire a substantial client in the face of rabid competition from other law firms than to lead that prize, once acquired, past the snares of law enforcement. Unless, that is, the client had attracted serious press attention. Or engaged in some category of conduct denounced in a recent speech by an agency notable. Or stupidly admitted his transgressions before retaining counsel. Then it takes more work.

Less conventionally, I bolted the law firm after a few years to become an analyst and legal advisor with a "short-biased" fund in California, Copper River Management. Among other things, I did research on companies suspected of cooking their books or otherwise misleading the investing public.

A short sale is a bet that a stock will decline because of negative facts not yet apparent to the market. Management is making up the numbers. Or the company's key product is a passing fad. Or its business sector is due for a fall. Soon others will see this and the stock will tumble.

Or not. That is the gamble.

Copper River—which at its peak managed almost two billion dollars of investor funds—made the gamble pay for more than 20 years, its survival a statistical improbability that ended at the very point the fund should, by rights, have enjoyed its greatest success. Like other "bear" funds, Copper River was positioned to profit from a market decline. Perversely, however, the largest decline in recent history left the fund's expectations brutally disappointed, its assets stripped away, offices closed, and partners and staff unemployed.

The events of late 2008 carried away a number of bears with the greater number of bulls. That was not how it was supposed to work. Those who believed the markets—however unpredictable in other ways—are subject to a single and revealed set of rules found, to their surprise, that a second set existed, housed behind a glass marked "break in event of panic." This lesson was learned at great expense by many who are no longer in a position to benefit from it.

★ ★ ★

An acquaintance whose political views line up roughly with those of the Unabomber once told me that my employment at the SEC placed me squarely "in the belly of the beast." I said he should be pleased. I would surely put the hurt on more corporate plutocrats, made rich from grinding the faces of cubicle-dwelling proles, than anyone else he would ever meet. He was not convinced and would probably have viewed my path from law enforcement to corporate legal defense as a further slide into infamy. As, for that matter, did many of my former colleagues at the SEC, where joining a private firm was referred to, not-altogether-jokingly, as "going over to the dark side."

My fall from grace became complete with my move from the law firm to a short-selling hedge fund. In America, the only thing less admired than our government is the hedge-fund industry, with its shadowy transactions and elephantine profits, and a particular enmity is reserved for those funds that bet on a decline in the market inimical to the hopes of others, and who celebrate when others despair. In the halls of Congress such creatures have been denounced as parasitic, vulpine, even unpatriotic: a secret society sworn to spread banana skins in the path of American business. They are allegedly given to "bear raids" on randomly targeted stocks and accused of spreading misinformation that unfairly contradicts the misinformation spread by the companies they short.

Richard Fuld, former CEO of the now-defunct investment bank Lehman Brothers, said: "When I find a short-seller, I want to tear his heart out and eat it before his eyes while he's still alive." *Many* corporate leaders, it seems, have harbored this dark appetite. Some have attempted to satisfy it—at least figuratively—by filing lawsuits and lobbying government agencies to pursue their short-seller critics for transgressions real or imaginary.

Copper River—known for getting all up in the face of corporate management it deemed less than credible—suffered such attacks to an unmatched degree. It was sued for hatching elaborate conspiracies with other people it had, in fact, never met or previously suspected to exist. It was investigated by the government for conduct that would have been incontestably legal if done by anyone other than a short-seller. When it appeared on the verge of profiting from the possibility that stocks of bad companies might actually go down, at least in a down market, the government prevented that unacceptable outcome through an episode of regulation by ambush.

All of this was what Copper River might have expected. After all, those who insult the gods of commerce by questioning their integrity earn their displeasure and tempt the lightning bolt. Few will trouble themselves over the firm's fate and many will think it well-deserved.

Looking back, I view my history as a sort of Rake's Progress. Taking me from government thug to corporate legal flak to minion of the great short-seller conspiracy, it traced a downward spiral through increasingly dark strata of the financial world.

But this did not make it a dead loss. The experience provided a broad if eccentric education in the ways our capital markets work and—quite often—don't. A worm's-eye view into the follies of the American financial behemoth as it marches boldly from crisis to crisis. The perennial frauds reborn for each generation, changing only in outward appearance over time. And the fables we are told to make us believe the dislocations and disruptions, from the most minor to the catastrophic, are in every case the fault of *others*—never ourselves and those we choose to lead us—and will not happen again.

Perhaps there is some small return to be gained from that.

Chapter 1

Rude Awakenings

The spring of 1987 stands as the bittersweet coda to my protracted adolescence. I was then 35. I had been happily ensconced at Harvard Law School working on an advanced degree of little practical utility other than to serve as an excuse for several years of scholarly lassitude. After getting my first law degree and enduring a year in a vertical lawyer ghetto in Century City, California, I made the discovery that I hated practicing law and could do without most lawyers. So I did what any sensible person would under those circumstances. I went back to school. My vague hope was to become an academic—like my father and grandfather and great-grandfather and God-knows-how-many other pedantic forebears—and never, ever go back to the billable hour treadmill of private legal practice.

The first year in the graduate program was a long slog of course-work, but after that I found I could freely indulge the attention deficit disorder I had previously struggled to repress. Poking around somnolent bookstores in Harvard Square...watching the squirrels outside my office window as they scampered across the Yard...plugging away on a doctoral dissertation on an obscure aspect of American economic history . . . and, in the late hours, writing a mystery novel that would eventually be ignored by the reading public. All the while, the school and my employed wife Eileen paid the bills.

This idyll, however, could not survive the news of a pending expansion of our family. While profoundly welcome, the prospect was unsettling. Academic bohemianism is all well and good when you don't have extra mouths to feed. Now responsibility knocked with brutish authority. Eileen seemed less concerned. Coming from a family of eleven, she accepted that children just sort of spring up around couples like mushrooms after a rain-storm. While I fretted daily over what would become of us, she would put on the purple bathing-suit that, as her pregnancy progressed, made her look more and more like an eggplant with feet, waddle cheerfully off to the university pool, and split a lane with an elderly gentleman she thought was John Kenneth Galbraith.

My plan, to the extent that I had one, was to find a not-too-demanding government job while I finished my doctorate and also dealt with the responsibilities of parenthood. I sent out resumes to a raft of federal agencies, not including the SEC. Its application form was onerously long and focused on the applicant's experience with the securities laws, of which I had none. The first to respond was the Federal Trade Commission's Bureau of Consumer Protection. Apparently the bar was not set very high. After a quick interview in Washington, employment was offered and accepted. We loaded our new son and old furniture into a U-Haul truck and migrated from Cambridge to a rented apartment in northern Virginia, across the Potomac from the imperial city.

Every organ of the federal bureaucracy has its own peculiar mores and practices related in some vague anthropological way to its regulatory goals, and which determine whether those goals are to any degree met. The Credit Practices Division of the FTC had a finger into every aspect of the nation's consumer credit industry. With a staff of less than twenty attorneys, it was in charge of so many rules and regulations that some attorneys had a statute or two they were expected to enforce all by themselves from one end of the continent to the other. This was on top of the division's duty to protect the public from every form of credit fraud.

Obviously, this presented the opportunity for chaos. The division was staffed, however, by mild-mannered government lifers, who had no tolerance for chaos. The issue was resolved by drawing constrictive lines around the rules that were enforced, buttressed by onerous procedural hurdles to frustrate any potential deviation from accepted practice, no matter how slight. In this, it was not unique among government agencies.

The FTC's effectiveness was further undermined when then-president Reagan inflicted on it an administration heavy with economists. Economists are like accountants, only more so. They do not count beans so much as argue over whether the beans exist and, if so, which among them deserve to be counted. The FTC economists conducted cost-benefit analyses to determine if Congress had erred in deciding certain practices should be prohibited. Mostly they decided it had. It has been suggested that, during this period, the FTC could see no harm to the American public in any practice not involving actual gunplay.

It might seem this situation offered the opportunity to draw a decent salary without really doing anything. But there is a fine line between not doing anything and not accomplishing anything. In government, the former is sternly frowned upon, but the latter not so much.

My indoctrination to this critical distinction came from a brush with a prominent Texas mortgage company. The experience also provided my initial exposure to the art, well known to large financial entities, of finessing, evading or simply ignoring inconvenient regulations.

In early 1987, the Federal Reserve Board, spooked by rising inflation, cranked up the interbank discount rate a full percent (100 basis points). This gave home mortgage rates a jolt, and lenders were caught between the rock of hundreds of millions of dollars in pending mortgage applications with rates contractually "locked in" and the hard place of a sudden rise in their cost of funds. In short, the loans would be unprofitable. The large Dallas lender Lomas Mortgage elected to shed its lock-in agreements by claiming they applied only when rates went *down*. This made them the equivalent of flood insurance that protects only against losses incurred during a drought. Other mortgage companies performed variations on this theme. Burned applicants eventually figured out that—under our fragmented, incomplete, and incoherent system of financial regulation—the sleepy little Credit Practices Division of the FTC had jurisdiction over the lending practices of some mortgage companies, Lomas among them.

Together with a younger attorney, who was fresh out of law school, I spent months trying to cajole the company into honoring its lock-in agreements. Lomas fielded a platoon of white-shoe lawyers in its defense. In lead-dog position was Harriett Miers, later nominated unsuccessfully by George W. Bush to the Supreme Court. Counsel was indignant that the government would attempt to tamper with bona fide transactions between corporate lenders and their borrowers, merely because the contracts *happened* to work out in favor of the (well-lawyered) lenders who drafted the contracts and—eschewing persiflage about items of small print—slid them past the (clueless) borrowers.

Lomas wouldn't budge. This meant the FTC either sued or dropped the matter. There followed months of meetings and memos. Much anguish was expressed over proposed legal theories. The FTC, by statute, is empowered to punish "unfair or deceptive" trade practices. But, it was argued, "unfair" could mean almost anything. That being unacceptable, it followed that it must mean nothing at all. And how were these contracts "deceptive" when one could, with careful reading, spot the lurking escape clause? Should people be excused from reading what they sign? Down that road lies perdition. But finally the commission agreed that, even in the era of caveat emptor, the company's conduct was beyond the pale. Shortly before I left the FTC in 1990, we gave Lomas the bad news: settle or be sued. I assumed it would be a matter of weeks before an action was filed.

Three years later, the FTC announced a settled action against Lomas. Nothing in the order indicated there might be anything unfair in drafting contracts so as to render them, in practical application, illusory, as I believed these contracts were. Lomas would pay a total of $300,000, trickled out to claimants in $1,000 increments, and agree that henceforth it would make sure its borrowers clearly initialed any weasel language Lomas put in its contracts. The amount paid for redress was likely less than Lomas paid its attorneys for copying and paralegal assistance. Ms. Miers, in her failed confirmation hearing, described the settlement with admirable modesty as "acceptable to Lomas."

In sum, much time and effort was expended to achieve a result of no real value to the public. But I learned from this a useful lesson. After being mired in this and other cases in which policy concerns trumped common sense, I determined to avoid "issue cases" and look for matters even an economist could love. This meant blatant frauds.

Fortunately, these were not in short supply.

In the days before the Internet, scam artists were largely dependent on the U.S. mail to hook potential marks. Boiler-room operators would send out postcards by the tens of thousands, offering impossibly great deals as part of a purported contest or market survey, and employ squads of telephone salesmen to field the leads that the mailers generated. The object was to extract the caller's credit card number. At that point, the fish was in the boat. The only question was how many times the person would be billed before he or she realized the charges were for unwanted goods. These operations infested beach communities full of transient young people desperate for employment and disinclined to ask questions.

Typical of these scams was a Venice, California, operation that pumped out mailers promising the recipient "a four-person outboard motor boat" in return for participating in a market survey. The boat, constructed of "pneumatically pressurized compartments," was described as "suitable for ocean fishing." Those who called to claim their prize were told yes, the boat was theirs. There was, however, the small matter of a $300 fee to cover incidental expenses: taxes, the cost to ship the boat "by commercial carrier," and charges for "transfer of title."

Tens of thousands of dollars had changed hands before the complaints began to pile up. The phrase "four-person outboard motor boat" had conjured in the minds of many trusting souls something other than an inflatable plastic dingy with an egg-beater motor. And they were pissed. A federal judge in Los Angeles saw their point and, without notice to the company, granted the application of the FTC for an order shutting the operation down and freezing its bank accounts. Judges were usually accommodating in this way—as I discovered after similar experiences in courtrooms across the country—especially once they recognized the defendants' social stratum (white trash) and the consequent near-certainty that no one would challenge the orders. The company was located a few blocks off Venice Beach. The building, when I found it, looked abandoned: paint peeling from salt breeze and sun, screens torn, litter decomposing in the alcove beside the entrance. But the sign on the door for American Nautical Adventures looked new and, inside, the place was jumping. Rows of young men in T-shirts and cut-offs slouched in surplused office chairs, each with a telephone cradled between shoulder and ear as he earned his rent.

An inflatable plastic dingy hung from the rafters, shifting in the draft from the open loading dock at the back of the large, uncarpeted room. However innocent in appearance, it was easily identifiable as the source of hundreds of complaints to the FTC.

From a raised dais at one end of the room, a man in his late 20s monitored the activities of the salesmen. His right leg was covered to the knee in a grimy cast and propped on a battered metal desk, an huarache sandal dangling from the exposed foot. His sun-streaked mud-brown hair bulged from under a backwards baseball cap and his T-shirt advertised a bar in Ensenada. The appearance of a suit and tie caused him visible concern. It could only mean trouble. His arms flailed as he righted himself and stood hunched away from his broken leg. He read the order slowly, moving his lips, and winced in dismay when I told him a federal judge had frozen all his assets, personal and corporate, including whatever loose change he had in his pockets.

But a true salesman is never at a loss for words.

A mistake had been made, he tried. Maybe there was another company by the same name. Or one of his competitors was slandering him. It was that kind of business.

Yes, those were his mailers. Sure, that was his boat. But so what? It wasn't like anyone had lied about anything here.

I mentioned a few points where he might have failed to reach a true meeting of the minds with his customers. That was too just much for him to take. Now he was upset. He pointed at the boat dangling overhead and offered to show me it could seat four people or more. If I didn't believe it was good for ocean fishing, there was an ocean just a few blocks away. I could try it for myself. Due to a skateboarding mishap—he knocked on the cast—he couldn't demonstrate the capabilities of the craft himself, but any of his employees would be only too happy.

He had answers for everything. The phrase "pneumatically pressur-ized" meant you had to blow the thing up. What else? And what he sought to convey by the phrase "the costs of transferring title" was, well, what you paid for the boat. The "commercial carrier" that tossed the boat onto your doorstep in its little plastic bag was the very reputable United Parcel Service. And it was also nothing less than the truth that the company was conducting a market survey. That is, it was a survey to determine if people would be more willing to buy a boat if told it was being offered as part of a market survey than if someone just called them up and asked if they wanted to buy an inflatable boat.

I told him he would have every opportunity to make these very compelling arguments to a judge or jury. He did not seem to find this reassuring.

The next day I went by to make sure no sales were taking place and found the office deserted and the local unemployment rolls swelled overnight by the addition of two dozen surfers, dopers and aspiring actors. The phones were gone, but no one had bothered with the furniture.

And the boat was still there, dangling in midair and spinning slowly like a big, clunky mobile.

When sued, these operations usually stole away with whatever was in the till.[1] The challenge was to find and freeze their bank accounts before they got wind of what was coming. That meant figuring out in advance which banks they used. Sometimes it was possible to get this information from the cancelled payment items of their victims, but not always. I tried driving in expanding circles away from the target company office to serve with a freeze order every bank within, say, a mile radius. But this too was hit-or-miss. Once, for a particularly egregious Florida scam, I hired private detectives to search its garbage for financial records.

The detective agency had its office in an old frame house in Daytona Beach. When I walked in to see the evidence it had collected, I found two burly ex-FBI agents jumping up and down, high-fiving each other and yelling as if they'd just won a football pool. They explained their euphoria by pointing to the image flickering on a video monitor. While hiding in a bush, one of the detectives had captured on tape the purportedly crippled victim of an auto accident in a game of beach volleyball, blithely spiking his claim against the insurance company employing the detectives.

---

[1] Such was the case with the rubber boat company. It received an injunction against future violations and lost what had been frozen in its bank account. Otherwise, it was in the wind.

They had also achieved solid results in their trash runs for the FTC. Among the pizza cartons and cigarette butts, they found bank statements that revealed where the company stashed its loot. The bulk of the garbage, however, consisted of letters of complaint from people the company had bilked. They were there in the hundreds: crumpled, coffee-stained, and all but a few unopened.

Chapter 2

The SEC Steps Out

October 19, 1987, is remembered on Wall Street as Black Monday. The New York Stock Exchange fell over 22 percent, the biggest one-day drop in its history. Other countries' exchanges also took a beating in a worldwide contagion of panic selling. Sales orders came in such torrents that the NYSE's order entry system was overwhelmed and the tape reflected prices from some uncertain point in recent history. For one day, everything was broken.

I owned not a single share of stock and my job then had nothing to do with the securities market. But the shock waves reached everywhere, even to my little regulatory closet. Little was done that day around the FTC as everyone watched the financial news and tried to gauge how badly their retirement accounts were bleeding and worried what this might mean for the American economy.

The day's distress was increased by confusion as to the source of the rout. The market had risen substantially over a period of many months—some thought too far to hold onto its gains. It had experienced some rough days in the previous two weeks, which made traders nervous. But few spotted the severe fragility that could lead to a full-scale collapse.

The impetus for the "market correction," as the government chose to call it, is still the subject of debate 20 years later. Plainly, there were certain developments kicking at the legs of a tiring bull market. Congress was fooling with an adjustment to the tax code that would have made certain business combinations less attractive. Specifically, the interest on debt used in leveraged buy-outs (LBOs) would, under the proposed bill, no longer be deductible. These were the late years of the mergers and acquisitions boom, so many stocks were fattened by takeover speculation. The proposed legislation caused some of those bets to be taken off the table. This was on top of the stress fractures opening in the junk bond world as a result of increasing prosecutorial interest in some of its major players, including the biggest, Drexel Burnham Lambert. Not to mention that there were simmering worries over the increased debt load carried by American companies as a result of the LBO craze—leverage and risk being always joined at the hip.

Also, the dollar was wobbly. It had weakened significantly during the previous few years—a boon to American exports (which became cheaper and hence more competitive) but not to domestic and international creditors—and the Reagan administration was making noises that the trend might be allowed to continue. This made our trading partners unhappy and invited repercussions, as well as raising inflation worries.

Whatever started the ball rolling, the momentum it developed has been blamed in large part on certain novelty items of financial technology. The double-edged nature of innovation is a theme that echoes through every boom and bust of modern finance. Here the two related culprits were "program trading" and what was called, with unintended irony, "portfolio insurance." Program trading is exactly what it sounds like: feeding buy and sell orders into a computer to be executed when portfolio positions hit specified price points. Although a helpful tool in managing a fund with numerous positions, its role in the 1987 crash has been portrayed as much like that of the evil computers in the *Terminator* movies. Take a long weekend in the Hamptons and what happens? Artificial intelligence takes over from the human variety and goes haywire. You return to your office to find a smoking ruin.

Portfolio insurance was one of those something-for-nothing schemes peddled by Wall Street technocrats that work wonderfully . . . until they don't. The idea was to build into money management a one-way ratchet that would limit potential losses without similarly reducing potential gains. The appeal was obvious: Heads I win, tails I don't lose much. Portfolio insurance came in different flavors. The most straightforward involved simply going to cash should the investor's positions decline to hit its predetermined loss tolerance and, conversely, moving increasingly from cash to equities as prices rose. Other varieties directed that the investor respond to market declines by writing futures contracts on the Standard & Poor 500 index. The cash received for selling the S&P futures would supposedly offset losses to the firm's equity positions. Should the market go up, on the other hand, the cost of honoring the futures contracts would in theory be more than offset by portfolio gains.

Whether this ever made sense at the firm level was probably beyond the knowledge of many of the money managers who gobbled up these wonky products. But it made them feel safer and, for that reason, many went more heavily into equities than they would have had they not been "insured." This arguably contributed to the market bubble. What these investors did not consider, however, was the systemic risk that occurs when many investors respond to a certain set of circumstances by doing the same thing at the same time.

Portfolio insurance—a "trend-following dynamic hedge"—responds to changes in portfolio value by trading in the same direction as the market. In a rising market, this means adding to the upward momentum, perhaps helping to inflate a bubble. In a falling market, such as that occurring in mid-October 1987, it means dumping equities. Given the widespread adoption of portfolio insurance, this resulted in a demand for liquidity that exceeded the market's capacity to deliver without significant price erosion. As Nobel laureate William Sharpe put it, "We learned in the 1987 market crash that if everyone wants the upside and no one wants the downside, then everyone can't get it."

Under the versions of portfolio insurance utilizing S&P 500 futures, investors sold futures as the market declined. The increased supply would cause their price to decline. The futures market is predictive of the short-term direction of equities. The sudden cheapness of S&P futures in October 1987, therefore, sent a signal to potential buyers to stand clear of equities, leaving the market to sellers. Further, when the price of futures on the index fell below the aggregate of its component stocks, an arbitrage opportunity was created. By buying S&P 500 futures (cheap) while selling short its component stocks, arbitrage funds could lock in the spread between two equivalent assets. The result of this linkage between the derivatives and equities markets was a tsunami of short sales by arbitrage funds that were exploiting a temporary decline in the price of S&P futures caused, in turn, by program trading in the service of portfolio insurance.

Admittedly, not everyone takes this view. While the SEC and others have fingered portfolio insurance, often operating on autopilot through program trading, as a primary cause of the crash, others point out that declines on exchanges in other countries did not correspond in size to the local popularity of portfolio insurance. This suggests to them that the root cause of the crash was the underlying fragility of a global market inflated to bubble proportions by speculative forces. What no one disputes, however, is the failure of the system to meet the challenge of Black Monday. Its inability to absorb the day's huge trading volume contributed greatly to the meltdown. Potential buyers stood on the sidelines, waiting for an indication that a bottom was in sight or at least for the return of reliable quotes. Uncertainty increased throughout the day and took much of the buy side out of the market.

The following day, the Federal Reserve Board (under its new chairman, Alan Greenspan) turned on the liquidity spigot and the market reversed course and began a lengthy recovery. Thereafter it became an item of faith that the Fed would come to the rescue to halt major market declines. This faith and the Fed's dutiful attempts to justify it are suspected by those sensitive to concerns of "moral hazard" to have encouraged a culture of indifference to some forms of financial risk, the painful consequences of which are very much with us today.

The regulators responded to the October 1987 market break by dealing with the mechanical side of the problem, providing "circuit-breakers" to halt trading during rapid market drops and measures to handle spikes in trading volume. There was no serious attempt to come to grips with the bigger issue: the destabilizing effects of widespread adoption of new investment techniques. The October 1987 calamity has not been replayed precisely, but the market has subsequently suffered different calamities that, in some respects, were not so very different at all. A common theme in each case has been the systemic risk presented by financial innovation. These unruly creatures have included the highly leveraged hedge fund and various new forms of derivates, including complex asset-backed products and credit default swaps. First out of the pen, however, was a simpler financial beast—the junk bond.

★ ★ ★

While the Federal Trade Commission (FTC) continued to earn its sobriquet as "the little old lady on Pennsylvania Avenue," the late 1980s were remarkable years for the SEC. Seen widely as a golden era for the agency, it witnessed the rise and fall of junk-bond king Michael Milken and a raft of splashy insider trading cases against Wall Street heavies. These matters raised the profile of the SEC and created a legacy of expectation that influenced its enforcement agenda for a decade.

The 1980s may be recalled without nostalgia as an era of strutting takeover kings who feasted on household-name companies with the help of Machiavellian bankers and their wicked weapons of financial destruction, of leveraged buyouts, downsizings and greenmail, when everything was in play and nothing secure. And the dark wizard most responsible for loosing these financial demons upon the land was a balding introvert from Encino, California: Michael Milken. If not a straight-up criminal like master pyramid-builder Bernie Madoff, he nevertheless played the capital markets and their regulations like a pinball machine, with the Tilt function disconnected.

It is a stretch to call Michael Milken an innovator. The financial empire he created from his X-shaped trading desk in Los Angeles rested on extensions and refinements of ideas appropriated from others. First among these was the perception that the risks and rewards of owning low-grade corporate debt become more predictable when spread across a number of different bonds. This was nothing more than basic portfolio theory applied to junk bonds. A similar insight—however misapplied—lies behind the recent boom and bust in subprime mortgage loans. It was contended by various academics that the average risk-adjusted return on "high-yield" corporate debt was disproportionate to that of other asset categories. Buyers were scarce, however, because of the serious likelihood of default—and the lack of reliable information—on individual bonds. Milken perceived there was money to be made in packaging these assets in a way that fit within the risk tolerance of major financial institutions and other potential buyers—or at least seemed to do so after the application of Milken salesmanship.

He began by developing a secondary market for existing debt issues, exploiting the large potential margins available to middlemen in an illiquid market, and enhanced the attractiveness of this market by providing analysts' reports though his firm, Drexel Burnham Lambert. Over time, he put together a network of compliant buyers, including insurance companies (traditional bad asset magnets) and desperate-for-yield S&Ls, that allowed his firm to bring out sizeable original issues. This provided greater access to capital to various struggling firms—mostly a good thing—and fueled the mergers and acquisitions boom of the 1980s—a mixed blessing at best.

Through its ability to quickly gin up enormous amounts of debt financing, Drexel became the investment bank of choice for some of the decade's most voracious corporate raiders. It also trafficked in management-led leveraged buy-outs that bled to death target companies by draining off cash to pay for their own acquisition. In theory, the corporate takeover provides a means of giving the shove to entrenched and complacent management. In practice, it has often eroded shareholder value through the short-sighted cashing in of assets to service debt or turn a quick profit, and was attended by job losses and other social costs. Here the "creative destruction" of capitalism had nothing creative about it.

Milken's influence grew until he dominated every facet of the junk bond market. This allowed him to control both supply and demand in particular issues, and thus their prices. The result was an increasingly artificial market. His ministrations imparted an inflated value to many of the bonds he bought, sold, brokered, and underwrote that could not be sustained forever.

In 1986, the government began to unravel a skein of criminal conduct associated with the M&A subculture. An insider trading ring had coalesced around plump and bumbling investment banker Dennis Levine and arbitrageur and Milken crony Ivan Boesky, built on swapping tips about pending deals and trading through offshore accounts. Nothing requiring much imagination. After flourishing undetected for years, it came to grief at last when the greed of its participants outstripped their caution. The SEC was alerted to Levine's suspicious trading by a call from Merrill Lynch compliance, which noticed that several of its brokers had been mimicking consistently prescient trades made through a client Swiss bank. Once the bank was induced to disclose that its customer was a U.S. investment banker, the dominoes toppled as members of the ring flipped on each other to curry prosecutorial favor. The SEC did the initial legwork. The U.S. Attorney's Office in Manhattan, run at that time by Rudy Giuliani, brought the muscle.

First to take the drop was Levine, a casualty of his own criminal ineptitude, in both senses. The trail then led through several lesser players to Boesky, who ratted out Milken in exchange for reduced jail time. Milken's misconduct was far more complex and sophisticated than the crude insider trading of Levine and his immediate circle. It was largely directed toward maneuvering companies into play and rigging their acquisition so Drexel could profit from the deal flow, with Milken personally raking off the bulk of those profits. Much of his conduct was unsavory but not illegal. And what was illegal was not easy to prove.

In 1988, nevertheless, Milken was indicted on 98 counts of stock fraud and racketeering. After much legal maneuvering, he pled guilty to six felony counts of charges of a technical nature, most of which involved facilitating the evasion of stock ownership reporting rules by other participants in his schemes. He paid a $600 million fine and accepted a ten-year prison sentence, served less than two, and left jail a billionaire.[1]

In 1989, the junk bond market Milken had done so much to promote collapsed, as did various S&Ls and other clients Milken had stuffed with risky bonds. Although this was not the fate of all his clients—some survive and prosper to this day—the number left face-down in the weeds was substantial.

A card sharp's adage has it that every game includes a mark. Look at the players around you and, if you can't recognize the mark, you're it. Milken constructed financial transactions rigged so the rewards would

---

[1] His subsequent career has been largely devoted to charitable activities, including providing support for research into prostate cancer, from which Milken suffered and survived, and other medical conditions.

flow to him and the risk of loss to those clients who did not see they were the designated marks in Milken's game of junk bond poker.

★ ★ ★

The most dangerous situation for a government attorney to be in is to be handed a high-profile case. It brings to mind the ancient Chinese curse, "May you live in interesting times." Credit-grabbing and blame-ducking are predictable companions to the spotlight of publicity, and whatever the final result of the case, there will be those who find it inadequate. The press has an ingrained belief that penalties should reflect the degree of public outrage at the defendants' conduct, as interpreted by the press, and has no patience with complicating factors. In the rush to roll up the trading network, settlements were reached on the fly, some of them less onerous than they might have been. After the Levine and Boesky settlements, the SEC was soundly trashed by the press for not leaving the perpetrators, as a later SEC chairman would phrase it, "naked, homeless, and without wheels." Once the media turned hostile, the SEC and the U.S. Attorney's Office fell out, SEC attorneys squabbled among themselves, and the commission harshly criticized its legal staff.

On Main Street, however, the whole episode proved reassuring. It was a morality play that had come to its proper conclusion. Good had triumphed over evil and the financial world was secure once more. Few worried about the details. And it helped that the primary villains could be seen as Wall Street intruders and interlopers, shady characters pushing dubious merchandise like hostile takeovers and leveraged buy-outs. It wasn't the old guard that was at fault. The established brands like Goldman and Merrill lost little of their cachet, despite having employees among the indicted.

Chapter 3

Short People

The media circus over Milken and his playmates thrust the SEC into prominence. It was seen as an exciting place to work and attracted a flood of resumes, mine included. Although the application form had not gotten shorter during my two years at the FTC, I risked rejection on the off-chance I might sneak in and be allowed to investigate *real* frauds—defined as frauds not committed by people whose primary means of locomotion is the skateboard. The boiler-room cases had begun to seem like exercises in cockroach-stomping, neither challenging nor greatly socially beneficial. The SEC, by contrast, did complicated cases. Cases that mattered. The *New York Times* said so.

A friend of a friend arranged an interview. I met a series of people in the SEC's general counsel's office, all very cordial until the last on my list. The most junior person I spoke with that day, he was by turns sarcastic, abrasive, and coldly dismissive. He stopped just short of tearing up my resume and showering me with the pieces. Later, it was explained to me that he had been under great personal stress. It had been his misfortune to be caught in a stairwell in an advanced stated of intimacy with another SEC employee. Twice. Both times by an elderly commissioner who apparently suffered from an aversion to elevators.

Although nothing came of that attempt, shortly after, as a result of L'Affair Drexel, Congress ponied up additional funds for the SEC. The result was a cattle call for new attorneys and in early 1990 I found myself rounded up with the herd and destined for the Enforcement Division.

The people in the group in which I landed were mostly either boring family types like me or young careerists looking for the next step up the ladder. The latter category included the occasional overachiever who wore his resume like a sandwich board and needed you to know that his inner child was an honor student. But most were simply bright young men and women who, as undergraduates, had come to the realization that for anyone interested in making a middle-class living, all majors in the liberal arts are synonymous with "Pre-Law."

Some had retained a frisky undergraduate mentality. One morning not long after joining the agency, I heard cries of distress from a nearby office so pitiable that I assumed a loved one had passed away unexpectedly. Two young attorneys were crammed into that office. The source of the outbursts, first name Chris, was sitting at his desk, madly flipping though a testimony transcript. He would stop, read a few moments, and then swear profusely. "No!" he shouted. "That's not right. That can't be right! I didn't fucking say that!"

His officemate, John, was staring at the wall with a constipated expression, breathing constricted.

Chris often pored over his transcripts as if reading a favorite novel. Although he had not been at this long, he considered himself a natural and liked to dwell on his achievements in questioning witnesses. Sometimes he read aloud passages he considered particularly adept, uninvited, to his officemate. Never again, however, after today.

When John's composure ruptured into uproarious laughter—joined by several neighbors who were in on the joke—the truth was disclosed.

John had grabbed an incoming transcript, undid the shoelace bindings, removed various pages and replaced them with his own creations, carefully typed on the lined paper used by the reporting service. In the substituted version, Chris made various admissions to a presumably startled witness about his legal abilities and mental state. "You must understand," he said, "that sometimes my mind shuts off. I forget where I am. What day it is. I ask questions that make no sense. I think they do but they don't. And sometimes I believe I am someone else. An entirely different person. I can't help it. If that happens, please call my supervisor and tell him I'm doing it again."

What the group had in common, as was true of the Enforcement Division broadly, was a meager understanding of the capital markets. With few exceptions, everyone had come to the commission straight from law school or, at best, after a few years of concentrated abuse as a law firm associate. That was to be expected. The ideal enforcement attorney combines the expertise of a seasoned litigator with that of a law professor, a forensic accountant, and a Wall Street trader. No such animal exists and, if it did, would not work for what the government can pay. So the SEC takes what it can get. In most cases, happily, this is a reasonably talented and motivated young attorney who in time gets more things right than wrong.

Like many of my new colleagues, I had never taken a course in securities law. I asked my immediate supervisor what I should read to begin mastering the field. She eyed me as if I were a very curious item indeed and said, "Don't bother. There's too much of it and, anyway, you won't remember anything you haven't actually used."

In retrospect, right she was.

The federal securities regulations fill a thousand pages, single-spaced, with opaque and convoluted legalese. Published court decisions fill rooms. And whatever architectural structure the securities laws once possessed has been obscured by decades of regulatory kudzu. Anyone trying to master it all by proceeding from beginning to end would resemble the "self-made man" of the modern French novel who read through the books in the public library in alphabetical order.

The commission churns out five or six hundred enforcement actions a year. While these numbers are inflated to impress Congressional appropriators, that's still a lot of cases. Many come down to paint-by-numbers exercises in penalizing hapless crooks whose schemes blew up in their faces. And the majority don't require great financial sophistication. Someone lied to someone about something or blabbed something he shouldn't have. The facts may take some effort to prove, but the legal issues are clear.

Yet if many cases can be handled by any decent lawyer, *some* violations—weighted toward the most significant—require specialized knowledge to recognize and prove-up. This is where the commission has often come up short. In theory, its enforcers can tap into the full resources of the agency, including the divisions that review corporate filings, regulate mutual funds, and inspect broker-dealers. In reality, these other offices function like separate agencies that happen to share the same building. Partly as a result of revolving doors into the entities they regulate, they have sometimes looked at their areas of the securities industry as their true clients, rather than the SEC Enforcement thugs who can be mean to prospective employers. The Enforcement Division is not immune to the same considerations but the incentives bend less in that direction, particularly for the rank-and-file, which is rewarded for bringing in scalps, not making friends.

As for spotting the next big problem before it results in headlines and red-faced congressmen, the record of the other divisions disappoints. The Division of Corporation Finance, which scrutinizes corporate filings, famously passed on reviewing Enron's filings because they were so long. It was much easier to meet the quota by reading only short filings. The Division of Investment Management failed for years to notice that some mutual fund complexes allowed select investors to "market time" their funds. Being able to skip in and out of funds in response to arbitrage opportunities, while mom-and-pop investors were in for the long haul, provided easy profits to the favored few. The discovery in 2003—by New York Attorney General and soon-to-be tabloid star Eliot Spitzer—that this practice had become widespread led to the biggest scandal in the history of the mutual fund industry. SEC regulators were caught by surprise, even though by then some funds were openly running "market timing desks" to handle this important client service. Then there was the partial responsibility of the office charged with inspecting investment firms for the failure to discover the Bernie Madoff Ponzi scheme until Madoff himself came forward and confessed.

Thus it behooves those who would effectively enforce the securities laws to look for leads beyond the confines of the SEC. But where to begin? The SEC receives complaints in the hundreds of thousands annually from both the temporarily and the congenitally disgruntled. Many are confused; others are insane. How to sift through all the dreck for the occasional nugget of useful information?

Also, communicating with the masses presents risks. This is not mere institutional paranoia, although that exists in abundance. SEC attorneys handle information that can move stocks. Not as often as the public believes, but now and then. A small indiscretion to an outsider can have serious consequences. Fear of such incidents is one reason that SEC attorneys often travel in groups, like nuns.

It happens, furthermore, that people with an interest in an investigation will try to lead the staff in a direction beneficial to themselves, and not always honestly. When it comes to tips from outsiders, SEC attorneys are taught to mistrust anyone who might have an interest in steering them wrong. But who in his right mind would go near a government agency *except* out of self-interest? Whether motivated by a desire to make a buck, get even with a hated former employer, or validate a theory of extraterrestrial infiltration of the capital markets, everyone who approaches the SEC has an ax to grind.

So the question is, Whose ax-grinding activities merit attention? Obviously, industry professionals are likely to be better informed about misconduct in the capital markets than, say, auto mechanics, musicians, or hairdressers. And, among them, unique in their interest in seeing bad companies get their comeuppance, are those deplored and abused denizens of the financial world, short-sellers.

★   ★   ★

In my first years at the SEC, I was wholly dependent on my superiors for cases. Like a baby bird with its beak open for the next parentally procured beetle, I gobbled up whatever came my way. Odds and ends from the cases of someone who had left the agency. NASD referrals about low-dollar insider trading cases. This, that and the other thing.

My first decent case came to me more or less by accident. An attorney in another group—Jim something—was sliding toward retirement and needed to offload part of his case inventory. The powers that be had decided to throw one at me.

The initial challenge was finding the guy.

At that time, the SEC was located in a dumpy 1960s-vintage building with an Arby's in the lobby, a few blocks from the National Mall. Space was limited, and the claustrophobic atmosphere was exacerbated by the towering columns of document boxes lining the hallways. Once, the chairman wandered by mistake into a part of the building where the hired help labored. He was outraged at the clutter and threatened to call the fire marshal if all the boxes didn't disappear immediately. A memo went out but nothing changed and, so far as I know, the chairman never returned, probably unable to find that hallway again. Making navigation even more of a challenge, the Enforcement Division was fragmented into blocks of offices on different floors, certain internal hallways were blind alleys, and office numbers were out of sequence.

My supervisor, a woman a few years younger than me, had referred to Jim as a "dinosaur": to her mind, anyone who had been at the agency more than five years without leaping up the hierarchy, or any male who got his hair cut by a barber rather than a stylist. Jim had been there *far* longer than five years and his hair showed no progressive tendencies. His office, entrance hidden behind a row of filing cabinets, was piled with stacks of loose documents. In those days you could still smoke in government buildings, and the corners of Jim's office were hazed with cigarette smoke.

Stocky and bearded, he moved heavily, as if the force of gravity had been turned up from a meter on his wall; but he livened up when he spoke about the case he was giving me. He had made an emotional investment he wished to see protected. Gauging my experience level as low, he gave me the remedial version. He stared at the ceiling, ran his thick fingers gently over key documents as if they were written in Braille, and spun out the story in fits and starts, occasionally doubling back and repeating to make sure I was following.

A public company on the outskirts of Philadelphia, HealthCare Services Group, had found a way to make money from providing minimum wage workers as janitors and maids to nursing homes across the country. More to the point, HealthCare was suspected of having goosed its numbers and hence its share price. Suspected, specifically, by a pair of short-selling brothers in Dallas named Joe and Tom Barton. They had developed an elaborate argument the company was engaged in a straight-up accounting scam with a Medicare fraud chaser.

Despite Jim's laborious tutorial, I came away from our meeting with only a vague notion of the Bartons' views. It had to do with paying bribes to quasi-bankrupt nursing homes in return for hiring the company's scut workers at inflated rates. The loop would be closed by passing the costs on to the taxpayers though excessive Medicare reimbursements. Or something like that. There were also various subtheories and related speculations.

Any fear that I would be left to muddle through the matter on my own, however, was dispelled when, at Jim's suggestion, I called Joe Barton to get the story from the source. I had been warned by my supervisor to treat speaking with short-sellers as an exercise in snake-handling, but her understanding of the species was more received than earned. She had never encountered any in person. Her attitude, however, was widely shared around the Division. The shorts were seen as occupying some dark fringe of the stock market: like gypsies camped at the edge of town, always presumed to be up to no good.

Given my novice status, I am unsure why I was allowed to speak with these guys unchaperoned. Partly, I'm sure, because no one cared much about accounting cases back then—everyone was looking for the next big insider trading scandal—and certainly not an accounting case involving janitorial services to nursing homes. So . . . go knock yourself out and let us know if you find anything.

Also, everyone around me was crazy busy. The division was responding to the latest market scandal. The investment banking firm Salomon Brothers had been caught rigging treasury auctions. The Treasury Department limits the percentage of any new bond issuance that can be purchased by individual firms so no one can corner the market and gain price control. Salomon traders got around this on a handful of occasions by using client accounts as straw men to supplement the firm's purchases. One trader also made an improper $1 billion purchase when a practical joke misfired. Because treasuries are the arterial blood of the economy, this was treated as financial treason. The head of the firm, John Gutfreund, was driven out of his position for not preventing the misconduct, and the firm was fined $250 million. Later, it was discovered that—oops—improprieties were fairly widespread among auction participants. The SEC dealt with the matter programmatically. It demanded *all* the major players sign orders—generated by the staff in assembly-line fashion—pledging never to do again what many insisted they had never done before. So much for that.

Thankfully, any worries about the Bartons leading me astray—easy as that might have been—were misplaced. As Jim promised, they were reliable bloodhounds. And that was invaluable. They operated *out there* in the real world of American business. They weren't stuck in some office with a computer and a desk and some filing cabinets and a bunch of other government employees looking for a clue. They *knew* things. They not only understood business dynamics but were decent lay accountants, with a nose for when something made so little economic sense that it might even violate the accounting rules. The result was the sort of field intelligence that the government rarely generates for itself.

The Bartons had acquired their expertise by working for the most notorious of all short-selling firms, the Feshbach Brothers of Dallas, Texas. The three Feshbachs—Matt, Joe, and Kurt—attired in matching jackets with "Fraud-busters" emblazoned on the back, had set a new standard—high or low depending on perspective—when it came to taking on public companies they thought had something to hide. Through the 1980s they kicked the tires of many suspect companies, sometimes until they popped. They called competitors, suppliers, customers, ex-employees—anyone who could give them an informational edge. And they were not shy about broadcasting their findings to anyone willing to listen.

They made (surprise) many enemies. Companies carped to the press, the SEC and Congress that the Feshbachs were in the self-fulfilling prophecy business, beating down good stocks with their blandishments. They claimed the Feshbachs had defamed them. The SEC, perennially receptive to such complaints, investigated. Its lawyers rooted through a truckload of documents and came up with nothing.

Over time, this has been the predictable outcome of short-seller investigations. It is unlikely any other type of case has proved so consistently unrewarding, while a surprising number of companies known for complaining about short-sellers later blew up from financial scandal. Nevertheless, allegations of short-seller conspiracy retain their power to beguile. The *story* is so compelling that the agency seems unable to resist. Like Charlie Brown with Lucy and the football, it always believes that next time will be the charm. Next time the shorts will be caught at their nefarious game.

Theoretically "short-and-distort" is as practicable a form of market manipulation as "pump-and-dump." It just doesn't happen as often. In April 2008, in an agency first, the SEC alleged an instance of such conduct. Compare this to the hundreds of penny stock scams busted by the agency over the years. Perhaps this is because short positions can be difficult to acquire and maintain. Or because company management, which often plays a role in pump-and-dump schemes, rarely sees an incentive to manipulate its own stock *down*. Or perhaps because every short-seller knows—merely from being what he is—that his name is on the roster of "usual suspects" meriting scrutiny from the government at the first suggestion of wrongdoing. And who would dare commit a crime with the police camped on his doorstep?

Many of the companies the Feshbachs shorted turned out to be as bad as they said, and their fund made solid returns through the 1980s. But all good things must end. What did in the good brothers was a dramatic rise in the NASDAQ, home to the small- and mid-cap stocks they targeted. This undercut their performance numbers, as did growing competition from copy-cat hedge funds. Also, a *Time* cover story depicting the firm as a bunch of Scientology freaks didn't help.

When the mothership collapsed, many Feshbach analysts tried the waters on their own. The Bartons were among them.

They made an odd couple. Joe Barton lived on the telephone. He had the ability to inform and—in a droll, good-old-boy way—entertain, while juggling several things at once. I pictured him tall and lanky, with a curly shock of rust-colored hair. I met him years later and he was short and had a brown pompadour like early Bruce Springsteen. Tom was abrupt and impatient and spoke with a Texas accent that made everything sound sarcastic. He doled out his time sparingly, so I rarely heard from him and I have yet to encounter him in the flesh.

I had some background in asset valuation, but no understanding of the multitudinous dodges, grifts, evasions, scams, contrivances, and studly frauds practiced to improve a company's paper performance. HealthCare Services went a distance toward remedying that deficiency in my education.

It makes sense that most accounting frauds involve bogus revenue. Phony sales filter down through corporate income statements to inflate other critical metrics, including operating income, net income, and earnings per share. The SEC and the Department of Justice would conclude that HealthCare played this game from several angles.[1] Before its initial public offering, it unwound an acquisition funded with its own stock and booked a profit based on the increased price of the returned shares. This served to double its income for the period preceding the offering. It also violated a basic accounting rule that companies can't realize profits from transactions in their own stock.

HealthCare, in addition, structured its housekeeping contacts to push income forward, making it look more profitable. Revenue from service contracts is supposed to be booked in increments over the period of the contract, rather than in a lump at signing. This keeps companies from booking revenue ahead of the related expenses, such as employee salaries. HealthCare cleverly avoided this stricture by bundling its service agreements together with contracts requiring its customers to purchase equipment from HealthCare. By inflating the charges for the equipment—which, if legitimate, could be booked up front—and reducing those for services by the same amounts, the company fast-forwarded revenue at no additional cost to its customers. Various software companies have run a similar scam by combining a sale of software with a contract for consulting and other services, and misallocated costs to favor the sale over the service component. HealthCare did it with mops, pails, and washing machines.

HealthCare never met a receivable (outstanding customer invoice) it didn't claim it could collect. This meant it rarely reduced its reported income to reflect the fact many of its customers had been letting the tab run with little hope of catching up. Some were in sad shape: financially strapped warehouses for the impoverished elderly. One, if I remember correctly, was above a bowling alley in an inner-city neighborhood. Another was at the end of an unpaved road in rural Georgia. After this investigation, I asked my wife, should it ever appear I needed to be placed in a nursing home, to please shoot me instead.

Lastly, the company made what the SEC referred to as "improper payments" to maintain certain client relationships. Nothing in the accounting rules says you can't provide cash inducements to customers, so

---

[1] HealthCare Services eventually settled actions brought against it by the SEC and the U.S. Attorney's Office in Philadelphia, with (as is typical in settled matters) no admission of wrongdoing by the company or its officers. Thus it is not certain the government could have prevailed on the allegations recounted here had the matter gone to trial.

long as you don't call them something they aren't. Yet few companies include in their financial statements a line-item for "bribes, pay-offs, and kickbacks." HealthCare did not disclose these payments.

All of this may sound technical, but it's the stuff from which financial fraud is made and, when detected, can send a company's stock into a death spiral. Everyone learned to care more about such technicalities a few years later when a raft of financial scandals led by Enron and WorldCom shook the country. It is a shame this awareness didn't occur sooner, or persist longer.

The possible Medicare fraud angle brought in the Philadelphia U.S. Attorney's Office. The FBI agent it assigned was alarmingly well-armed at all times—even when questioning witnesses in a high-security federal building. That may have been strategic. White-collar types who shrug off SEC penalties as a cost of doing business experience bowel-loosening terror at the thought of criminal charges. A holstered automatic is a reminder of how much worse things can get.

The agent hailed from a place where people pour corn liquor on their cornflakes. In his 40s and tired of the ways of the big city, he was considering retirement. He said he hoped to find an unspoiled corner of the American outback where he and his "sweet gopher-shootin' mama" could live the life bucolic, rural tranquility disturbed only by the occasional shotgun blast.

He regarded all lawyers as placed on earth for his personal amusement, and I was never sure when he was having me on. But he had a clear-eyed take on the realities of law enforcement. When I complained that placing witnesses under oath merely focused their attention on the importance of lying well, he advised me that "bullshitting the SEC is the most popular indoor sport in this country." He discounted, also, the odds that the Medicare case would pan out. The term "Medicare fraud," he said, was redundant, and the regulations rarely enforced.

He was right on the Medicare issue, which got dropped along the way, but the financial fraud case paid off. The company and several of its officers settled out by, among other things, paying fines totaling $850,000—modest by present standards but the largest penalty paid in an SEC financial fraud case to that date. Congress had granted the SEC the power to fine bad actors only a few years before, and the agency was taking baby steps in using it. Indeed, I had to lobby to keep my superiors from giving back some of the money the defendants had agreed to pay. They were afraid the size of the penalty would ratchet up public expectations and make future cases harder to settle. The U.S. Attorney's Office took what I gave it and, unconcerned about raised expectations, dinged HealthCare for an even million. It expressed satisfaction with the outcome.

I looked at that as a pretty fair accomplishment for my first real case for the SEC. The Bartons, however, were of a different mind. The company was still in existence and its officers not in jail. What sort of bang for the taxpayers' buck was that? Pathetic!

Indeed, HealthCare Services still operates today and has grown substantially. It employs many people and appears to have done decently for its investors, with no additional scrapes with the law that I've seen. I'm not sure what would have been accomplished by putting it out of business, even had that been legally possible, other than to indulge a sense of righteous retribution.

And? the Bartons might respond. Something wrong with that?

Short-sellers, as a group, have approximately the same willingness to forgive and forget as the Almighty in the Old Testament. The wages of financial sin, in their view, should include, at the very least, the career death that comes of banishment from the industry. Also, penury would be good: all assets seized and auctioned in the public square.

If this seems harsh, consider. The Bartons have long since given up shorting stocks, finding it too punishing a way to make a living. Many other short funds have thrown in the towel for a variety of reasons. Some come quickly to mind: Corporate disclosure failures that continue for years, blatant pump-and-dump schemes ignored by regulators, manipulative trading by company insiders and cronies, institutional analysts pimping for investment banking business for their firms with bogus "buy" ratings—not to mention companies that use lawsuits and smear campaigns to play whack-a-mole with their critics.

Add all these together and it should be clear why short-sellers may grow a tad vindictive.

Chapter 4

Belgian Waffles

The Orange Line of the D.C. Metrorail System carries weekday swarms of lawyers, accountants and office managers from the aging suburb of Arlington, Virginia, to the granite honeycombs of the District of Columbia. During the morning rush, trains like giant tin caterpillars follow each other at three-minute intervals, more crowded at each stop. They slide along Route 66 past block after block of redbrick Cape Cods and center-hall colonials as uniform as monopoly houses, before slipping into the earth for the passage under the Potomac. On their return journey, they rise to the surface beside a park where, on summer evenings, kids play pickup soccer in the gathering dusk.

One morning in 1995, fortunate to get a seat on the train, I read in the *Wall Street Journal* about an obscure stock that had gone on a gravity-defying run, jumping 15-fold in a day. The company, Comparator Systems, had "fingerprint identification" technology that it claimed would be the next big thing in corporate security, but had yet to rack up serious sales. Management had no explanation for the run-up and seemed eager to have the incident go away.

Thinking it might be a market manipulation gone berserk, I flagged the matter as mine on the commission's computer system. By then I was a bottom-rung supervisor with attorneys who needed cases. The system didn't work purely on a first-dibs basis. Anyone covetous of a particular matter could bitch to the front office that their position—geographic or political—made them more suitable to do it than whoever got there first. The SEC's Los Angeles office was obviously much closer to this Orange County company than I was. But the matter seemed so weird and the company so tiny that it was possible the locals wouldn't make a play for it.

Within a few days, the company was a national curiosity, having beaten the NASDAQ volume record three days running and taken its market cap from nothing to over a billion dollars. All on no news. Inquiring minds of the financial press wanted to know how this could be. By that time, fortunately, I was deep enough into the case to convince the front office I should keep it despite the protestations of my Southern California colleagues.

A visit to Comparator's premises by two staff attorneys, Karen Mincavage and Chris Ehrman, had revealed what appeared to be a front behind which management cranked out shares to sell through straw-man accounts at fly-by-night brokerage firms. The woman in charge of the otherwise empty office, a former pornographic film actress, said she thought her bosses were crooks. The company's warehouse contained no "fingerprint ID" technology and, indeed, nothing more valuable than a box of old LPs, including the work on vinyl of Iron Butterfly and Grand Funk Railroad.

At that time the NASDAQ required that a company have assets of at least $2 million to be listed on its SmallCap system. Comparator had purported to reach this threshold by throwing onto its balance sheet some unusual items. Biggest in dollar amount was a bunch of patents and licenses. Intangible assets are always good for pumping up a balance sheet because they are hard to value. Comparator's patents and licenses were quite easy to value, however, because they had all expired or passed into the public domain. Comparator had put a price tag on its interest in several private companies, none of which, it turned out, were engaged in any business activities or had real assets. The company had a claim against a former employee for Comparator stock it alleged she had stolen. She said the company had given her the stock and, anyway, she was broke so just try and collect. There was another chunk of stock provided to a consultant, no longer on the scene, for assistance in locating business opportunities in Russia.

The company did have a physical prototype of the fingerprint device. Unfortunately, its claim to ownership was tenuous. A Comparator executive had been entrusted with the device by its inventor, a Scottish gentleman, for demonstration purposes and absconded with it.

All of these "assets" were clearly worthless and the company's auditors—a small local firm located in a strip-mall—had some splainin' to do.

We obtained an asset freeze from the federal court in Los Angeles in the dim hope that the company might have some cash after selling 65 million shares of stock to the public, albeit at pennies a share. But Comparator was strictly a hand-to-mouth operation. There was nothing in the till and the principals were broke.

Trying to establish the commission could act quickly in a financial fraud case—by doing it once—we wrapped up most of the legal aspects in a month or so. The company's stock was kicked out of the public marketplace and several of its officers barred from ever running a public company again. The auditors had their tickets pulled. Because none of these people had the wherewithal to litigate with the government, there was about all this the feeling of using a cannon to kill a gnat. But at least the gnat was dead.

Due to the outrageous spike in share price and the bizarre cast of characters, the press clung to Comparator like Ishmael to the coffin of Queequeg. *USA Today* ran stories that took up several pages, lovingly describing each of the pathetic mopes implicated in this fiasco. *The Orange County Register* won an award for business journalism for its tenacious coverage. The SEC got laudatory marks for its aggressive enforcement actions. Victory was declared and everyone went home happy.

Except, of course, the Comparator people, who must have felt *very* ill-used indeed. They had never asked for anything other than to be left in peace to now and then crank out a few million more shares of stock. Was it their fault every idiot in the country suddenly wanted to buy *their* stock rather than the many equally worthless stocks on the NASDAQ?

As for the cause of the startling run-up, no one really knows. Pumping by longs on Internet message boards probably played a role. Momentum buys by day traders may also have contributed. But all that falls short of explaining why lightning happened to strike this particular company one sunny day in May 1995.

This was a lesson in itself. Most of what happens in the market is a puzzlement even (or perhaps particularly) to the people who regulate it. From its deep waters, things now and then float to the surface that can be identified as requiring a certain treatment under the law. Other pieces of market flotsam, when seen, are harder to classify. But what lies beneath the surface for the most part remains unknown.

To belabor this metaphor, the financial regulators stand in the shallows and peer into the depths, wondering what they may contain. Little comes of this. From time to time, however, someone comes along who, in a remarkable gesture, hauls forth from below a grand curiosity and drops it on the shore at their feet.

Such people are rare but useful indeed.

★ ★ ★

Some time before the turn of the century, I began getting calls from Northern California short-seller Marc Cohodes. He had been sicced on me by his friend Joe Barton, by then out of action after getting pummeled by the bull market of the late 1990s. In this, Joe had much company. For short-sellers, the second Clinton term could be dubbed "the great extinction."

Cohodes was the portfolio manager for the hedge fund Rocker Partners, named for its founder David Rocker. The firm, with offices in Manhattan, New Jersey, Boston, and Marin County, California, had a 15-year history of sparring with companies it thought were crooked or at least terminally lame. David Rocker had a Navy background and two Harvard degrees and wrote macro-finance articles for *Barron's*. He was the suit of the firm. Then in his late-50s, he had the chip-on-the-shoulder intensity of a man whose talents and efforts have brought less recognition than he believes warranted. Being a short-seller will do that to anyone with a sensitive ego.

Marc Cohodes was a different breed altogether. Raised by a single mother in Chicago, he was a beefy guy in his 40s who bore a passing resemblance to the actor John Goodman. His wardrobe favored Bermuda shorts and well-seasoned T-shirts. He would later become an early adopter of Crocks footwear in a rainbow of colors. His tonsorial upkeep consisted of running an electric clipper set at "fuzz" around the circumference of his head. He loved the Oakland Raiders, stock car racing, and the R&B band Southside Johnny and the Asbury Jukes. A diehard fan, he hit more Southside Johnny concerts than anyone except the man himself. While Rocker could be intense and outspoken, he was a conventional money manager next to Cohodes, with his disarming candor and high-octane mouthiness.

The two men complemented each other in an odd way: Rocker measured and severe and Cohodes proudly eccentric. There was a hint of the good-cop, bad-cop strategy to their approach and, despite their obvious smarts, of the comedy pairing of straight man and amiable goof. The Bartons had a similar dynamic. As did the Smothers Brothers.

The investment model for Rocker Partners was expressed in the motto "frauds, fads, and failures." The three Fs. The idea was to buck the giddy bullishness rampant in the market by shorting companies so utterly porcine no amount of hype could long delay their dates with insolvency. This was no easy task. In those years, before the tech-bubble burst and the NASDAQ shed 80 percent of its value, no one remembered the market had a reverse gear. People still believed sell-side analysts truly loved every profitless dog they hyped. Few considered the possibility these arbiters of corporate value might be influenced by the hope grateful companies would reward their effusive praise by throwing business to their investment banking colleagues, some of which would ooze back to the analysts. The absence of "sell" and scarcity of "hold" recommendations might have been a tip-off. When the New York Attorney General found internal emails in which analysts dissed in private the same stocks they kissed in public, all doubt was eliminated.

It took stamina, self-confidence, and a discerning eye for a bear to avoid getting flattened by passing pump-and-dump schemes or general market lunacy. As these guys approached their chosen line of work, it also took a willingness to mix it up with company management. Rocker was known for asking blunt questions in conference calls. Cohodes, in one legendary episode, appeared at a shareholder meeting in a striped referee shirt and, after every management statement he deemed misleading, blew a whistle and threw a red penalty flag. More than money managers chasing profit, they, like other short-sellers, saw themselves as stock-market vigilantes out for truth and justice. As the *Financial Times* put it: "for a group that is supposed to be composed of deeply cynical, self-serving, sharp calculators, short-sellers tend, in their eccentric way, to be the most idealistic class of portfolio managers. They take corporate malfeasance and incompetence personally."

At the time, I knew none of this. I trusted the Bartons but had no idea whether their social circle consisted of solid citizens or raving freaks. Cohodes, however, was incredibly persistent. There was no limit to his desire to convert me—and the financial world at large—to his views about particular companies. He was the hardest-working man in the hedge-fund industry, so eager and palpably sincere that hanging up on him would have felt mean-spirited.

More importantly, I was by this time a mid-level administrator with fifteen attorneys to feed. I was hopeless when it came to suck-ing around the division's front office for whatever might trickle down from above, most of which turned out to be junk anyway. Friends in other divisions came through once in a while, but that really wasn't their mind-set. The financial press had produced a few strikes, and I had learned how to milk journalists for tips when they called about some breaking story and wanted to check the "SEC declined to comment" box, by responding with questions like "Well, maybe if you could tell me a little bit more about the matter you're writing about." But the strong possibilities were usually taken before they got anywhere near the media.

I needed challenging cases to motivate staff attorneys who tended to wilt in their chairs when given routine crap. Good cases were not easy to come by, so I could not afford to be picky about sources. No one would confuse a short-seller slamming a stock with an impartial third party. But it is a rare thing for anyone to rat out a company from pure public-spiritedness, and no one with a long position ever does so at all. I had learned years before that self-interest did not preclude good research. To the contrary, the one often led to the other.

Cohodes was a guided missile directed at the Belgian software company Lernout & Hauspie. It was, he assured me, the fraud of the century, a "dastardly," "despicable," and "demonic" operation run by evil Euro-crooks. He was convinced the company's numbers were phony "beyond belief." His descriptive efforts started at the hyperbolic and ascended from there.

Lernout made voice-recognition products to allow people to communicate with computers through a microphone rather than a keyboard. Its technology also translated spoken words between various languages. This was apparently hot stuff. According to its hype, Lernout was the Microsoft of Belgium. I wasn't sure this wasn't like being the Yao Ming of midgets, but it sounded good.

Cohodes had stumbled onto Lernout by chance. His son Max was born with cerebral palsy and Cohodes was always looking for new technology that might help Max cope with the challenges of his disability. Voice recognition had obvious potential. When he heard about Lernout's products, he hustled to check them out. He went to trade shows, read industry publications and bought whatever was on the market. He was not impressed. The technology didn't perform and he suspected the company's public demonstrations were rigged. That led him to question the company's claims more broadly.

As a foreign company with a U.S. listed stock, Lernout was subject to relatively loose reporting standards. Its annual reports, for example, were not due until six months after its fiscal year-end and omitted information that is required of U.S. companies. We allow foreign companies to file stale and incomplete information because otherwise they might not grace our markets with their securities, depriving the NYSE of a revenue source, and denying our investors the opportunity to make ill-informed investments in companies they probably can't sue if things go wrong.

Analyzing Lernout was therefore an exercise in financial tea-leaf reading. But Cohodes was committed. He pawed through what was available. He noticed that Lernout's CEO, Gaston Bastiaens, had run another software company and it had gone bankrupt—after buying product from Lernout. Everywhere he looked, he found complicated, poorly described deals.

Lernout was a serial acquirer of other companies. Acquisitions are a fertile ground for abuse because the accounting rules are squishy, making it possible for management to stash bloated reserves (booked as liabilities), which can later be reversed and bled back into income as needed. Roll-ups of software companies present additional temptations to earnings chefs because the assets acquired are mostly intangible and their value subjective. On top of this, a big chunk of the Lernout's sales came from related parties, specifically private companies it helped finance. This gave rise to the suspicion Lernout was buying product from itself through circular transactions, or parking product with compliant third parties.

I was not Cohodes' first stop in his evangelical campaign against this company. He had already bugged a bunch of financial reporters. So far, however, only *MarketWatch* columnist Herb Greenberg had written skeptically about Lernout. Rocker Partners had a solid reputation for spotting bad companies, but the case against this name still rested largely on intuition.

Cohodes at that time ran an Internet radio program with the ungainly title "The Facts from the Other Side of the Tracks." He and his California partner Mark "Monty" Montgomery, in a sort of Wayne and Garth format, would rag on companies they thought were bad news, while venturing into broader issues in response to listener questions. They blithely invited the companies they razzed to send someone on the show to debate them. *As if.* That was before companies with dirty laundry learned to sue their critics to shut them up.

Naive as it may sound, the show wasn't bad. Cohodes conveyed an infectious passion for his views. Montgomery, a former college football player with an ebullient personality, had a talent for making complex financial issues both understandable and entertaining. And the shows strove earnestly to provide a public service.[1] This led, for example, to the following exchange between Marc and his mother.

"So, everyone," announced Marc, "we're going to do something new and unusual here. I had my mom out for Christmas and we were talking about stocks and she happened to have bought a stock we were

---

[1] They included various guests on the show. At Cohodes' invitation, I joined him and Montgomery for one session to answer generic questions about the SEC. The head of the SEC's Internet unit guested on a later program.

short. And I threatened to call her up and discuss it with her. So sure enough, I'm going to see if I can call up and surprise my mom."

Sound of telephone connection being made.

"Hi, Mom."

"Hi, honey."

"Mom, we have you on the radio program and I want you to tell the listeners why you bought Black Box. The symbol is BBOX."

"Because I think it's supposed to be a great company."

"Mom, now! You should know better. Did you do any research on this company?"

"I did not."

"How did you hear about this company?"

"I cannot divulge my sources."

Marc sighs in exasperation.

"Part of the show is, as you know, for educational purposes, and I was very troubled to learn that you bought a stock off a friend's tip and did no research on it."

"Well, if you would give me more tips then I wouldn't have to do that."

Monty chortles.

"Mom, in this year ahead I will hopefully try to give you more tips but, as you know, it's not an easy market."

"I know that."

"I love you dearly but I was a little disappointed to know that you were buying stocks blindly in this treacherous market."

"Then you have to pay more attention to your old mother and give her some good advice."

So much for trying to tell Mom what's what.

Lernout got kicked around a lot on the show. Marc and Monty mocked the company, its products, and its management—their tone much like that of a right-wing talk show host bashing Barney Frank.

Then there was Marc's presence on Lernout Internet threads. He posted under his own name and made no secret of his firm's short position. At least here he drew a response: taunts and insults from the Lernout faithful and one death threat. Upset over some ugly slurs, he sued to get a court order to identify the worst of the anonymous posters. The court held that no one could take seriously statements floating unclaimed in cyberspace. That meant, in its view, Cohodes had suffered no harm. So the message board *lumpenproletariat* was left to snipe, smear, and threaten to its heart's content. As it does to this day.

★ ★ ★

My initial reaction was tepid. I had never done an international case and didn't know what it would involve. It sounded like biting off a mouthful. Also, Marc was a voice in the wilderness on Lernout. His views had found little support in the financial press other than Greenberg's pieces, and no attention from the sell-side, save one negative report from a Lehman analyst. I was not about to start throwing subpoenas at a big foreign company based on the unconfirmed musings of a short-seller.

Still, it wasn't a walk-away. The phony product angle was intriguing. One of my early cases as a staff attorney involved a satellite television operation that had regaled potential investors with the clarity of its purported satellite feed. In fact, the images came from a tape machine located in another room and hard-wired into the demonstration monitors. No one can claim such conduct falls into a gray area. Also, the more unorthodox and complex a transaction, the more likely it will be accounted for incorrectly. Whatever else might be said of Lernout management, it displayed great creativity in structuring its deals.

And, damn, Marc was persistent.

The odds quickly mounted that whenever the phone rang, it would be him with a new fact or insight. Without asking, I assumed his fund had a big short position in Lernout and he resented the buoyancy of its share price. From early 1999 to March 2000, it went from a few bucks to $65. This was a short-seller's worst nightmare. While a long buy can never result in more than a 100 percent loss (should the stock go to $0), losses on a short position are theoretically infinite. A short that goes on a wild run can turn into a black hole sucking down the fund's assets to meet escalating collateral calls.

Which was not my problem.

In later days, Marc would opine that the SEC was woefully derelict in its obligations to the short side in general and himself specifically. He would call with what he considered great information and want instant love. He would get instead: "thanks for the call . . . anything else?" His reproaches were couched in terms of how often in the past his fund's research had been on target, as if the Kafkaesque obstacle course of the commission's internal process could be made to vanish simply because the matter came from *that* Marc Cohodes. In his comparatively rare calls, David Rocker would complain more bluntly that the agency should act more quickly on tips from the street, particularly theirs. He was vinegar to Marc's honey.

This being before the Google era, information on foreign companies was even more elusive than today. I wandered by the SEC's Office of International Affairs to see if help was available there, and thus began what would become a lengthy tutorial in the vagaries of international law enforcement. There are some countries whose regulators are sufficiently tight with the SEC that they will provide assistance without a lot of red tape. Others require a request under a treaty (approved by the U.S. Senate) before handing over anything to a foreign government. International treaties often address criminal violations exclusively and are therefore useless to the SEC, a civil agency, unless someone at the Department of Justice can be persuaded to take an interest, real or feigned. Finally there are countries that will provide information to U.S. law enforcement at about the time that curling becomes the official sport in hell. Some are fraud havens whose economies are based on hiding assets for crooks and tax cheats. I was also cautioned that, merely by calling into some countries without permission, I, as a government official, could face criminal charges should I thereafter be caught within their borders. France was a case in point.

It looked like it would take a treaty request to get anything out of Belgium. Not good. Even if we could arrange this, it might take years before we got the first piece of paper. We tried the International Office at Justice to see if its people had any suggestions. Over the phone, it sounded as if it were staffed by one career employee who didn't get out much, slouching around an office piled high with dog-eared reports and moldy coffee cups. The guy had a few ideas but was pessimistic about getting much from the Belgians. We called the U.S. Embassy in Brussels for whatever it could provide. This eventually arrived in the form of a folder of articles about Lernout & Hauspie from the European press. Not exactly John LeCarré material.

It seemed from its press coverage that Lernout & Hauspie truly *was* the Microsoft of Belgium. The company was the creation of computer technician Jo Lernout and tax accountant Pol Hauspie. Having acquired cheap software from someone else's failed company, they set up shop in Ieper, Belgium, and, in 1987, began growing speech recognition technology. This was an area of the country not known for much other than complaining about people from other areas of the country. Certainly not for technological innovation. The two men became local notables even before they made their first sale.

After years of development-stage purgatory, everything clicked for the two entrepreneurs around 1995. Lernout products—and its *story*, marrying regional pride to profit potential—began to sell. The local investors who had carried the company though its lean years were joined by major financial players. From there it went straight up. Acquisition binges kept the company's revenue growth on an upward tangent. Stairstep increases in reported profits and endless product promotes made it a flash stock in Europe. By 2000, the company's market capitalization topped $10 billion.

It became the anchor for the "Flanders Language Valley," a "campus" of speech technology companies planted in the rolling cow pastures of North Belgium and projected to be Europe's answer to Silicon Valley. The project reeked of vision. Its roadways were laid out to mimic the anatomy of the human ear. The Belgian prime minister presided over its dedication. The persons of Mssrs. Lernout and Hauspie were now symbols of a shining information-age future for the Flanders region. They graced magazine covers, won investments from Microsoft and Intel, and conversed intimately with the King of Belgium.

I have struggled to reconstruct the chronology of our early attempts to come to grips with Lernout & Hauspie. My group had several other big accounting cases going; so, as usual, we were thin on the ground. In the early phase of the investigation, most of the work was done not by any of the group's line attorneys, all otherwise occupied, but by an administrator, Deb Heilizer, while she oversaw a dozen other cases. This was typical of the workload carried by Deb, generally unrecognized and always without complaint.

We hesitated before contacting the company, fretting that investors might decide to vote with their feet if news of our investigation hit the market the wrong way. Lernout was under no legal requirement to disclose an inquiry from the SEC. But many companies choose to do so, if for no other reason than to protect their executives from charges of insider trading if they sell stock while an undisclosed investigation is pending. It also seemed possible we might trigger an international incident if the Belgian government accused us of harassing its celebrity business. Deciding we had seen enough to justify going forward, however, we sent Lernout a request for a pile of documents.

We needn't have worried about the potential repercussions. Lernout would feel no need whatsoever to inform the public of our interest. Nor were its officers shy about dumping Lernout stock without disclosing the pending SEC inquiry. Jo Lernout, for example, sold $25 million of his stock in July 2000 alone.

The company took the familiar hedgehog approach. Its lawyers did what securities defense lawyers do best: stall and evade. When we asked for documents, we were told the amount requested was unmanageably large. When we asked about specific transactions, we were told that would violate confidentiality agreements with customers. To increase our leverage, we obtained authority from the commission to issue subpoenas. Because Lernout had a U.S. office, we could serve it without going through an international treaty. Its lawyers said they would start looking and keep us informed of their progress.

Finding that the company's CEO, Gaston Bastiaens, was in the United States, we brought him in for questioning. His demeanor was surly and his denials comprehensive and categorical. We had nothing on paper to dispute his statements and wrote off the meeting as a frustrating first pass. We would never get our hands on him again.

The company's auditors were also no help. KPMG Belgium flatly refused our request for their work-papers (the files auditors must keep to prove they really did an audit), citing Belgian client-confidentiality laws. In the United States, auditors are prohibited from releasing client files without a subpoena or the consent of the client. We badgered Lernout management into providing a letter of consent. KPMG Belgium, however, claimed that wasn't enough to protect it from liability. Someone else might decide to sue them. A customer perhaps. We asked a Belgian law firm for its opinion and were told the law was unclear. I would eventually form the opinion that *all* Belgian law is unclear and therefore there is little to be gained from hiring local attorneys. Subpoenas made no difference. KPMG, like other international accounting firms, is legally compartmentalized on a national basis, like fifteenth-century Medici banks. We were told there was no formal legal relationship between KPMG Belgium and other national offices, including the U.S. operation. That they share the designation "KPMG" is little more than coincidence. Try to get documents from KPMG Belgium by serving a subpoena on anything in the United States—other than a partner on a family vacation at Disney World—and prepare for a lecture on the sheer ignorance behind such a wildly ill-considered and legally inappropriate action.

Thinking the Disney World angle might actually be worth a try, we set up a "border watch" with U.S. Customs in hopes of tagging a Belgian partner coming into the country. Nothing came of it. These guys were not into The Mouse. Or they realized they were better off with an ocean between them and us.

Because Lernout & Hauspie filed reports with the SEC, its auditors were required by a rule of the accounting profession to have their work reviewed annually by an American CPA. A KPMG U.S. partner performed this task. You might suppose this would represent an opportunity to capture Belgian audit documents. You would then be mistaken. The U.S. review was limited to major audit issues and didn't involve grubbing around in piles of work papers. And the small amount of paper sent to the United States for review was promptly bounced back to Belgium, storage space apparently being at a premium here.

   Notice of an SEC inquiry will sometimes send a company's auditors scrambling to determine if and how badly they screwed up. This is not a matter of professional pride but a necessary prerequisite to damage control. Once they understand the problems, they can take credit for making the company correct them and, further, get a head start on fashioning an argument that they were all management's fault and not theirs. The auditors were lied to or at least given faulty information. Management, also scambling to get a grip on things, will of course claim that the problems *were so* the auditors' fault or, failing that, the fault of previous management or, failing that, the fault of lower management.

   This situation is pure joy if you're a government investigator. Everyone fingers everyone else in individualized variations on the SODDI defense ("some other dude did it") and you get a good idea of the story early on. This allows you to guide the investigation without false starts and wasted effort and puts important witnesses in the bag. It didn't happen with Lernout & Hauspie. KPMG Belgium internal e-mails, as later churned up in private litigation, reflect some tentative finger-pointing, but no real attempt to look behind the curtain and face whatever was lurking there. Nor was management quick to start any such painful process.

   The initial exposure of what would soon be seen as the biggest financial fraud in European history would come from an altogether different source.

★ ★ ★

In early 2000, Lernout purchased two American companies, Dragon Systems and Dictaphone Corporation. The sales were largely financed with Lernout stock, then priced at a nose-bleed level. As a result of these acquisitions, the bulk of its assets by balance sheet value were located in the United States. This meant Lernout no longer qualified for the relatively lax disclosure standards otherwise applied to foreign companies, and had to comply with the same rules as U.S. companies. When, in June 2000, Lernout filed reports under the more exacting standards, it disclosed for the first time the geographic distribution of its sales. And the house of cards that was Lernout & Hauspie began to tremble.

From these reports it was apparent the company owed its continued revenue growth, the biggest factor in its surging share price, to massive sales in, of all places, South Korea. Lernout's Korean sales had gone from less than $100,000 in the first quarter of 1999 to $59.9 million in the same quarter of 2000, and now made up more than half of its worldwide sales. Business everywhere else was anemic, and indeed even declining in Europe and North America.

Why would anyone care? What difference did it make where Lernout made its money as long as it made more of it each quarter?

It mattered because these figures defied common sense. It was not plausible South Korea could gobble up as much of the company's speech-recognition software as the entire rest of the planet. What's more, a huge percentage of the company's sales from the previous year had come from Singapore. This, too, made little sense.

The first people to notice this absurdity were Marc Cohodes and Monty Montgomery, who studied the company's reports as if poring over the will of a rich relative. They scratched their heads and called someone they knew at a different software company in South Korea and asked if Lernout was some sort of national fad, like pet rocks or hula hoops. He said he could see *no* market for Lernout products there. Marc and Monty concluded the numbers were phony and conveyed this view with great conviction to anyone they could buttonhole. *MarketWatch* columnist Herb Greenberg, already a Lernout skeptic, jumped on the issue first. Crediting Marc for the catch, he pounded on the weirdness of Lernout's Asian numbers. This enraged Lernout supporters, who in web postings denounced Greenberg as a shameless belly-crawling shill of the short-sellers, whose continued existence was a blatant affront to the integrity of the capital markets.

Close on Greenberg's heels came a team of *Wall Street Journal* reporters led by Jesse Eisinger and Mark Maremont. In early August 2000, they questioned Lernout's claim that its Korean sales boom was attributable to its purchase of a small local company. They contacted some of Lernout's purported customers. A few said they had never heard of Lernout—others that they had bought its products but in smaller amounts than the company claimed.

The stock dropped precipitately with the article's publication, wiping $1 billion from Lernout's market cap.

The company fought back, as companies will. It denounced the *Journal* article as riddled with errors, claiming its reporters "did not know how to question Koreans." Its CEO accused Rocker Partners of being behind a smear campaign. One of the *Journal* reporters, Eisinger, had previously worked for an Internet publication in which Rocker Partners owned a minority interest. This gave Lernout an opening to attack his credibility.

Despite the continued loyalty of most sell-side analysts, Lernout could not stone-wall indefinitely. The *Journal*'s continuing coverage and the SEC's demands for information finally caused the Lernout board to emerge from hibernation. It asked its auditors to do a special review of the company's financials and hired an American law firm to investigate its Asian sales. By the end of August, CEO Bastiaens had "resigned" and been replaced by John Duerden, former head of one of the American companies acquired by Lernout with its pumped-up stock.

Cohodes was quoted as predicting this was the "beginning of the end" for his nemesis. If the company actually made its income projections for the year, he said, he would go to its headquarters and "serve them all lunch wearing a dress." This was more a threat than a promise. Had they been personally acquainted with Cohodes—an individual with the physique of a shot-putter—they would likely have found the thought of him invading their sanctuary in women's clothing highly disturbing.

That prospect, however, vanished in early November when the company announced it would amend its financial statements for the previous two and one-half years to fix "errors and irregularities." This is accountant-speak for "okay, yes, the books are cooked." There was no longer any doubt Lernout & Hauspie was in trouble. The question was whether it was a real company that had done some bad things or a complete fraud destined to vanish under a scrim of lawsuits.

John Duerden's first priority as the new CEO was to run down the real story behind the Korean bonanza. The company's balance sheet reflected $100 million from these sales, all of it supposedly on deposit in Korean banks. Lernout desperately needed that cash to be in Belgium but, for reasons that were unclear, it was stuck in Korea. Duerden flew to Seoul to pry it loose. His trip was not a success.

On his return journey, Duerden stopped in Washington to brief us on what he had learned. Sitting in one of the SEC's drably oppressive testimony rooms, looking like he had not slept in days, he told a strange and alarming story. The head of Lernout's Korean operations, Joo Chul Seo, had been a difficult man to pin down on the whereabouts of the $100 million in sales proceeds so crucial to the survival of the company. The sales at issue, incidentally, had prompted the payment to Joo of a $25 million performance bonus the previous year. When pressed by Duerden, Joo admitted the money was gone. He said he had given it back to the customers.

This profoundly unsatisfying answer was to receive no elaboration from Joo. His interview with Duerden ended in melodrama when three men stormed into the room, yelling and gesticulating wildly. They grabbed the struggling Joo and frog-marched him into an adjacent office. From the shouts and bangs that came through the wall, Duerden concluded Joo was being soundly thrashed by the intruders. Finding himself an unwilling character in an Eric Ambler novel, he paused only long enough to urge other employees to call the police before he scampered for the airport.

Upon reflection, Duerden wondered if the altercation had been staged as a means of covering Joo's abrupt departure from the country. Joo was later spotted in mainland China, living with a brother who ran a necktie factory. Presumably he took his performance bonus with him. It also seems the wily Joo had pilfered another $30 million by pledging as collateral for a loan the assets of the Korea branch of the Flanders Language Valley Fund, an investment company closely linked to Lernout & Hauspie.

The American law firm retained by the company would confirm and add detail to what was by now widely assumed: the Korean business was a sham. It sent a squad of lawyers to Seoul to go through company documents, something the SEC was not able to do. They eventually pried enough paper from the clutches of hostile Korean employees to conclude that most of the Korean sales were contingent on the "customer" reselling the product to someone else, or had been paid for with disguised loans from Lernout Korea. The lawyers also confirmed what we had learned separately though contacts with the Korean banks. Although the company claimed it had "factored" (sold at discount) receivables to these banks, in truth the company had guaranteed the receivables with blocked deposits at the same banks. A factoring with recourse against assigned assets is, in substance, a secured loan and not a sale. At the very least, the company should have disclosed these transactions for what they were.

Meanwhile, evidence piled up that Lernout's accounting abuses were not limited to Korea. The Singapore Securities Commission told us that the majority of Lernout's purported customers in that country shared one mailing address. A stringer for the *Journal* visited the address and confirmed it was a letter drop. Corporate documentation from Singapore showed these companies had no operations there and were run from Belgium.

It became apparent the company's sales to a multinational constellation of start-up companies were also tainted with fraud. These "language development companies" had supposedly paid Lernout to use its software to build speech-recognition technology for a variety of regional languages. But questions abounded. The dollars were large to be coming from start-ups and the commercial rationale dubious. If Lernout was having trouble selling its major language products, who was going to buy software to translate Farsi into God-knows-what? As became increasingly clear, no one. A Bahrain bank that had played a pivotal role in some of these deals unaccountably decided to hand over its documents to the SEC. In the "sales" they described, the customer could get its money back if it couldn't sell the Lernout products to others. Some digging showed that the "language development companies" were barely more than shells, staffed by Lernout employees and partly funded by its friends at the Flanders Language Valley Fund.

Years later, the European press added a cloak-and-dagger wrinkle to this aspect of the Lernout story. According to the Belgian newspaper *De Standaard*, one of sponsors of the language development companies was a German agent. The paper asserted that the start-ups were partially funded by German intelligence in hopes they would develop language technology helpful for monitoring communications in countries that, well, needed monitoring.

By the end of 2000, Lernout was in bankruptcy in the United States and Belgium, its share price had fallen by 99 percent, Mssr. Hauspie was hospitalized for depression, and the Belgian authorities had announced a criminal investigation. Unfamiliar with the Belgian justice system, I called the U.S. Embassy in Brussels and spoke with its legal attaché, a friendly FBI agent. I asked which of the various Belgian law enforcement agencies was involved. As near as she could tell, she said, it was all of them. This was the biggest scandal to hit Belgium since King Leopold's misadventures in the Congo. Everyone wanted a piece of it.

That sounded great to me. People on the ground getting to the bottom of things.

The "legat" set me straight. She said the last big Belgian financial fraud was 10 years ago and was *still* nowhere near trial. Something involving a carpet company. The Belgian government, she said, is completely incompetent. The Belgians will admit this when drunk. Many want to go to America, where things work most of the time. Of course, they hate us too. What do you expect from a country whose only major artist was a surrealist? And as for expecting any help from the authorities—ha!—they don't even know how to help themselves.

I had no idea what to make of this. Had she been dumped by a Belgian boyfriend, or perhaps gotten a bad plate of mussels for lunch, and decided to hold it against the whole country? I was later to meet Belgian officials who were anything but incompetent. The legat's prediction of problems in dealing with them on this case, however, was dead on. Our repeated attempts to set up a dialogue were ignored. I offered to come to Belgium and meet with whoever was in charge. The reply was always the same: the time is not yet right. And when would it be right? We'll let you know.

By early 2001, we were spinning our wheels. The major witnesses and critical documents were an ocean away and under the control of a foreign government unmoved by our need to conclude our investigation. The only significant player in the United States was former CEO Bastiaens. When he was picked up by the FBI on an extradition order and shipped back to Belgium, we were left with only small fry. They told us about revenue scams by the U.S. operation. Most were in small dollars and came down to booking sales before the company had any reason to think it would get paid. All the real action was abroad.

Without the help of the Belgian authorities we were, in short, screwed.

★ ★ ★

In the spring of 2001, I attended a conference on financial crime in Cambridge, England. In a jet-lagged haze, I awakened halfway though a rainy afternoon barely in time to give a paper on Internet scams. I listened to several other papers as boring as my own, then killed part of the evening wandering the "backs" behind King's College. This was much like stepping into a Constable landscape: arched bridges across meandering streams, with here and there a picturesque cow, and the spires of Cambridge in the distance. I was completely alone in the mist and drizzle—not counting the cows—when there appeared a man in a wheelchair pushed by an attendant. As they passed, I recognized physicist Stephen Hawking. He was wearing a rain hat.

I was tempted to tag along for a quick tutorial on the workings of the universe. But I resisted. Who knew what profound insights he was about to grasp in his twilight perambulations that I might be responsible for spoiling? *Damn!, I almost* had *it and then this stupid American tourist comes bouncing up and breaks my chain of thought.*

That night I picked up a phone message that the Belgians had finally agreed to a meeting and wanted to hold it immediately. I was as ecstatic. I assumed this meant we would soon be allowed to tap into the deep vein of evidence the Belgian authorities were mining. A day later, I took the Chunnel train across the softly rolling fields of northern France to Brussels, and arrived in the early afternoon at the address I had been given on Waterlooand Road, little knowing that I was about to learn a painful lesson.

I expected to meet with a handful of prosecutors in shirtsleeves: a working meeting to discuss how to coordinate our efforts and share information. No such thing. The meeting room was packed from end to end with representatives of the Belgian legal and political establishments, the table that ran its length barely big enough to hold them all. The State Department was well represented. The local and national prosecutors' offices attended in mass. In the French fashion, there was an investigating magistrate (*judge d'instruction*) to oversee the prosecutors. He was very young and the only person in the room who spoke no English. Whether all these bodies were working a single investigation or several was unclear.

It was their country but—they quickly let me know—my meeting. The assembled multitude eyed me with a bland curiosity, as if encountering a new biological species of uncertain utility, and left it to me to engage them. I expounded on the joys of trans-Atlantic cooperation and the expertise the SEC could provide to assist their efforts. I pretended that much of the action would take place in the United States. They listened indulgently, from time to time prodding me with skeptical questions.

It became evident they were here today not to join hands with the U.S. government in common cause, but rather to gauge how intrusive we intended to be into what they saw as a peculiarly Belgian matter. The legat had said they would consider it a matter of national pride that the locals punish those responsible for the implosion of their most prominent business, rather than leave it to foreigners. Not to mention the havoc that could be created by a busload of Neanderthal Americans tromping around the countryside poking into relationships between Lernout & Hauspie and various prominent Belgians who had been its political and financial supporters.

I could understand their attitude. Doubts about the sensitivity of our government to the concerns of other nationalities were not unique to this group and hardly irrational. Still, I was not in a position to say: go for it and, if you get a chance, drop us a line and let us know how it turns out. Lernout & Hauspie had cost U.S. investors hundreds of millions of dollars and bought large U.S. companies with worthless stock. The SEC would be expected to do more than sit on its hands for the decade I had been told it would take the Belgians to resolve things.

The dance went on for two hours with little ground gained or lost. When the top dog from the Belgian State Department, a lovely dresser with impeccable English, finally called it a day, and I had shaken a long parade of hands, I found myself accompanied to the train station by the head of the Ieper police. He seemed to have some use for me, unlike everyone else. A railroad workers' strike in France had backed up trains across Northern Europe. He sat with me in the station bar while I waited for my long-delayed train. His English was weak but I gleaned from the conversation that the political situation was tense. Wheels within wheels. There was conflict within the Belgian delegation as to who would be in charge. He was afraid he would be left by the wayside as more powerful interests directed the case.

I thought: If so, you should probably count yourself lucky.

Due to the rail strike, I arrived at Waterloo station well after midnight. The London cabdrivers had their own strike going and would pick up only previously arranged fares. So I walked from the station, south of the Thames, to my hotel by Hyde Park in new shoes bought for the Cambridge conference. There were no lights in the park and the night was moonless. I hobbled along through the inky dark, each step more painful than the last, following one path, then another.

When I reached my hotel, my socks were red with blood.

★ ★ ★

Eight years later, little has changed with Lernout & Hauspie.

In the summer of 2001, the Belgian police arrested Mssrs. Lernout and Hauspie and two other officers of the company. These former masters of industry languished in jail for three months without being charged—as permitted under Belgian law—and without, I've been told, giving up anything to the prosecutors.

Lernout, at least, made the most of his period of confinement. He designed a robotic guinea pig responsive to voice commands. It was not reported whether his efforts were commercially motivated or spurred by a desire to arrange companionship for what might be a long term in prison.

Eventually boxes of paper began making their way across the Atlantic. Most of the documents, fortunately, were in English and, between what we could gather from them and what we learned from other sources, we were able to quantify the company's fraud. It was enormous. Phony transactions with related parties in Belgium had been good for $60 million. The litter of "language development companies" to which Lernout gave birth in the late 1990s added another $110 million in fictional revenue, supporting the false impression of exponential growth.

Reported revenues from Korea were $175 million. The bulk came from contingent sales or sales financed indirectly by Lernout. It is an open question how much of the fraud was directed from Ieper and how much was a side project of Mr. Joo. Given that it was a crude fraud that must eventually have been detected—unlike the more elaborate and opaque devices favored by the Belgians—it was quite possibly the latter. Joo may have planned from the outset to skip to the PRC, pockets bulging with Lernout cash, the moment he could no longer stall demands from Belgium to unlock the Korean bank accounts. It has been suggested that, rather than a rogue operator, Joo was the front man for a Chinese gang that cleverly contrived to fleece Lernout while it, in turn, fleeced others. If so, it was a good plan. Joo grabbed quite a pile and Korean attempts to prosecute him *in absentia* for bank fraud and embezzlement were dropped for (get this) lack of evidence.

In 2003, we drafted a district court complaint against Lernout. The result was an order against a defunct company requiring that it not commit fraud again. It had no practical effect other than to provide an official version of what ranked as Europe's biggest financial fraud until, several years later, it was outdone by the Italian dairy company Parmalat. That was hardly satisfying.

Early in the Lernout investigation, I tried to convince a prosecutor at the U.S. Attorney's Office in Manhattan to open a parallel criminal inquiry. It was, after all, an historic fraud with huge losses to American investors. When I told him how much of the case was overseas, he laughed. He understood what I had yet to learn. For U.S. regulators, the map of the world beyond our shores should bear the legend "terra incognito," and sometimes "there be dragons." Paper agreements mean little in the face of *real politic* concerns. If, in pursuing foreign malefactors, you obtain the assistance of the local authorities, you might just cover yourself in glory. Without it, you will likely cover yourself in something else entirely.

In May 2007, Belgian prosecutors opened the criminal trial of Lernout, Hauspie, and other former executives of their company. As of this writing, no verdicts have been announced. Private litigation remains pending in the United States and Belgium. Perhaps these court proceedings will add to what we know. But that would be cold comfort for those defrauded by a company once heralded as ushering in the financial future to a formerly neglected part of northern Europe.

Which, in fact, it did—if not in the sense expected. Considering the procession of corporate scandals witnessed over the following years—Enron and WorldCom, Sunbeam and Conseco—Lernout & Hauspie was indeed ahead of its time.

Chapter 5

AremisSoft and the Deemster from Hell

I n early 2001 there was a loud buzz about a possibly crooked software company run out of Cyprus, India, London, and New Jersey. Marc Cohodes had it in his sights. So did his next-door neighbor, Dave Scially, then of West Highland Capital. Scially is the anti-Cohodes, as measured and understated as Marc is outspoken. I also received calls from a few people I'd never heard from before and never would again. Bringing up the rear was investigative reporter Herb Greenberg, formerly with the *San Francisco Chronicle*, at this point doing an online column for *TheStreet.com*. He was also lit up about this company.

Herb in high school was the kid who looked years younger than he was, played a good game of tennis without coming close to being a jock, and would be dislodged from the honor roll when dogs play the accordion. The cynicism that marks many reporters never took with

Herb. His open personality displayed not a hint of guile and his devotion to his trade was unwavering.

So it goes without saying Herb was one of the most hated figures in financial journalism. He had popped too many bubble stocks not to have acquired passionate enemies. They had coalesced into something of a cult. Herb was always on the verge of being sued by some company whose dirty linen he had exposed. And it sometimes seemed the Internet was invented primarily so that message-board trolls could accuse Herb Greenberg of being an ignorant—if not indeed consciously corrupt—shill for short-sellers.

Herb, in fact, provided a ready ear for the likes of Scially and Cohodes and whoever else he thought might give him fodder for his column. That much was true. It was also his job. He was an investigative journalist. Talking to potential sources is what such people do. That does not mean they are part of a conspiracy to prey upon innocent companies.

The same goes for government investigators. They have to start somewhere. Nothing comes from nothing. No one finds anything from cold readings of SEC filings, which amount to millions of pages a year. Without leads from outside the bureaucracy, ignorance reigns. So the door is left open to the plaints of disgruntled employees, pissed-off investors and repentant corporate stooges. Even short-sellers. Much of what rolls in is junk. But ignore the lot and you also miss out on the occasional rare find that elevates the job beyond routine into an adventure charged with a genuine sense of purpose.

So it was with AremisSoft Corporation.

Whenever I question whether my 13 years at the SEC were well spent, I think about this company and decide, yes, I could have done worse with my time.

★   ★   ★

In 1999, AremisSoft announced a $37.5 million contract with an agency of the Bulgarian government. It had something to do with automating the country's healthcare system. Together with a general upsurge in reported revenues, this deal, which the company touted for a year and a half, pushed the price of the NASDAQ-listed stock up 10-fold until the company boasted a market cap of $1 billion. All the while, corporate insiders were unloading. By early 2001, stock sales by the two top executives, both Cypriot nationals, totalled half a billion dollars. This, however, was not fully apparent from their SEC filings.

The Bulgarian contract was an exhibit to an AremisSoft SEC filing. Dave Scially, gifted with a long attention span, did what no one on the sell-side had attempted and actually read the thing. Its language didn't jibe with the company's press release, the contract coming out at more like $3.75 million than $37.5 million. That was the amount AremisSoft was sure to get paid. Then there were two "letters of intent" that might be worth something someday. No way to tell. Scially found articles in Bulgarian newspapers and spoke with officials of other Bulgarian agencies to confirm that the contract was for the smaller amount. After making some of the same calls as Scially and trying unsuccessfully to get answers out of the company, Herb Greenberg started writing skeptically about the deal. AremisSoft claimed falsely that Greenberg hadn't called it for its explanation, and then said it didn't matter anyway because the deal accounted for only about 5 percent of its expected revenue for the year.

That spring I struggled to staff a raft of accounting cases I knew were winners. Involving, as it did, one transaction lost in a fog of claims and counterclaims, AremisSoft, by comparison, seemed a marginal prospect. Also, I cringed at the idea of seeking information from Bulgaria, a country I envisioned buried deep in the shadows of Eastern Europe, with one foot in the middle ages. The prospect brought to mind the scene from *Dracula* in which the young lawyer is driven through the wild Carpathian night to the count's waiting castle. I could see some poor SEC attorney, possibly me, stepping from the coach in cap-toed Oxfords, briefcase in hand. Wolves howl in the nearby forest. Lightning flashes and the sign above the castle entrance lurches out of the darkness: "Bulgarian Health Sector Reform Project."

The thought gave me chills.

If the company had sprung a decent explanation for the apparent discrepancy in its numbers, I would have passed on it, at least until more dirt came to light. But its response to Greenberg was so lame it rang an alarm bell. It was like seeing the first cockroach. If a company has one deal that bad, it's a good bet there are others.

I asked one of my staff attorneys, Richard Rosenfeld, and his immediate supervisor, Rob Keyes, to dig around and see what popped out.

Rich was among the division's more remarkable young attorneys, impossible to ignore if anywhere in the vicinity. Heavy-set but bouncy, Rich occupied rooms like an invading army. He was incapable of a private conversation. The building's papier-mâché walls were no match for his resonant voice. A sort of benevolent manipulator, he always had some creative approach to indulging his personal objectives while at the same time contributing to the agency's agenda. His ability to dodge boring assignments was legendary. And should things get slow around the SEC, he would find a back-door way of being loaned to some U.S. Attorney's office to do criminal securities cases.

When Rich hurt his foot in a skiing accident, he milked the situation to wear sandals and Bermuda shorts around the office for a good six months, much to the chagrin of elements in the Division's front office. I let him get away with stuff for the simple reason that, like everyone else outside *uber*-management, I liked Rich. Plus he accomplished things. He was smart, energetic, funny, and fearless. He would go up against anyone, including his supervisors, and generally prevail.

Rob Keyes, then in his late 40s, had been with the commission about five years. In previous life phases, he had been a Catholic priest and a partner in a San Francisco litigation firm, demonstrating an unusual combination of gentle soul and tough mind.

At first they both wondered what had possessed me to waste time on some offshore deal involving the Bulgarian healthcare system, which I wondered as well.

But not for long. Within a month, the cockroach theorem proved a winner. When we contacted other purported AremisSoft customers, we found few solid sales. Some of the entities could not be located. Others had no business activities that would justify major purchases of software. A few had never heard of AremisSoft. It was now obvious we had a probable fraud on our hands, and we contacted the company for a load of documents.

Meanwhile press coverage intensified. Greenberg banged away. Financial reporter Alex Berenson, later to become a best-selling author of spy novels, raised questions about the company in the *New York Times*.

AremisSoft, for the moment undaunted, took the battle to its detractors. In a press release it claimed its stock "was undervalued in the marketplace due to the concerted activities of unscrupulous short sellers who have been spreading false and misleading information. . . ." In early July 2001, it brought suit in federal court in San Francisco against Dave Scially, his fund, Rocker Partners, and Greenberg's employer, *TheStreet.com*. The complaint charged defamation and market manipulation. It would serve as the prototype for later retaliatory actions by public companies against short-sellers and obstreperous reporters. AremisSoft opened an additional front through its largest shareholder, corporate raider Irwin Jacobs. In Internet posts he accused Rocker Partners—which had been publicly critical of AremisSoft—of conspiring with Herb Greenberg to defame the company.[1]

This pugnacious stance, however, was short-lived. As July progressed, smoke started to pour from under the hood. AremisSoft failed to file its SEC report for the second quarter of 2001. That meant, at the very least, someone inside the company had serious questions about its numbers. And it led to the de-listing of AremisSoft stock from the NASDAQ. One of its cochairmen and a primary stock-dumper, Lycourgos Kyprianou, resigned abruptly, along with two other directors.

The board responded to the negative publicity and SEC inquiry by hiring a former SEC Enforcement director, Gary Lynch, to conduct an internal investigation. A patrician figure—tall and thin, with sharp features under a crest of gray hair—Lynch headed the division during the Milken-Boesky years. He was at this point an elite article of the defense bar. Having been burned a few times, I viewed company-initiated investigations as presumptive exercises in stalling, if not outright misdirection. But Lynch justified his princely rates with a memorable report.

He'd sent teams of accountants and lawyers to AremisSoft offices worldwide, including those in Nicosia, Cyprus, and Bangalore, India. They'd questioned every warm body and rooted through every file in sight. On August 6, 2001, Lynch presented his findings to a half-dozen SEC attorneys assembled in a conference room. He seemed to enjoy the

---

[1] To his credit, after it became apparent that AremisSoft was a blatant fraud, Jacobs apologized to Rocker Partners. He was quoted in the *New York Post* saying: "Look, I was wrong. Rocker and the short-sellers were right. Guys like them are part of the solution in addressing financial fraud."

drama of the situation. "This is going to be one of the most interesting days of your careers," he began. "The company can't find any support for $90 million in revenue."

It was, by this time, no surprise that AremisSoft had some bad sales. But the magnitude of the problem Lynch laid out was stunning. Ninety million dollars was three-quarters of what the company had booked the previous year through its "Emerging Markets" division, which provided the bulk of the company's total revenues and all its growth. And the admission that it "couldn't find any support for" these sales was unambiguous to those who knew the jargon. It meant they were a complete fiction.

Lynch elaborated. Supposedly major AremisSoft customers were, in fact, marginal businesses with no use for expensive software. One was a meatpacker in Eastern Europe. Other purported customers simply didn't exist.

The company's accounting records should have been available for inspection in its Bangalore office. But a squad of accountants drafted by Lynch from the local affiliate of Deloitte & Touche found the office in the process of abandonment, nearly denuded of people and furniture. As they came in the door, the manager of the office was talking on the phone in a dialect used solely by residents of one small Indian town, and which he surely assumed the interlopers would not understand. By chance, however, one of the Deloitte auditors was among the tiny fraction of the Indian populace native to that town. When the AremisSoft manager assured his listener that all the office documents had been destroyed, she caught every word.

And he had spoken too soon. A boy supporting a banker's box on each shoulder strode past and out the door. One of the Deloitte auditors had the presence of mind to follow him at a distance. Two blocks away, the boy emptied the boxes onto a roadside garbage heap and walked away.

Rescued from the makeshift dump, the several thousand pages of torn and coffee-stained documents told quite a story.

Included were serial drafts of AremisSoft financial statements that progressively inflated purported results without relationship to the actual performance of the company. The scribbled edits, as we would learn much later, were in the handwriting of Roys Poyiadjis. Nothing in the documents indicated the company had any real business.

AremisSoft, moreover, claimed to have rolled-up several hot Indian software developers at substantial cost. Rather than the thriving computer code factories it described, however, they were now revealed to be profitless items of subcontinental corporate flotsam, booked at absurdly high values to add heft to the company's balance sheet. One $100,000 acquisition, for example, was valued at $10.9 million—over 100 times its actual cost. Not exactly a rounding error.

Now, this was all well and good. A big bold fraud is always more interesting than the tentative sideways kind. But while everyone else was thinking about how they would soon become famous, at least inside the building, and couldn't wait for Lynch to leave so they could start leaping around and high-fiving one another, I experienced a sickening sense of déjà vu. The company's operations were mostly offshore. All its documents either destroyed or in far-flung corners of the world. Its primary honchos were in London, Cyprus, and Bangalore, and unlikely to accept an invitation to come the United States to explain just how they'd managed to pull off such a big-ass accounting fraud. And if we got a judgment against them, who knew if it would be enforceable in whatever countries they had, by then, come to roost?

So, in short, was this Lernout & Hauspie all over again?

It was an ugly thought. My mind wriggled and twisted like a bug on a pin trying to find some means to escape what might be my personal *Groundhog's Day*. But there was no going back. Now that we knew the company was a major fraud, we would be expected to do *something* about its gross abuse of our markets. Even if, ultimately, we could do no more than get empty judgments against a bunch of foreigners and educate American investors in exactly how badly they had been screwed, we would have to make the effort.

The matter was set to follow the standard SEC process of however-many-months filling up files, a few more months writing up a recommendation to the commission, and still more months for tag teams of bureaucrats to scrutinize the proposed action, all before anything definite would be allowed to occur.

In this instance, however, it was not to be.

The usual obsessional exercise was abruptly derailed. And the immediate cause of this development was a phone call from an island in the Irish Sea.

★ ★ ★

Up to this point, the Isle of Man was to me simply the residence of "Happy Jack" in the Who song of that name. I couldn't have found it on a map and had no idea it is a sovereign nation with its own financial system and regulators.

Then one day in August 2001 one of these regulators cold-calls the SEC, gets bounced around, and is finally routed to me. He wants to know if we have any interest in bank accounts held in the Isle of Man by an officer of a company reported to be under SEC investigation.

The company is AremisSoft and the officer is its president, Roys Poyiadjis.

Maybe. Depends. How much money are we discussing here?

"About two hundred million dollars."

He must wonder if he's lost the connection. "Yes, um, well, yes, that could be, eh. . . . Tell me, where are you located exactly?

In the ocean, he says. About halfway between Liverpool and Dublin. It's an island.

Okay, good. That sounds plausible. And the guy is very professional. Cordial and articulate. But he doesn't know anything about the SEC. He asks if we are a criminal agency. When I say no, strictly civil, his tone is regretful. Their laws only permit them to render assistance to foreign *criminal* agencies. So there probably isn't much that can be done.

If it's a criminal agency you want, I tell him, we've got lots of those. Give me your number and I'll find one that fits the bill.

The one I find is the U.S. Attorney's Office in Manhattan, a primary outpost of the Department of Justice. The attorney I go to, Steve Peikin, though still in his early 30s is somewhere close to the top of its securities fraud unit. I know him from another case and remember him as extremely able. None of the assistant U.S. attorneys I've dealt with are exactly party animals. You don't get those positions without being a full-blown workaholic with a minor in delayed gratification. These guys live on the edge—of obsession. So it is with Peikin. He has the relentlessly terse approach to conversation of someone who is trying to get more done in a day than is humanly possible. In his silences you can hear the wheels turn in his head. But a nice enough guy—as long as you don't try to jerk him around.

He jumps at the opportunity the situation presents. The company is a total fraud. Good start. That the crooks are offshore might have been fatal to his interest, but the Isle of Man element is unique. Typically, once money has gone offshore, it is in the wind. It can be moved electronically from country to country in an instant, while tracing a single transfer can take months or years. So funds easily can be sent many jumps ahead of anyone chasing them. But here—glorious luck—we know at the outset where a big chunk of the cash is parked. At least for now. If we can freeze the Isle of Man funds, we can then go through the necessary legal process to recover them for the company's victims. However long that takes. What a glitteringly beautiful prospect that is.

And it all begins so well.

The local ("Manx") authorities are as helpful as can be. An officer in the Isle of Man Constabulary explains informally that his government wants the country to be seen as a legitimate financial center, not a hideout for hot money. Cooperating with international law enforcement is part of the image makeover. In fact, a wave of reformist zeal is now hitting various countries long known for strict bank secrecy laws. This follows U.S. efforts to push the international banking community to shun countries on a fraud-haven list, potentially strangling their most lucrative industry. The real action, in any event, is in tax avoidance, not in laundering money for crooks. So this is a sensible move by the Manx. And in keeping with tradition. Their national emblem, a "triskelion," depicts three running legs radiating from a single point, like spokes in a wheel. I am told the meaning of this odd motif is "However we are thrown, we always land on our feet."

The constable sends us a lengthy memo about the local legal system and connects us to a very nice young lawyer in the Office of the Attorney General. Her name is Lindsey and she is English, not Manx, but the British and Manx legal systems are joined at the hip, so people can move back and forth between them. As explained to us, the Isle of Man generally adopts British legal standards, but on specific issues the process can take decades.

The AG's office assures Pekin it can obtain a freeze of the funds as soon as it receives official notice that criminal proceedings have been or soon will be filed. But this is not something Pekin can pull out of the air. He will need to be close to presenting evidence to a grand jury for an indictment. At this point he is just learning about the case. The fear, of course, is that Poyiadjis will get wind of our interest and, bang, move the whole two hundred million to Switzerland, Grand Cayman, Luxembourg, or any one of a number of Pacific island nations with few inhabitants but well-developed banking systems. After the AG discusses the matter with the relevant bank officials, we are promised a few days notice before the funds are transferred, but that is not enough to matter.

Building a case against Poyiadjis will, we realize, be no easy thing. The hard part of most financial cases isn't proving the company's numbers are wrong—that's often apparent from the outset—but tagging the responsible individuals. If there are bad sales, the financial people blame the sales people and vice versa; supervisors blame underlings and underlings experience selective memory loss. However intuitively obvious it may seem that a company can't manufacture the bulk of its revenues without the knowledge of top management, intuition and evidence are at most distant relatives in court.

Although Kyprianou and other officers went to ground at the first serious whiff of trouble, Poyiadjis is still hanging in with the company. He was on the board when it hired Gary Lynch to conduct an internal investigation, which hardly suggests a guilty mind. His office is in London, and the fraudulent transactions centered around Cyprus and India. No witness has fingered him as a culprit. So, as things stand, he can claim to have been kept in the dark by duplicitous colleagues without eliciting laughter.

Nor does the mere fact he dumped stock at a fortuitous moment prove his guilt. He can shrug and say he was diversifying his assets. Wouldn't you if you suddenly found you owned a paper fortune in one NASDAQ stock?

The stock angle leads to another, potentially fatal, complication. We are told the Isle of Man courts will expect proof the money in Poyiadjis' accounts came from sales of AremisSoft stock. One might ask, How else would he come up with a quick $200 million? But to freeze the accounts and keep them frozen, the Manx courts will require more than rhetorical questions.

All this is most depressing. What we imagined would be a straight road to an historic result we now see twisting away up the side of a procedural mountain.

As August slides into September, we struggle desperately to fill in the blanks. It is like defusing a ticking bomb without let-up for weeks on end. We know the money might vanish from the Isle of Man in a day. We also know we can do nothing to stop it. Not now. Maybe not ever.

But the more our goal takes on the hues of fantasy, the more necessary the effort seems. Government lawyers squander much time on projects of questionable value—for example, getting orders telling people to stop doing whatever bad thing it is they got caught doing years ago when the case was new. Orders that are often meaningless because either the person would never do *whatever* again under any circumstances or because he surely will do *whatever* at the first opportunity, order or no order. That spring we'd gotten an injunction on a man who croaked the day after the order was entered. This was considered a coup because, had we acted with less alacrity, the commission's stats for the year would have been reduced by one and all our efforts in that case been for naught. That our order was in place for less than a day before this person was enjoined, so to speak, by a higher power, permanently and completely, was beside the point.

Very rarely do we ever get the opportunity to truly right a wrong. And, given what we are paid in salary, capturing this amount of money would allow us to say with confidence that in hiring us the agency received a solid return on its investment.

I tell Rich that I don't care what he does, how many hours he spends, how many toes he squashes, so long as we bag the $200 million. The money has to come home. That will mean a lot. It will make up for a lot.

★　★　★

One Tuesday morning in September, I notice a standing-room-only crowd in what is anachronistically known as the Enforcement "ticker room," and squeeze in to see what the deal is. Above the Bloomberg terminals that long ago replaced the room's stock tickers is a TV monitor tuned to CNN. A clip of an instantly recognizable office tower runs over and over. A small silver object drifts across the screen and pierces the tower's side, which bleeds smoke upward into an empty sky. The program runs it again and again, like film on an editing machine. The announcer is trying to make sense of the event. How can an accident this bizarre happen in the middle of New York City?

Then a second object enters from the right edge of the screen and traces a path to a second tower, and it is clear that nothing is happening by accident.

We lose Peikin for over a day. His office is in St. Andrew's Plaza in lower Manhattan. Communications and traffic are in chaos. He has to walk from his office to his apartment far uptown.

Nevertheless, things continue apace as we attempt to piece together the money trail. We know from the Isle of Man police which Swiss banks wired funds into the Manx accounts. The problem is tracing Poyiadjis' AremisSoft stock sales into those Swiss accounts. From documents obtained in the United States without, we believe, setting off any alarms, we know Poyiadjis transferred millions of AremisSoft shares and options into the names of various nominees.[2] The options were exercised and all shares sent to agents in Europe, who ran them through foreign banks and then into corporate accounts with a New York City bank.

So far, so good. The next and we hope final stage requires tracing the money out of New York and into the specific Swiss banks that, in turn, transferred it into the Isle of Man. That will close the loop. But our luck does not extend that far. The New York bank effectively slams the door in our face. It makes hundreds of thousands of transfers into the Swiss banking system, it tells us, but *not* to individual Swiss banks. Instead, the funds go into a general clearing service—much like the Depository Trust Corporation in the United States—and the New York bankers have no way of knowing which Swiss banks are credited with particular transfers into the pool. We might eventually get this information from

---

[2]Kyprianou followed a similar process to dump his AremisSoft shares. The money from the sales went into accounts in Greece and the Caribbean but could, by this point, have been anywhere in the world.

the Swiss authorities, but the turnaround on such requests takes years. We will be lucky to have weeks.

The story from the bankers doesn't make perfect sense. Surely there has to be some identifying information accompanying each transfer to indicate who gets the money? Yes, yes, comes the response, but it is lodged in a numeric code to which only the Swiss are privy.

Still far from satisfied, we demand everything the New York bank has on its transfers of client funds to Swiss banks. We are told this is hundreds of thousands of pages of computer print-outs, most of it irrelevant to our investigation, and would be indecipherable to us anyway.

We obtain documents from the NASDAQ giving precise times for large sales of AremisSoft stock we suspect were made for Poyiadjis. Assuming the proceeds went straight through the New York account, as we have been told, this drastically narrows the time window for identifying the Poyiadjis transfers.

In response to a more specific directive, we receive several reams of partially redacted computer print-outs that, as we were warned, mean nothing to us. It is worse than looking for a needle in a haystack because the needles are indistinguishable from the hay. And that's where this aspect of the case might remain, but for the timely intervention of an SEC intern named Mike Wallander. Told to look at the documents up, down, and sideways to see if he can pull anything out of them, he takes the job seriously. One morning I arrive to find him asleep on Rich's floor.

It seems a thankless task until he comes to Rich with something he thinks might be significant. He noticed that the 30-digit code for each transfer has, imbedded toward the middle, a series of five numbers that follow certain patterns. Each of the transfers corresponding in amount to suspected Poyiadjis stock sales contains, in the position spotted by Wallander, one of four five-digit number sets. He and Rich question whether they reference the recipient banks. This would mean the transfer codes are like the routing numbers on personal checks, not the constantly mutating product of an algorithm known only to a few Zurich gnomes. If so, the question is which five-digit numbers correspond to which Swiss banks.

Rob and Rich barge into the headquarters of the New York bank demanding to know if it can provide an answer to that question. Bank attorneys decline to let them past the lobby, but bring out some back-office personnel to hear them yell. The back and forth goes on for some time with various threats made and denials offered until one of the lawyers says: "If you have what they want, give it to them."

What they have is precisely what we need: a single sheet of lined paper, pulled from someone's desk drawer, containing the handwritten names of Swiss banks and their corresponding five-digit identifying codes. The banks that received the funds from the Poyiadjis stock sales are the very banks that effected the transfers into the Isle of Man, and in approximately the same total amounts. The loop is closed.

★   ★   ★

On October 1, 2001, Peikin submits a declaration to the Attorney General of the Isle of Man stating that Roys Poyiadjis is the subject of a criminal investigation and his indictment is expected in the near future. Rich, who is rarely impressed by anything, is ecstatic about how well he has presented the case. "This guy is good," he says.

Three days later, an Isle of Man court grants the freeze application with the admonishment that the U.S. Attorney's Office must bring a criminal prosecution by January 4, 2002, or lose the freeze. It is the largest asset freeze in SEC history, albeit obtained through the good offices of the Department of Justice and the Isle of Man AG.

On October 4, the SEC files an action in federal court in New York City against AremisSoft, Poyiadjis, and Kyprianou, charging multiple counts of securities fraud. The suit was authorized a month before but held back until the Isle of Man freeze could be put in place. The court grants our motion for an asset freeze against the defendants, sought in the speculative hope we will eventually find assets belonging to these guys someplace where a U.S. court order matters. The commissioners, when voting out the action, were as jazzed as I've ever seen that crew. For once the agency could say it had been proactive. One commissioner was particularly emphatic. "I love this case," she said.

This is good because it means we will be less vulnerable to outbreaks of administrative cold feet when the bills started coming in. There is already cause for concern. After first being informed of the situation in the Isle of Man—a huge but potentially complicated opportunity—I trotted down the hall to inform the division director of this development. I brought Rich with me—thankfully no longer in his shorts-and-sandals phase. The director, lying on a couch in his office, listened to the story, one hand on his forehead. Arranged around him were other division notables.

When we had finished sketching out the situation, the director offered the suggestion that we simply get an injunction against the defendants and leave it at that. That way the division would get its stat without having to spend any more time or money on the matter.

There was a long silence as I scanned the expressionless faces flanking the director. I heard a sort of choking gargle from my immediate right and saw that Rich's body language signaled an imminent departure from standard institutional etiquette. To avoid a worse incident, I said something to the effect that I didn't think that was necessarily the best idea I'd ever heard. The temperature in the room dropped noticeably but, after some hemming and hawing, we emerged with our case intact.

The freeze order takes Poyiadjis by surprise. Normally as discreet as a charging hippopotamus, the government has for once successfully snuck up on someone. The day he learns of the enforcement action, he bolts from his London apartment to join Kyprianou in Cyprus. And there both will stay, confident Cyprus will not extradite two of its own citizens, but vulnerable to being picked up on an Interpol "red notice" should they leave the island. Neither, of course, will live in penury. Kyprianou made as much as Poyiadjis from pumping-and-dumping AremisSoft stock and, not having made the mistake of parking it in the Isle of Man, remains in control of his ill-gotten gains in whatever fraud haven they have come to rest. He is reputed to be the richest man in Cyprus. I hear he can be seen every night in the clubs, dancing on tables. Poyiadjis is also wealthy, independent of the frozen funds, although he will state otherwise to any court he thinks might respond with sympathy.

Our elation at obtaining the asset freeze is short-lived. The next month is spent supporting Peikin's case for an indictment. Like most people who don't practice criminal law, I thought grand juries hand out indictments whenever the government asks politely. Apparently not. At least not in the Southern District of New York. Peikin runs us ragged for a month—filling in this, explaining that—before he goes before the grand jury. In early November he obtains an indictment on a single count of securities fraud. This is much less than he intends to charge when the matter is fully developed but enough to satisfy the Isle of Man statute.

With the bank accounts frozen and the indictment in place we breathe a collective sight of relief. We've come a long way and believe the hard part is behind us. Isle of Man law enforcement has been supportive of our efforts so why not its judges? It seems a safe bet the island folk are of one mind on such things. Everyone there has to be at least a second cousin to everyone else.

In point of fact, the Isle of Man does not have judges. It has "Deemsters." This Dickensian appellation derives from their function of "deeming" things to be true or false, legal or illegal. We are told much of a Deemster's day-to-day involves disputes over competing claims to sheep. Whether or not this is said seriously, it seems certain our matter will test the legal acumen of whoever pops up on the bench to hear it.

And that test isn't long in coming.

The two "trustees" who are the nominal owners of the Poyiadjis accounts quickly file a raft of motions challenging the freeze and the standing of the U.S. government to bring an action against the accounts. As best we can tell, these two do nothing but launder money for people like Poyiadjis and beat away whatever competing claims might arise. One is said to be the richest man on the island. We seem to run up against the richest man on every island we hit.

Unfortunately, they know their profession well. The legal onslaught is immediate and effective. Any hope the Manx courts will quickly hand us the Poyiadjis millions dies in a volley of motions followed rulings hostile to our side. The Deemster could not be less deferential to the U.S. government or more sympathetic to the trustees. In a series of orders he treats the Manx AG—carrying water for the Department of Justice—like a chronic local nuisance, best ignored.

The trustees, first, request they be allowed to tap the frozen accounts to oppose this outrageous assault upon the rights of Mr. Poyiadjis. The Deemster gives them $30,000 a month. Each. And, of course, they will need to hire attorneys to assist them. Certainly. Take whatever you want and let me know from time to time how much it's running. They want to make sure the Bentley kept by Poyiadjis on the island will not be interfered with by any bumptious Americans. Hard on the upholstery. Motion granted. The Deemster also suggests arguments the trustees might have made but had somehow neglected. They thank him for his legal insights.

When the news of this debacle reaches our shores, the lamentations are loud. "We're getting our asses kicked," as Rob puts it. Rich is even less sanguine. He's certain this Deemster will never accept *any* order of an American court. So we will end up bringing an action there. "We're going to end up litigating this in the Isle of Man in front of this character," he moans. "And we're going to lose." The Manx AG, licking his wounds, has reached the same conclusion. He suggests we give it up.

The suddenness of this reversal of fortune leaves everyone stunned. Apparently this Deemster missed the memo saying that henceforth the Isle of Man does *not* want to be seen as a refuge for dirty money. I imagine him as a gnarled, wizened creature, living in a cottage at the end of a dirt lane, driving an ancient truck into town once a week to hear legal arguments through an ear trumpet.

But clearly we shouldn't give up just because of one bad Deemster. Lots of things could happen. He might die. Or at least retire. Or we could think of some way around him.

But that will not be simple.

I have been badgering the Cyprus authorities for whatever information they can provide on our two fugitives. They regard Poyiadjis and Kyprianou as very bad boys and have been trying to prosecute Kyprianou for an earlier securities scam, so far without success. So why not let the United States do it for you? Allow their extradition and your problems are over. Our contact at their justice ministry asks their Attorney General. The answer comes back "not a chance." When a country starts serving up its own citizens for prosecution in foreign lands, where will it all end?

By this point, we are lawyered up in England and the Isle of Man, anticipating much legal maneuvering from the Poyiadjis crew that will have to be met by people who know the legal terrain. In London, we hire the venerable firm of Herbert Smith, with partner Campbell McLaughlin in charge. Campbell, although a New Zealander, fits the stereotype of the Oxbridge-educated British solicitor. Someone who thinks in full paragraphs, he can, with unfailing erudition, lead stumbling American minds through thickets of British legal precedent, all the while maintaining an attitude of languid objectivity. His associate Justin D'Agostino is a young Scot with liquefied hair rising from a squarish head. He displays the earnestness of the young professional who breaks up 80-hour weeks with the occasional pub crawl. We have also retained Queen's Counsel, the privilege of making court appearances being reserved, in the Isle of Man as in England, for those who have "taken silk." Murray Rosen, QC, is easily the oldest member of team and notable for a certain measured tenacity of approach. Finally, we have a Manx lawyer to keep us apprised of the lay of the land in his quaint outpost. DOJ has retained its own squad of foreign attorneys.

It is a reassuringly solid legal team, but the ground now seems so tilted against us we no longer indulge in episodes of giddy optimism. Our U.K. attorneys are initially encouraging about the SEC's prospects, then progressively less so. Various avenues are explored. Perhaps the Manx court will recognize a U.S. court order on summary judgment—that being, more than a default judgment, a decision on the merits of the case. Or perhaps it will allow a U.S. receiver to take control of the assets. If worst comes to worst, we might file an action in the Isle of Man and prove our case there. Meanwhile, we can backstop the DOJ asset freeze with a "Mareva injunction," a creature of British common law that will operate like the freeze already in place but be less vulnerable to legal challenge.

By the spring of 2002, however, every tactic considered has been discarded. Our U.K. lawyers have concluded the Manx courts will not recognize any U.S. court order obtained by the SEC unless Poyiadjis submits himself to the court's jurisdiction, say by making an appearance at a hearing. That, of course, is the last thing he's going to do. Indeed, he and Kyprianou are likely to stay hunkered down in Cyprus as long as they risk getting picked up by Interpol the moment they set foot elsewhere. It gets worse. Because the SEC did not *itself* lose any money to Poyiadjis but, rather, is pursuing money taken from private investors, our U.K. attorneys advise us we will not be considered by the Isle of Man courts to have standing to bring an action there. As for the Mareva injunction, a total waste of time. The Manx courts will know we have no realistic prospect of capturing the Poyiadjis accounts. So why freeze them while we try and fail? And by making the attempt we'd risk being ordered to pay the legal bills Poyiadjis runs up in scotching our effort.

From what we've seen, those bills would be astronomical. Poyiadjis is letting his attorneys gorge themselves out of the frozen accounts—filing motion after motion—hoping to improve his chances of keeping whatever remains at the end of the day. A dream situation, obviously, for his legal team. His lead trial attorney, sitting next to one of our team in an airport bar, Guinness in hand, marvels at his good fortune. "What a trough," he says.

Thus do we find ourselves shoved offstage in an historic drama we were responsible for bringing about. At best, the SEC will be allowed to tag along in the matter as an "affected person." But even that is no certainty. It is a situation not previously encountered by the Manx courts. We must make application and see what happens.

So for the time being the full weight of the matter falls on Peikin. However, DOJ may be no better able than the SEC to get a judgment it can enforce in the Isle of Man. As long as Poyiadjis remains in Cyprus. He can't be hauled before a U.S. court, and it is uncertain a conviction obtained *in absentia* will stand up under challenge in the United States, much less the Isle of Man.

Looking for ways out of this box—while Poyiadjis' legal team pleads with the Deemster to lift the freeze—we contemplate increasingly imaginative (i.e., desperate) schemes to tighten our grip on the funds. Peikin obtains an order directing Poyiadjis and Kyprianou to repatriate to the United States the proceeds of their stock sales. The question is whether the Manx courts will *care*, given Poyiadjis' success to date at eluding U.S. legal process. Lindsey, in the Manx A.G.'s office, thinks they might. Our U.K. lawyers doubt it. Either way, it will take months or years to litigate. Meanwhile, the SEC and DOJ will exhaust their budgets for outside counsel, watching in disgust as the other side's lawyers pig happily from the $200 million "trough" scammed from American investors.

The bank holding the bulk of the Poyiadjis funds is a seventh-level sub of a U.S. financial institution. We consider whether the American parent can be induced to move the accounts to the United States, finally giving up on that scheme because we can see no way it won't be frustrated by the asset freeze we went to so much trouble to obtain. If the freeze is lost, it is possible we can then jack the money through the parent bank before it can be sent to Poyiadjis' fraud-haven of choice, but we hope it will not come to that.

The trustees apply to the Deemster for permission to convert the dollars in the account into "any other currency," arguing that other currencies earn more interest. Whether this makes sense as an investment matter, it suggests another scheme for grabbing the money. We are advised by people who are supposed to know such things that the only way the trustees can convert that much U.S. currency into something else is to wire it through one of two banks in New York. During the six seconds the funds exist only as electronic impulses clearing the New York banking system, it might be possible to seize them under the SEC's asset freeze order. This approach has been used successfully in drug cases.

Officials of the clearing system confirm the possibility of pulling individual transfers from the rushing tide. Much, however, will depend on knowing when and through what channels the conversion is to take place. We are able to determine which bank in New York will handle the conversion. We ask the Manx AG's office to find out what it can about the mechanics of the conversion, saying we need assurance the funds won't be diverted out of the country.

At the end of April, we are given notice that the conversion will take place in two days. The question of whether our scheme can be made to work, however, is mooted when DOJ decides against interfering with the transfer, concluding that to do so would likely be seen as an underhanded way of short-circuiting the Isle of Man legal process and might cause an international incident. Given the strong assistance we have received from the island's government, this seems the right decision. The transfer takes place without a hitch—details unknown to us—and the funds are now held in euros.

The trustees continue to howl that the American government has no legal right to the Poyiadjis accounts and so the freeze should be lifted. Reflecting teacher's pet treatment from the Deemster, they are increasingly arrogant and disdainful toward our representatives. And it can't be denied we've experienced some setbacks. The Manx AG advises Peikin it's quite unlikely the repatriation order will be recognized by the island's courts. So don't bother to try. Then the Deemster rules the SEC has no practical interest in the frozen funds and therefore can't participate in the proceedings in any capacity. We obtain the authorization of the commission to appeal his ruling to the "Staff of Government House," the Manx appellate tribunal, and wait for its decision.

The bills from our U.K. legal team are running about £140,000 a month. This is more than Enforcement's budget for all matters involving foreign litigation for the entire year. In light of our dimming prospects, it is becoming hard to justify this sort of expense, none of which the agency will get back under any circumstances. Worse, the AG is now making noises about being indemnified by the U.S. government for his office's potential liability to Poyiadjis. Under the British system, the loser in litigation pays the winner's legal expenses. Should Poyiadjis prevail in this matter, the AG as nominal plaintiff will be on the hook for the bloated legal fees of Poyiadjis and the trustees. Although we agree his office should not be exposed to that cost on our behalf, there is no legal means to indemnify it. By statute, government agencies are prohibited from taking on any sort of open-ended liability without authorization from Congress.

Suggestions we drop the whole thing are dribbling down from above and begin to sound almost reasonable.

But we aren't there yet. A happy alignment of legal authorities opens another prospect for resurrecting our legal fortunes. Rich and an attorney in our international office hatch a theory that, under the Isle of Man statute on foreign judgments, an asset forfeiture order obtained by the DOJ Civil Division might get better traction than anything from the criminal side. American case law suggests a civil forfeiture order can be obtained by default. So Poyiadjis won't need to be brought into a U.S. court—an obvious impossibility. Lindsey finds an English case giving effect to just such an order. She believes the Manx courts will accept it as controlling. As icing, she comes up with an Isle of Guernsey decision that, in medieval legal prose, follows the English precedent. In London, Campbell and Justin see this as the most promising approach yet.

Peikin runs the idea past the U.S. Attorney's asset forfeiture people for their take. They also think it might work and assign Kevin Puwaoski to handle it. As it turns out, this is good news. Adding someone new to the mix is always hazardous, but Kevin is solidly capable, tenacious but self-effacing, the opposite of the prima donnas occasionally found in U.S. Attorney's offices.

In March 2002, Kevin files a civil forfeiture action in federal court in Manhattan. Poyiadjis is easily found in Cyprus and served with the complaint. Kyprianou proves more elusive. He lives in a gated and well-guarded beachfront mansion. The process server comes away from his first attempts to tag Kyprianou frustrated, but scores after several more tries.

The matter goes by default. Poyiadjis and the trustees make no effort to oppose entry of the judgment. Apparently they assume it will fare no better before the Manx courts than the previous default judgments. But in July Kevin files an application to "register" the judgment in the Isle of Man and they abruptly wake up to the seriousness of this development. They rush to petition the Deemster for funds from the frozen accounts to hire U.S. lawyers to attack the default judgment. This involves much whining about Poyiadjis' inability to pursue his profoundly desired legal vindication due to the jack-booted American thugs having fastened their rapacious fingers around his life savings.

The Deemster's decision will be a major event in the case. If he denies the trustees access to the frozen accounts, Poyiadjis must either let the United States default judgment stand or drop his pretense of having no other funds to hire attorneys. Courts are always reluctant to strip a person of *all* his money, no matter that he stole it from widows and orphans. If it becomes apparent Poyiadjis is a very wealthy man apart from the Isle of Man funds, he will lose a big sympathy chip. He may also give us solid discovery on where to find the rest of his stash.

We feel we are building momentum at last. Our appeal from the Deemster's decision denying the SEC "affected person" status is granted.

Also, we are getting a remarkable amount of help from various foreign authorities. Switzerland coughs up two boxes of documents in what is, historically speaking, record time. This material helps in tracing the money from Kyprianou's stock sales, including $25 million he sent to the Netherlands Antilles and a bigger chunk routed through a bank in Athens. Of course, by now it all could have been moved any number of times through any number of countries. Only the sort of outrageous good luck we experienced with the Isle of Man or placing a judicial headlock on Kyprianou will allow us to find it.

From the Cyprus authorities we learn that Poyiadjis recently arranged the transfer of $100 million through Cypriot banks, though where the money is now they can't tell. This surely puts paid to his claims of indigence. We would like to use this information to oppose his plea for funds to hire U.S. counsel, but the information was provided to me informally and we must go through the usual bureaucratic obstacle course to obtain it in the signed-sealed-and-delivered form we can use in court.

Finally, Rich and Kevin trace $10 million in additional Poyiadjis funds to a Guernsey account. When we contact that island's financial regulators, we are told the account has already been frozen in anticipation of our interest.

We begin to see indications of disorder in the Poyiadjis camp emerged. Their lead attorney appears in a European body art magazine, elaborate tattoos covering his well-muscled body. The trustees prove intolerant of his artistic endeavors and replace him. The Isle of Man Constabulary begins making noises about pursuing a money laundering case against the trustees. The more prominent of the two puts his house on the market. It is the most lavish property on the island.

In November 2002, I hear from Poyiadjis's Cypriot attorney. In disturbing news for the Cypriot Board of Tourism, it seems that Poyiadjis is so unhappy about being bottled up on that island he is willing to pay for the privilege of leaving. How big is not clear from the initial feeler. But he may be finding his current refuge less hospitable. The Cyprus criminal authorities are warming to the idea of pursuing a money-laundering case against him and Kyprianou. They want us to come to Cyprus and go over the evidence with them.

Meanwhile, we have our own issues. Rob leaves the group to join the SEC's New York office. November 15, 2002 is his last day and it feels like a wake. He will be missed on many cases but none more than AremisSoft. His command of the record is almost as good as Rich's. I realize how much I've relied on him to oversee the day-to-day development of the case. For the time being, he will continue to provide support from New York—but it is clear he is for us a wasting asset.

Rich is also getting antsy. A criminal case he has been working on the side for a U.S. Attorney's office in Texas is wrapping up and he's thinking this might be a good time to bounce—possibly to a permanent position as an Assistant U.S. Attorney or a staff gig with a Senate committee. Or even something in private practice. The alternative of working his way up the ladder at the SEC lacks appeal.

The market for Enforcement attorneys has recently exploded. After Enron, WorldCom, Adelphia, Sunbeam, and various other black eyes to corporate America, the SEC received Congressional largess to beef up its enforcement efforts. DOJ is also putting more bodies on the line to fight financial crime. This means more work for the defense bar and many firms are building out in this area. For the first time, I'm getting regular calls from headhunters. I'd settled into seeing myself as a career government mope, but with so many of the people I like jumping ship, I begin to wonder if I'm missing something. Like the possibility of making serious money. Between my SEC salary and what my wife makes as an elementary schoolteacher, we barely break even each month. But I put off thinking this through while AremisSoft and three or four other cases in which I feel heavily invested remain at critical stages.

By the end of 2002, the remaining hurdles in the Isle of Man have been clarified. There are now two proceedings before different Deemsters, one lined up behind the other. The first will resolve whether the Poyiadjis trustees may raid the frozen accounts to finance an attack on the asset forfeiture order. The second will determine whether that U.S. judgment will be recognized in the Isle of Man, even though obtained by default. If the first goes our way—*and* Poyiadjis doesn't come up with funds from another source to hire U.S. lawyers—we go straight to the second, with optimism it will lead to the Poyiadjis money being wired into the registry of the U.S. District Court in New York. On the other hand, if the trustees are let loose to frolic through the U.S. courts on what we have come to think of as our money, the ultimate resolution in the Isle of Man will be put on hold until they conclude that adventure. This could take years.

The Deemster who will hear the application for legal fees is not a local product but someone being shipped special delivery from England for the occasion. Our hope is we will get a person with a less parochial outlook than our current Deemster. Someone with no ear trumpet.

The hearing is scheduled for early February 2003. It will involve a full-blown presentation of the case by both sides. The critical nature of this event demands an all-hands response and we gather in London several days before the hearing to prepare. Rich has handled the hotel arrangements, working around the government per diem. I've adopted a "don't ask, don't tell" policy concerning his logistical machinations, thinking what I don't know can't hurt me. Usually, in fact, it works out very well. But when I find myself standing beside Catherine Zeta-Jones at the registration desk of the Savoy Hotel, I wonder if I should be more inquisitive.

I arrive a day before Rich and Kevin for a meeting on another case. At loose ends for the evening, I ask about seeing a Premier League match. After years of watching my son play in youth soccer leagues, I'm curious to see the game played by people over five feet tall.

The hotel concierge says—my bad luck—tonight is a London "darby" between Arsenal and West Ham United, a major local event sold out months ago. But a cab driver tells me it can still happen. There should be "touts" around the Arsenal stadium scalping tickets. Take the tube out to North London, he advises, and just follow the crowd. But be mindful. Parliament recently saw fit to ban touting, so there's a *minor* possibility of arrest.

But then all good things involve risk.

From the underground station, it is easy to follow the flow to the stadium, most of the fans wearing the red and white polyester shirts of the home team. The human stream swells as it makes its way through Highbury Park, the evening sun dipping below the tree-line. But with the stadium now in sight, I haven't found any touts. Also, there are many policemen around—some on horseback—to prevent confrontations be-tween fans of the opposing teams. I fear my contemplated criminality is evident as I furtively dart around looking for someone behaving in an equally suspicious manner.

As a last hope, I try a man selling programs from a portable stand. He is reassuringly scruffy with a promising absence of teeth. A likely guide to the particular stratum of the London underworld that I seek. And he does not disappoint. He jerks his head sideways and says: "Go one block up, one block right ("roit") and look out for two dodgy-looking characters. They'll set you up, mate."

And, indeed, there is no mistaking these two for solid citizens. Dodgy is the word. One tall, the other short, both in loud plaid jackets, they are dead ringers for the Cockney dog-nappers in *101 Dalmatians*. Peering around to be certain we are unobserved, the taller tout slides a ticket from his jacket pocket. The price is over a hundred pounds but it's worth it. It buys the memorable experience of being squashed in the middle of thirty thousand drunken Englishmen as they leap up and down shouting "All Hail Arsenal!"

★   ★   ★

We had envisioned an orderly process of briefing our Queen's Counsel, Murray Rosen, and DOJ's QC David Farrer, so they will be as effective as possible in dispelling whatever fictions are thrown out by the Poyiadjis attorneys. There should be a convivial dinner or two—within the per diem, naturally—and a few pints at the Frog and Peach.

Instead, we have a three-day fire drill.

Poyiadjis files a 70-page affidavit the week before the hearing. He loudly proclaims his innocence and implies we—both the SEC and DOJ—are mere fronts for the CIA. Also that we intend to keep the money for ourselves and not give it back to investors. He complains he can't return to the United States to fight the government without being clapped into jail and deprived of any assets he might use to defend himself or even to pay his bail. This part is mostly true. Peikin and his colleagues at DOJ are taking a hard line, at least until Poyiadjis obeys the court order to repatriate his money to the United States.

It is quite a document and if the Deemster buys any of it our task will be significantly complicated.

The chambers of David Farrer, QC, are tucked into a block of red-brick townhouses east of Hyde Park. The bland facade opens on a series of well-appointed offices that continue back into another building, invisible from the street, that was once a carriage house. Our first task is responding to the Poyiadjis screed. We must do so immediately or risk postponement of the hearing. Any delay means additional costs that we are less able to bear than the other side. They surely know this—hence the last-minute wrench in the works. We sift through a mass of half-baked arguments and flat misrepresentations, responding to any that might seem plausible to a Deemster who doesn't yet know what's what. David is visibly hassled. His speech is clipped and movements abrupt as he races against the looming deadline, giving directions to everyone else. But he manages. The document is finished and shipped off with the final express mail that Friday night.

The weekend is spent at the Herbert Smith offices preparing a "skeleton argument"—a sort of summary legal brief in outline—to be submitted to the Deemster on Monday. The team works together smoothly, with the Brits running the show. Rich and Kevin have developed a close relationship though constant phone calls and a few all-nighters. The jittery nerves from Friday are soothed as the skeleton argument comes together well. On Saturday night we adjourn for dinner at an Italian restaurant by Covent Garden. David, a man with the distinguished profile of a Roman senator, plays host. He likes his wine and becomes voluble on subjects including his son's musical career and his family's summers in Provence. Then the conversation skitters loosely around what we can expect in the Isle of Man, but there's little left to say.

I feel that for now we've done all we can do.

★   ★   ★

On Sunday, the flight from Gatwick to the Isle of Man. As we land, the sun is dropping in the general direction of Ireland. The island, from the air, looks like a child's first jigsaw puzzle, the pastures cut into odd blocks by lanes and hedgerows. In the dusk of evening, a sprinkling of lights traces the coast.

We all pile into a cab that takes us along narrow roads twisting through a bucolic landscape. The air smells of grass and ocean. Clearly heaven on earth, especially if you happen to be a sheep.

The driver instructs us solemnly that when we cross a certain small bridge we *must* greet the fairies who live beneath it or invite bad luck.

Sideways glances, then we do as instructed. We've had all the bad luck we can take.

Rich has made the trip before and knows where to stay. He learned from painful experience that the local Hilton has no association with the American hotel chain of that name, but does have a close association with bedbugs. He takes us to an old hotel on the strand like something out of a BBC production of an Agatha Christie novel: plaid carpeting, creaky stairs, doors not quite square, and an ancient Otis elevator with an accordion gate. But the staff is friendly and the bar warm and well-stocked.

That this is the place to be while visiting the island is confirmed when the Poyiadjis legal crew checks in behind us. Surely, for them price is no object. We greet each other with distant courtesy.

In the morning, the strand is deep in fog. Opposite the hotel, the statue of a World War I infantryman looks across the seawall into the milky harbor, bronze rifle at the ready, a single seagull perched on his soup-plate helmet. At first I think the bird is part of the statue. Then it straightens and hops onto the breeze, carving through the fog with rigid wings. At the end of the quay, a spit of land supports a tiny castle. From a distance it looks like a stage prop—the joke castle from *Monty Python and the Holy Grail*. Or a backdrop from *The Mouse That Roared*.

We spend the day in a flurry of meetings with Manx law enforcement and final preparations for the hearing the following day. Everything is in place. It simply remains for our QCs to convince the English Deemster to see one legal issue our way.

We have dinner at a restaurant far out a country road. The fog is gone and the sky crowded with stars. In the parking lot, Kevin points out Saturn and Jupiter to Campbell, while Rich chats up David Farrer about English legal practice.

It strikes me that this is what I wanted to get out of law, whenever I've allowed myself to think it could mean more than a paycheck. Working on cases that matter with people who care about what they're doing and do it well. Now if we can just get this bedeviled case to come out right. To justify all the time and expense. So it doesn't turn out to have been a tragic farce.

But how likely is that, really? I can't quite make myself believe it. The Law so often disappoints those who think themselves its rightful beneficiaries. A game of snakes and ladders that will give a tumble to those it first pretends to favor ... just to show it can. Its process feeds upon itself, and prefers those with the money and time to indulge its worst proclivities. Here that is not us. The cost of this litigation is straining the budgets of our agencies and the issue of indemnifying the Isle of Man AG looms large in the background. A few more delays and reversals and we may be forced to throw in the towel.

The courtroom where we gather the next morning is small and modern in decor. The Deemster is an English QC, well-tended and stern in middle age. According to our QC, Murray Rosen, she is smart but has no background in any relevant area of law. When not moonlighting as a Deemster, she handles real-estate transactions. Better that, I suppose, than disputes about sheep. We are instructed to bow to her whenever we enter or leave the courtroom.

The Poyiadjis lawyers employ a simple tactic, supported by much legal blandishment and misdirection: put the United States on trial in place of their client. They understand that the Manx courts *can* award the Poyiadjis accounts to the U.S. government. And things are headed in that direction with Kevin's civil forfeiture action. But the Manx statute contains a loophole. Such a result must be determined by the court to be "in the interests of justice." The plan is to argue that the American government has been so arrogant, grasping, overbearing, and dishonest that it would be against the interests of justice to reward its conduct with their client's hard-stolen money.

First up for the trustees is a prominent but ancient trusts-and-estates lawyer. Stooped and white-haired, he leans his shrunken figure against the podium for support. His voice is brittle and his speech achingly slow. One can almost hear the sands of time sifting between his words. His role is to impart an air of legitimacy to his clients. Tedium is his chosen instrument. The trustees, he opines at length, are dedicated fiduciaries protecting the interests of their clients. Not—perish the thought—money launderers helping a crook hide money from his victims.

The heavy lifting, however, is done by counsel for Poyiadjis. Murray has described him as a thug but an *effective* thug, and he does look like an aging soccer hooligan stuffed into an expensive suit. His previous reference to the frozen accounts as his personal "trough" provided a succinct statement of his professional philosophy.

He presents his client as an innocent abroad who wandered unawares into the brutal and sordid world of the American capital markets. By sheer good fortune, he came into a certain sum of money from selling an interest in a company that—who knew?—turned out to be of limited value. That he happened to be the president of that same company is a mere detail. Mr. Poyiadjis, of course, was not allowed to depart, pockets full, from the back-room craps game that is American finance. A less trusting soul would have known what was in store. Waiting in the alley, sleeves rolled, blackjacks in hand, were the American financial police, ready to relieve him of his gains.

His oratory fastens on our supposed deviousness in obtaining an order from a U.S. court requiring Poyiadjis to return his money to the United States after first freezing it in the Isle of Man. This bit of trickery, he says straight-faced, was designed to put Poyiadjis in contempt of the U.S. court so that he will be arrested the moment he returns to the United States to defend himself. He suggests we must have misled the district court to induce it to lend itself to such a nefarious scheme.

The idea that Poyiadjis would cheerfully release his $200 million were it not for the freeze is, of course, ludicrous. He went to great trouble to hustle his cash out of the United States, through the blind of Switzerland and into the Isle of Man, quite obviously to place it beyond the reach of American justice. Had he been willing to let go of the funds, moreover, the U.S. Attorney's office would have been happy to accommodate him by lifting the freeze. Also, contrary to the hyperbolic assertions of his counsel, the Manx freeze order was fully disclosed to the U.S. court, which treated it with great deference in structuring its repatriation order.

Listening to this crap is aggravating in the extreme. I can feel Rich vibrating in his seat. He is breathing like a pole-vaulter about to make a run. And the situation deteriorates when we see that the Deemster is not about to respond with a well-merited horse-laugh. To the contrary, she is all sympathy and concern. In formulating her questions, she refers to DOJ and the SEC—and she throws in the Isle of Man AG to the extent that he supports us—by the dismissive shorthand "the Americans." The term is said in a slightly querulous tone, as if referring to ill-trained house pets. On the other hand, she seems to regard Poyiadjis as little worse than an amusing scamp, cleverly tweaking the nose of "the Americans."

The idea that Poyiadjis has been maneuvered into standing in contempt of court, she finds wholly credible, and deeply disturbing. She sprinkles her comments with references to the "draconian" American legal system. It is, in fact, true that Poyiadjis would face a tough time of it in New York. He would likely be arrested, although for securities fraud and insider trading, not contempt of court. And he would have to convince a judge that he should have access to the proceeds of his stock sales to pay for bail and lawyers—something well within the court's discretion but no sure thing. If this seems harsh, however, the English practice in such cases—as the Deemster seems wholly unaware—is no more lenient. We briefed this point but I wonder if, after digesting the 70-page Poyiadjis rant, filed at the last moment, the Deemster had time for more than a passing glance at our papers. If not, Poyiadjis' lawyers deserve credit for their crude but effective tactic.

Or perhaps she just hates Americans.

When, in rebuttal, Murray describes the U.S. justice system as a model for other countries, she snaps at him for his rhetorical excess, then sniffs and concedes that, yes, America is in its way "a civilized country."

But this costs her some effort and she is not so generous in her other comments.

★ ★ ★

The early morning cab ride to the airport is a grim affair. No one feels like talking.

We get a different driver but he is as jovial as the last. Hoisting a suitcase, he says, "You're for the metal budgies, then?" The accent is East London.

As we bounce over a certain small bridge, I ask him whether there really is a local belief that greeting the resident fairies brings good luck. I'm skeptical. They don't seem to have done well by us so far.

His laugh is noncommittal, "Strange breed, the Manx."

During the rest of the ride, I brood over our next move. It's clear the Deemster will rule against us. She probably jumped up at dawn to begin writing her thoughts on "the Americans." This means either selling the commission on taking an appeal or letting Poyiadjis and the trustees open another front in their war of attrition. Not a happy situation. What was supposed to be a quick legal smash and grab is turning into procedural purgatory.

"Here you go," the driver says at last. "Isle of Man Airport. Terminal One."

The place is unprepossessing in the morning light. I peer around and ask: "How many terminals are there?"

"One," he says.

Chapter 6

Taking Out the Eurotrash

*M*ay 13, 2002.

The Port of Antwerp stretches in all directions as an end-less maze of docks and access roads, warehouses, cranes, and grain elevators. The sky is the color of mussel shells and the River Schelde pocked with rain. We are gathered on the dock looking at a city-block-long cargo ship, smoke rising in desultory exhalations from both stern and bow. "We" being me, three of the attorneys in my group, and the Antwerp Chief of Police.

The local fire department has lined up several trucks beside the ship, each patiently playing a thread of water into its open hold. The weight of the accumulating water makes the vessel list heavily toward the dock. Behind us, a parking lot perhaps a quarter of a mile deep is jammed with used cars collected from all over Northern Europe and destined for African ports. Freight intended for the ship we now watch burn.

That morning, I flew over from London after a meeting with our U.K. counsel on the AremisSoft case. We are at this time in our early struggles with the Isle of Man judiciary and most of a year away from our encounter with the broomstick-riding Deemster. Thus our hopes of recovering the $200 million frozen in bank accounts in that quaint island nation have not yet been turned upside down.

At this moment, however, AremisSoft is not my first concern. That would be the Belgian auto importer ACLN Limited. Two months ago we suspended trading in its stock on the New York Stock Exchange—the first time in a quarter century the SEC had taken such an action against an NYSE stock. ACLN claimed to make fat profits from shipping cars from Europe to Benin and other parts of West Africa, but there is much reason to believe these profits exist only on paper. It also appears that its heavily touted distribution deal with a Korean automaker is a fabrication, like its purported ownership of the three-thousand-ton car carrier the *Sea Atef.*

In April, with the help of various local authorities, we found and froze ACLN bank accounts in Denmark, Luxembourg, Monaco, and the Netherlands. Together they hold about $51 million.

What we haven't done is sue ACLN or its people anywhere in the world. We are still working on that—frantically trying to upgrade what we damn-well-know about the company into what we can actually prove in court. Although a Cyprus corporation, ACLN operates—to the extent it has operations—out of Antwerp. Its partially shredded files have been seized by the Belgian police, who are being so helpful to us I can almost forgive the country for Lernout & Hauspie. Also, they have frozen $7.5 million in ACLN funds deposited in Belgian banks that arguably should go to defrauded investors.

So for us Antwerp is the place to be.

It was a sunny day in London and the weather held through the short flight to Brussels and the brief train ride from there to Antwerp. But by the time the cab dropped me at the police station the clouds were sliding in from the coast. The driver said I'd brought the bad weather with me.

SEC attorneys Heidi Mayor and Charlie Neal and their branch chief, Michael Moore, arrived two days before and have settled in a conference room with boxes of documents rescued by the police from ACLN's premises. Walking through the station, I passed the open doorway to a small interrogation room. A thin, 40-something man twisted around in a straight-backed metal chair to look at me like a lost soul seeking redemption. I wasn't it. His face collapsed in disappointment.

ACLN is the creation of three men: Joseph Bisschops, Aldo Labiad, and Alex de Ridder. Bisschops, the aging chairman of the board, fled the country when the Belgian police began executing search warrants, but not until after he shredded quantities of the company's financial records. When last seen he was in France and still on the move. Labiad, the CEO, is somewhere in Belgium, but no one knows quite where. Wanted on an old Tunisian warrant for criminal fraud, he is unlikely to show up in any country where his Belgian citizenship won't protect him from extradition. The unhappy person here in the station is de Ridder, ACLN's chief operating officer. He is being held for questioning in connection with the Belgian money-laundering inquiry, which, by good fortune, dovetails nicely with our securities fraud investigation.

Police chief Rudi Arnauts, whom I've previously known only as a voice on the telephone, is fluent in English, as well as several other languages, and a handsome, outgoing 40-something—as far as possible from the no-neck specimens Americans seem to type-cast into police chief positions. When I was introduced to the detective working the money-laundering case, Patrick Vervaet, he looked exhausted. He had been up since the early hours, he said, pursuing escaped prisoners. They'd bribed the jailer to let them out and it fell to Patrick to round them up again. He didn't seem particularly surprised, but also didn't comment on whether this had happened before.

The Antwerp police are also investigating an attempted car-bombing that occurred a few weeks before. We care because the car belongs to one of our prospective witnesses, Merhi Ali Abou Merhi, a business associate of ACLN CEO Aldo Labiad. Merhi avoided a fiery death thanks to the fortuitous intervention of a young couple who, driving home from dinner, observed someone crawling under his Mercedes and reported it to the police.

The detective on that matter, an older man with a mass of pewter-gray hair falling over the collar of his bomber jacket, told us the device found by the bomb squad—a plastic explosive with mercury detonator—is the sort currently popular with certain Middle Eastern terrorist groups. He didn't expound further upon it that day, however, interrupted by the news that a car-carrier was on fire in the harbor.

Our first thought: is this the ship ACLN claims to own? Perhaps torched for the insurance. Insurance fraud was one of the many allegations swirling around this company.

Chief Arnauts was out the door instantly, leaving Patrick, bleary-eyed from his night of chasing self-paroled prisoners, to follow behind with his American charges. It was a long drive in the rain. Miles of gray harbor went past before we came to the source of the smoke, all the while assuring ourselves this must be ACLN's ship, the Sea Atef.

But now, standing on the dock watching the fire trucks douse the flames, we find it is not that ship. It is, rather, a similar vessel owned by a (much larger) competitor of ACLN, the Grimaldi line. Grimaldi, also, has provided information about ACLN to certain California hedge funds. So maybe this is payback. Or maybe someone dropped a cigarette in the wrong place.

Or maybe a lot of other things.

★   ★   ★

The first thing I saw about ACLN was a 12-page "Eyeshade Report" from the Maryland research firm Forensic Advisors. Although its analyst surely suspected the company to be a fraud, he limited his observations to pointing out issues with its basic performance ratios. Accounts receivable, for example, were increasing at a rate more than twice that of revenues. This is a red flag to financial analysts. It often signals poor quality earnings: invoices the company has booked but can't collect. It is of less concern if the company has reserved against the possibility that some of its receivables will never be collected. ACLN had no such reserves.

The company was seeing less and less cash from operations despite an increase in net income. There are many reasons this can happen, some innocuous, others not. Most obviously, the company could be booking phony sales that never turn into cash.

The "Eyeshade Report" also noted crude inconsistencies in the company's public information. Its figures for new car sales were inconsistent between company documents. Oddly, in some quarters ACLN listed two CFOs and in others none. A company that can't get basic stuff like this right probably has, at the very least, internal controls problems that will surface in other areas.[1]

I don't remember who sent me this report, but within weeks it had been supplemented by information from other sources. Northern California hedge fund manager Dave Scially and analyst Jim Carruthers had each found additional discrepancies in the company's public statements and noted that the current CFO was 27 years old, not an accountant, and located in Los Angeles, far from the company's operations. Previously he had been a fledgling investment banker at Cruttenden Roth, the firm that took ACLN public.

ACLN's geographic distribution of sales—the item that proved Lernout & Hauspie's undoing—also raised suspicions. The company reported an explosion of car sales to Benin beginning in 2000. In the first six months of 2001, its take from that small and impoverished African nation was $52 million, about twice the amount of *all* exports from the United States into Benin during that period.

Scially contacted the company's Gen-X CFO and asked for information on the dealers to whom ACLN delivered cars in Benin. He was told there were none. The company sold directly to individuals. That made it impossible to check further without access to the company's records.

ACLN claimed to have a deal to resell 31,000 new cars from a Korean manufacturer. Its SEC filings stated it had sales contracts for each of the cars, with full payment in advance of shipment. But according to the CFO, ACLN merely shipped the cars on behalf of a middleman acting, in turn, for three Korean car companies. The agent kept title to the cars until they were delivered to port agents in West Africa. Neither approach jibed with the company's financial statements. If ACLN simply schlepped around cars owned by someone else, it should not have booked the sales

---

[1] A few years later the "Eyeshade Report" was the target of a particularly deplorable episode of "issuer retaliation." The patent medicine company Matrixx Initiatives sued "The Eyeshade Report" after it reported possible side effects from the company's nasal spray. The litigation costs put "The Eyeshade Report" out of business. In 2009, however, the FDA confirmed that the company's product was hazardous to the human proboscis and its stock collapsed.

as revenue—only its fees. On the other hand, if it took title to the cars and received cash up-front from the buyers, the cash should have appeared on its balance sheet. It didn't.

Scially also noticed that ACLN's chairman, Bisschops, had reduced his holdings of ACLN stock by an amount worth $100 million at then-current prices, without filing the appropriate forms with the SEC. Finally, his examination of shipping records raised doubts that the company owned the cargo vessel it had valued at $6 million. In a letter Scially sent the SEC in late October, he observed that ACLN—with its third-world transactions and funky financial reporting—would make an excellent blind for a money-laundering operation.

This was more than intriguing. It cried out for investigation.

And for caution. The company has operations on at least four continents, including many countries that might not cooperate with U.S. law enforcement. We could easily end up spending our lives on this one with nothing to show for it. But the damn stock was on the NYSE and pretty frisky, taking the company's market cap to $700 million in September. It was hard to ignore.

Deb Heilizer was jammed up with a dozen other matters, including litigation against the Sunbeam Corporation and its former CEO, "Chainsaw" Al Dunlap. Rob Keyes was also more over-committed than usual. So I picked on my other branch chief, Michael Moore. Mike was fluent in French, having a French mother. That, as it turned out, would be hugely helpful because many of the transactions we were interested in took place in French-speaking areas. Mike's father was not French. He was African-American from inner-city Baltimore and career military. Perhaps reflecting his father's military experience, Mike had an attitude toward the power structure that was wryly dismissive, but only in private.

Mike had two attorneys he could pretend had time to work on this matter, Heidi Mayor and Charlie Neal. Heidi was the daughter of some sort of socialite without the benefit of being rich, and had tried this and that in various parts of the world before ending up at the SEC. She had an amiable directness and zero bullshit tolerance, in high contrast to the more cagey persona typical of government attorneys. She lived a quasi-bohemian existence in a small house in northwest D.C. with several highly coddled dogs and, in her spare time, helped promote a local rock band. A perfect fit for my group.

Also helping out when he could get away from other cases was Charlie Neal, whom we'd stolen from the Texas AG's securities division. Charlie was so unassuming he might have been thought-disengaged—until drawn out with direct questions. It would then be apparent he was not only up to speed with you, he was several steps ahead but too considerate of your feelings to show it. He would work late every night for a week, devote the weekend to driving his grandparents to the Appalachian crest to see the autumn foliage, then show up early and eager on Monday morning. A supervisor's dream if it didn't bother you to be *indulged* by someone who recognized your worst ideas for what they were, but rarely said so.

In December 2001 we subpoenaed the company for documents on its sales, assets, and stock issuances. At about the same time, Herb Greenberg started knocking ACLN in *TheStreet.com*. His columns poured cold water on a message-board campaign of hype centered around rumors the company would soon acquire, with financing from J.P. Morgan, three cargo vessels in addition to the one it already purported to own. I assumed he was pointed in this direction by Scially and Carruthers. Greenberg not only scoffed at the J.P. Morgan deal but retailed many of the shorts' insights about the company's financial disclosure, including its unexplained ramp-up in receivables and lack of allowance for doubtful accounts. When the company failed to respond to his questions, he wrote tartly: "Maybe this is what happens when the company's CFO is in one part of the world (Los Angeles), its attorneys are in a second (Cyprus), its headquarters is in a third (Belgium), and it does business in yet another (Africa)."

Greenberg's columns kicked the legs from under the stock. Its price fell 65 percent after he began coverage. These were the heady days after Enron and WorldCom when questions about a company's financials could panic investors. This atmosphere invited short-sellers to look for shady companies and call them out in public, while knowing they could find themselves in a world of pain if they were wrong—and maybe even if they were right.

By airing the issues floating around ACLN, Greenberg took some of the pressure off us. At least the stock was no longer ratcheting up on the basis of rumors and potentially false financials while we squared our shoulders to the investigatory wheel.

In early January, ACLN disclosed the SEC inquiry and promised its full cooperation. This is a phrase defense lawyers have macroed into their word processors, like "the suit is without merit and will be defended vigorously by the company." In fact, the cooperation we received was of such poor quality it felt more like obstruction. ACLN's board hired U.S. counsel and someone from PricewaterhouseCoopers to fob us off with whatever the company wanted us to see. The PWC accountant was blithely clueless. He attempted to engage us in a game of mutual discovery about what it was, exactly, his client did to make money, most of his understanding pieced together from public documents. The U.S. lawyer wasn't much more helpful. He had been fed scraps of information that he passed on to us—none very reassuring. The company, he told us, had only four employees. It was, in effect, a "virtual company" that outsourced its operations to a Belgian management company, "MFT," which ACLN paid in the low millions every year for its services. And who owned MFT? That would be ACLN chairman Joseph Bisschops. The lawyer said he didn't know what the initials stood for. I would come to remember it through the mnemonic "Many Fraudulent Transactions."

We asked him to bring in Bisschops and Labiad for testimony. But that, it seemed, would be difficult. Each was hiring personal counsel, so he couldn't say when they will be available. What about speeding up the delivery of documents? Again, problematic. He represented *only* ACLN's board, and all the documents were with MFT, a separate Belgian entity we had not served with a subpoena. Nor did it look like we would be able to do so, unless by way of a treaty request going through the Department of Justice. That, of course, could take months or years.

But before we started yelling, he wanted us to know the company had paper on its shipments into West Africa to prove to us it was not making up its sales. He slid a stack of invoices across the table, along with a list of vehicle identification numbers for new cars the company claimed to have sold in Africa. The invoices were on the letterhead of "Danish Car Carrier, Ltd." and made no reference to ACLN or its "management company." On their face, moreover, the invoices indicated the cars shipped by Danish Car Carriers belonged to a number of companies, including some of ACLN's competitors. Counsel had no explanation for the apparent discrepancies.

★ ★ ★

Despite the lack of cooperation from the company, things soon started to fall into place. And the story that emerged was distressing. From the response of the Spanish police to an Interpol notice sent out at our request, we learned Labiad was wanted in Tunisia for embezzlement. In the early 1990s, he'd raised money to establish a shipping company, sold the company two boats at grossly inflated prices, then skipped with the cash. He was arrested in Monaco in 1999 but released for reasons not immediately apparent. As a naturalized Belgian citizen, Labiad was safe from extradition so long as he stayed put. The arrest warrant was somehow omitted from ACLN's SEC filings.

Truly, the man carried some brutal baggage. We spoke with the daughter of one of his former business associates, a woman he should clearly never use as a reference. She described him as a career conman. "He's cheated everyone who's ever had anything to do with him," she said. Another Labiad acquaintance would speak to us only anonymously, afraid that Labiad, if he learned of the contacts, would have him killed.

However intriguing, this stuff didn't get to the core issues in the investigation: phony revenue and overvalued assets. The biggest item on the company's balance sheet was $117 million in cash, supposedly on deposit with BNP Paribas Luxemburg. Going over the documents we received from ACLN's counsel, Charlie noticed that the BNP Paribas bank statements looked to have been altered. The numbers on the documents sometimes used periods and sometimes commas to separate every third decimal place, as if reflecting a mid-Atlantic sensibility. We contacted the Luxembourg financial authorities to see if they will tell us, at least, whether the documents are genuine. There was little reason for optimism. We had been told by our international office that Luxembourg has particularly tight financial secrecy laws. Once funds go into that country, they become untraceable.

Then there was the *Sea Atef*. The ship was registered in Malta as owned 50 percent by Danish Car Carriers and 50 percent by a certain

Merhi Ali Abou Merhi. Danish Car Carriers, upon further inquiry, was found to be a private company owned by Bisschops. But that's not the same as being owned by ACLN and, anyway, who was this Merhi guy who owned the other half of the boat? From documents ACLN's attorney handed over, moreover, we learned the *Sea Atef* had cost its present owners $3.95 million. But ACLN valued *its half* of the boat at $6 million. The company seemed to have a problem with basic arithmetic.

ACLN's counsel identified the Korean car company that provided new cars to his client as Daewoo. He knew that much. In its SEC filings for the first three quarters of 2001, ACLN had reported revenue of over $123 million from this line of business. We contacted Daewoo U.S. to check this out. Its people professed ignorance of what deals were made in Korea. So Heidi began making early morning calls to Seoul. There was much dodging around, but on March 9, 2002—the day Rich Rosenfeld was pitching the U.S. Attorney's office on filing a civil forfeiture action against AremisSoft—she got through to a Daewoo executive. He said his company had sold *no* cars to ACLN. He had met with Labiad and his Korean associate, Gary Hwang, to discuss the African market but nothing came of it. Labiad and Hwang had struck him as less than pillars of the business community. But he demurred from confirming this in writing. Daewoo was in bankruptcy, he said, and he couldn't do anything that would complicate its legal situation.

We managed to find a phone number for Hwang. In broken English he told a disjointed story about the "gray market" for international car sales. The idea was that Daewoo was making clandestine sales through Hwang's company to ACLN. He wouldn't explain why it would want to do that. He said he couldn't go into detail for fear of damaging his source of supply. But apparently even this was more than he'd intended to tell us. The following day, Heidi received an email from Hwang claiming he was drunk during the interview. He could prove this with a bar bill and a witness who would testify he had "more to drink than the legal limit." Therefore, we should simply forget everything he'd told us.

We also tried to get information from Africa. A contact at the State Department told us that might work—assuming we were prepared to wait two or three years. Michael had a friend who knew someone who knew someone who knew the president of Benin. He started to work that angle and eventually reached, not the president of Benin, but a local lawyer supposedly capable of getting things done in that benighted country. His price to check out ACLN's business dealings there would be $500,000. When asked what method he used to set his fees, he said: "The French method. I charge what I think it is worth to you." We passed.

We were not contacted by attorneys for Labiad or Bisschops—no surprise—and so tried to reach the two men directly to get their response to the tide of evidence flowing against them and their company. There were many phone calls to Belgium and Cyprus. From the Cypriot attorney we'd retained in the AremisSoft matter we learned that ACLN's Nicosia office was nothing but a mail drop and phone machine. When we called its Antwerp office, the evasions were blithely absurd. We would be told Labiad was in a meeting in their conference room, then a few minutes later that he was in Africa. Eventually we got him on his cell. Between broken connections he said he was on the way to the airport but looked forward to speaking with us at a time to be arranged by his Norwegian lawyer. The lawyer, when we called him, said he didn't represent Labiad but would nevertheless arrange a conference call with him. He didn't and from then on evaded our calls.

We approached people at the U.S. Attorney's office in Manhattan to ask if they would provide help in pursuing treaty requests. They had no interest in going after a group of foreigner nationals they would probably never be able to bring to trial, but were willing to facilitate our efforts as a form of charity.

We now were gifted with a major lucky break in our investigation. Merrill Lynch self-reported some questionable transactions in ACLN stock made through its London office. Its lawyers brought in a 50-something broker of Middle Eastern extraction, Kamal Sadak, to tell us about his former understudy. Merrill had a buddy system in which the newer hires were teamed with more experienced brokers. Sadak's misfortune was to be coupled with a young broker named Christopher Pan.

Pan had looked, at first, to be a solid prospect. He brought in significant brokerage business from the father of a personal friend, who seemed to have set up the account for the sole purpose of selling ACLN stock. The father's name was Aldo Labiad. As an officer of ACLN, Labiad was restricted in the amount of stock he could sell and had to comply with SEC reporting requirements on his trades. Kamal told Pan to be sure Labiad was following the rules.

After this admonishment, the account went quiet for some time. Then a new brokerage customer trotted in, referred by—yes—Labiad. The client was the Panamanian corporation Pearlrose Holdings and the human being on its papers a woman of purported means named Francis Perez. Someone with a substantial net worth—most of it in ACLN stock—who could be expected to do big trades. In truth, she was a secretary for a Panama City law firm that operated as an offshore corporation mill. Later, when her testimony is taken by the Panamanian authorities at our request, she will admit that the account-opening documents (written in English, which she did not understand) were inaccurate and she couldn't remember Pearlrose as distinct from hundreds of other companies cranked out by her law firm.

In July 2001, Pearlrose sold through Merrill London a million shares of ACLN stock for $38 million. The money was wired several months later to banks in London and Luxembourg. The account continued to be used for ACLN sales, with Sadak handling the trades when Pan was out of the office. Everything went along nicely until Sadak, hoping to keep the proceeds from the Pearlrose sales in house, suggested they try to interest Perez in Merrill investment products. And then things went the shape of a butternut squash.

According to Sadak, Pan took him aside and said: "Don't you get it? This is Aldo [Labiad's] money." This, of course, meant that all sorts of SEC regulations had been violated—most obviously those requiring corporate insiders to disclose their personal transactions in securities of their companies.

Sadak, stunned by Pan's casual revelation of serial wrongdoing, piped: "Do you realize what you've done?"

"They'll never find out," Pan replied. "And you're involved too."

What a guy.

After what must have been a bad night, Sadak did the right thing and told his supervisors the whole story. Merrill also did the right thing in picking up the phone to us.

We learned from Merrill, furthermore, that a million share transfer of ACLN stock had occurred through its Monaco office. The client was a Liberian corporation controlled by Belgian lawyer Edwinne Mannaerts.

With a little digging, we found that the company was incorporated by Steven Blum, a young man with the financial sophistication of a garden implement who happened to be the nephew of ACLN employee Anny Bormans. Of the approximately $32 million realized from the sales, $2 million went to Bormans and the rest to banks in Monaco. Bormans' name was already known to us as the incorporator of a British Virgin Islands company used to sell stock for Labiad.

In March, ACLN's three U.S. directors quit, apparently feeling the heat from our inquiry and the press coverage. None of them, so far as we could tell, had played any role more significant than collecting fees for attending telephonic board meetings. ACLN's U.S. lawyer also walked. There's only so much you can do for a virtual company that isn't paying your fees.

The day the directors quit, the NYSE halted trading in ACLN stock with a "news pending" designation. Its staff told us vaguely they weren't satisfied with the company's explanation for the resignations. But when the company put out a press release promising a conference call later in the week, the NYSE allowed the stock to resume trading. This seemed to reassure the market.

We had still not met the Commission's risk-averse standard for bringing a fraud action, particularly one that will mean spending time and money all over the globe. Very little of what we knew was documented. Even simple things like getting copies of shipping documents were frustrated by procedural obstacles. But it seemed reckless to let the stock continue to trade on the NYSE with little beyond rumor and Greenberg's columns to warn investors of the company's problems.

If we weren't ready to prove fraud, there was no doubt ACLN's disclosure was seriously defective. The SEC has the power to halt trading on a stock based on the lack of reliable public information about a company. It lasts for ten days only, with another ten if the Commission decides to reload. But it tells investors to handle the stock with gloves and tongs and prevents securities firms from making a market in the stock until the company cures its disclosure problems.

The market analysts in the Enforcement Division told us that the SEC *never* suspends trading in NYSE stocks and probably lacks the power to do so. When shown otherwise, they got excited about being involved in such a novel action. None of the other divisions that got to weigh in did more than minor fretting and the Commission approved the action without lengthy discussion. The atmospherics were simply overwhelming.

The trading halt began on March 18, 2002. It was the first time the SEC had suspended trading on an NYSE stock in over 25 years and it caused a storm of criticism in the press, all directed at the NYSE for not properly vetting a foreign company that it listed. A *New York Times* article connected ACLN to AremisSoft and Lernout & Hauspie, questioning whether accounting fraud had moved offshore.

The Internet buzzed with assertions that, after the halt expired, ACLN would reopen at twice the previous price. Hope springs eternal. So does hype. Then the NYSE delisted the stock—apparently stung by the press coverage—and the boards went silent. ACLN stock languished in the pink sheets at pennies per share.

I got many calls and e-mails from distraught investors. Victims of chat room promotions, some had put substantial chunks of their life savings in ACLN. One man, voice cracking, said, "I'm not stupid. I'm college educated. Although this was on the raw edge of aggressiveness for me, I thought it was okay because it was listed on the NYSE and had supposedly audited financial statements. Who would have known?" The calls were divided between people who said ACLN was a great company the government was trying to destroy for reasons that varied with the conspiracy theory of choice, and those who now believed it was a total fraud the SEC should have shut down long ago—before, that is, they bought the stock. This is always a problem. There's never a good time to pull the plug. No one is more loudly critical of the SEC than an investor in a pyramid scheme the agency shuts down before he can cash out and leave others holding the bag.[2]

A man with a thick Chinese accent told me he had lost most of his family's savings on Enron. Then he put their last $125,000 into buying ACLN on margin. Now he was getting margin calls from Merrill Lynch and wanted to know how they could sell him out if the stock wasn't trading. Shattered by this experience, he insisted despairingly that America "is the most evil country on earth."

---

[2]This leads to damned-if-you-do, damned-if-you-don't situations. If the SEC pulls the trigger early on a possible fraud, uncertain it can back up its allegations, it may cause huge investor losses. But if it waits too long, it becomes responsible for the losses of later victims, at least in their opinion.

★ ★ ★

Whatever its other effects, the trading halt raises the public profile of ACLN dramatically. This puts us under pressure to sue the company quickly so that no one can claim we acted in improper haste with the trading halt. Now we work in double time.

The only ACLN officer in the United States is the erstwhile CFO. When we hustle him in for testimony, we meet a baby-faced 27-year-old with a pink tie. Despite his title, he says he does nothing with the company's books. His remote access to its computer system doesn't include any part of its accounting records. He lives close to the little office ACLN rented in West L.A. and commute to work—wouldn't you know it—by skateboard. As the session goes on, he becomes increasingly distraught. It dawn on him he has been used as a front. When we show him the Tunisian arrest warrant on Labiad, he dabs at his eyes with a napkin. "My whole world is turning upside down," he blurts. "Now I don't know what to believe."

Heidi feels bad about making him cry. I tell her it might have been worse. I've had witnesses throw up.

To our surprise, we receive assistance from the Luxembourg banking authorities. This is a first. Either they've changed their policies or no one ever asked them nicely enough before. They confirm that the BNP Paribas account statements we were given are phony. They also tell us that the account held $56 million until all but $3.9 million was transferred to a bank in the Netherlands three days after we first served a subpoena on ACLN.

We hear through an intermediary that former Labiad associate Merhi Ali Abou Merhi is willing to speak with us. We have heard that Merhi, the 50 percent owner of record of the *Sea Atef*, is a major player in the car transport trade. But he is also rumored to be a bad lot who traffic in arms, drugs, "and human beings." Apparently this mean supplying product for the international sex industry, perhaps through coercion. These rumors may be complete fiction, nothing will ever be confirmed, but they add to the lurid atmosphere. When we reach him in Antwerp, Merhi, in very weak English, agree to speak to us on the record in Belgium.

Soon after, Merhi's assistant contacts us with the news that an attempt has been made on Merhi's life—a car bomb, discovered and disarmed by the police. Merhi contends that Labiad is involved with Hezbollah and ordered the bomb in the belief that Merhi had in some way assisted Israeli intelligence.

Then, on April 5, we are pitched into crisis mode. The Luxembourg authorities tell us ACLN has given BNP Paribas transfer instructions for the $3.9 million remaining in that account. They can delay the transaction for a few days. After that, it will take a court order. Once this money is out of Luxembourg, we will probably lose sight of it forever. But the commission never does anything quickly. Certainly not file an action in a foreign country concerning a complex financial fraud. And if we jump on money in Luxembourg and not in other countries where Labiad and Bisschops have accounts, it seems certain they will promptly move whatever they still control beyond our reach.

We consult local counsel in Luxembourg. In a resonant, French-accented voice that conveys authority, he assures us that procedures exist to freeze the money rapidly. We also contact an attorney in the Netherlands about the accounts in Dutch banks into which Labiad and Bisschops have sent money. He describes the process for blocking those accounts.

We spend the weekend writing an emergency memo to the commission asking for authority to freeze accounts in Luxembourg, the Netherlands, Monaco, and also Norway, a country where we have "soft information" there's another ACLN account. We know the ACLN principals have used certain banks in those countries but, with the exception of BNP Paribas in Luxembourg, do not know if any have current balances.

The authorization is granted on Monday, April 8, and, working through local counsel, we obtain civil attachments in Luxembourg and the Netherlands. But the money is fairly small. There's only the $2.9 million in Luxembourg and another $3 million in the Netherlands. Also we hear informally there's very little in the Norway account.

That leaves Monaco. Given the heavy use of banks there by the ACLN principals and our ability to identify several of their accounts, we are hopeful of finding some serious money in that country. But snagging it may be problematic. Local counsel has told us that, to initiate proceedings, the Monegasque courts require plaintiffs to pay a "judgment tax" that represents a hefty portion of the amount sought in the suit. He doesn't think that being an agency of the U.S. government will get us a pass from this requirement. If not, this will be fatal to any hope of capturing Monaco accounts—the mechanism simply doesn't exist for the SEC to put up this sort of litigation bond.

But while we are figuring out our options, the Monegasque authorities, it so happens, block a number of ACLN-related accounts based on a "suspicious activities report" filed by a local bank. They contain about $15 million. On the phone, the investigating magistrate is supremely cordial. Unsure which transactions are of interest to us, he faxes a list that goes on for many pages. We arrange to meet with him in Monaco.

The information from Monaco pays immediate dividends. We see that $25 million in ACLN money went from HSBC Bank in Monaco to Jyske Bank in Denmark. The transfer took place the previous week, so perhaps the money is still there. Danish counsel advises we can freeze the account, but only if the commission posts a $600,000 bond, which it will forfeit if it loses the case. We don't have the ability to post the bond so, rather than see the funds vanish into the ether, we alert the Danish police to the tainted source of the funds and suggest they freeze the account on their own. They do.

Now all we need to do is figure out how to claim it.

On April 17, while preparing to scramble a crew to visit local counsel and government agencies around Europe, I get a call from the Chief of Police in Antwerp, Belgium, Rudi Arnauts. His staff is investigating money laundering by Bisschops and Labiad and has frozen $7 million in ACLN bank accounts in Belgium. They are in the process of attaching a "castle" in central Belgium purchased by Bisschops with suspect funds. Chief Arnauts also mentions a $25 million account in Bisschops' name in Monaco, which they may attempt to seize.

Any transfers of money in Belgium not for a "legitimate economic purpose" may be considered money laundering. The funds need not derive from illegal activities. The Antwerp police have no idea how Bisschops and Labiad got this money; what matters to them is that it was moved around between banks for no apparent reason. The police have arrested ACLN's COO, Alex de Ridder, and are searching for Bisschops and Labiad, who are proving elusive.

Although Chief Arnauts offers his help with our investigation, including giving us ACLN financial documents grabbed by his detectives,

I am unsure whether to regard him as friend or foe. Are we going to be fighting over ACLN assets, with the Belgians having home field advantage? I leave this an open question for a face-to-face meeting in Antwerp.

★ ★ ★

The day after my arrival in Belgium—and our field trip to the Antwerp docks—is spent sifting through ACLN documents at the police station. Most of the material is useless but there are bank statements that give us additional links in the money trail. Patrick Vervaet mentions they also found some sexually explicit pictures of Bisschops and his male lover. We take a pass on examining them.

At lunch with Chief Arnauts, who has succeeded in charming the hell out of my attorneys, I broach the subject of the money frozen in Belgium. Shouldn't it go to the investors these guys ripped off, rather than into the Belgian treasury? The distribution we intend to make at the end of the case will not be limited to U.S. investors. Any screwed Belgians can queue up too. He seems amused by my proposal but is too considerate to tell me I'm dreaming. He says the decision will be made by people above him in the hierarchy.

In the later afternoon Patrick drives us out into the country to see "the castle." Everyone piles into his car except Charlie, who is buried too deeply in the documents to be extracted. On our way out of town, Patrick points out the jail where de Ridder is held. From the outside it looks like a typical office building, distinguishable from the structures on either side only by address. A model of European discretion.

It is quite an unusual residence the police have seized, and an unusual household they have put to flight. In a huge and isolated structure outside Antwerp, worth many millions, Bisschops and his lover raised twin boys fathered by one or the other—it is unclear which—with an American woman who rented out her uterus for purposes of commercial propagation.

The driveway winds between nodding, rain-soaked trees to a broad iron gate. We can't enter because the magistrate has yet to sign the order giving full possession to the local prosecutor, who is working to prove the property was purchased with laundered money. Patrick believes the twins and their nanny are still there, alone, waiting for whatever will happen. We prowl along the high fence skirting the property to glimpse, behind clusters of trees, an eighteenth century manor house, once owned by the local gentry, now by a reputed financial fraud artist on the run. A few bedraggled peacocks, scattered across the grounds, are the only visible signs of life, their harsh cries the only sound above the rain.

A joke of history and a perfect setting for a low-budget horror film.

That night I receive a message to call Labiad's Norwegian lawyer. On the phone, he says Labiad knows we are in Europe and wants to speak with us. I suggest Labiad give testimony at our embassy in Brussels. The building is legally U.S. territory, which means an embassy official can administer the oath and make it all official. It also means we will have complete security. The message comes back that Labiad wants to confer with U.S. counsel before he decides. Perhaps he is afraid we'll roll him up in a rug and throw him on a plane back to America. Next we hear he wants another week to think about it. By that time we will all have departed, so it isn't going to happen. Not that it was ever likely to in any event.

The Antwerp police arrange for us to speak with the only ACLN employee still in town, Annie Bormans. My sense is that they made her an offer she couldn't refuse, but I don't ask for details. She has agreed, under whatever duress, to meet us in the lobby of a small hotel, next door to what we have been told is the residence of Labiad's ex-wife. She declined to come to the police station for the interview and has insisted we meet in a public place.

A once-beautiful woman with a personal history of transient employment and absent husbands, Bormans is the most flagrant and unconvincing liar I have ever met. A chain smoker with flighty mannerisms, she says whatever pops into her head and then tries to cover up obvious contradictions with new contradictions, all with an air of being overwhelmed by the vagaries of life and the inscrutable conduct of other human beings. Beneath the outer layer of ditz, however, is something else that seems like fear bordering on panic. I wonder if she is wearing a wire or under observation from elsewhere in the lobby. She seems determined to be as brazenly unhelpful as possible.

Her role at ACLN, as she describes it, was to provide minor ministerial services around the Antwerp office as directed by Bisschops—the word Labiad is not in her vocabulary—and with little understanding of what she was doing or why she was doing it. She obtained manifests from the stevedores who loaded the boats and generated from them bills of lading which she then left at the ACLN office for whatever use anyone might make of them. She can't remember seeing summaries of the company's transactions, bank documents or customer payment items. Rarely did she speak with anyone else at the company.

She has no explanation for the two million dollars in ACLN stock she received from Bisschops and sold through a Merrill broker in Monaco, a person she claims she met at a party and decided on impulse to have sell her stock. Bisschops gave her the stock "for personal reasons." That's all she will say about that. She previously told the Belgian police the stock was a reward for her help in getting Labiad out of jail in Monaco. Either she's forgotten the earlier story or, more likely, doesn't care about being consistent, so long as the word Labiad doesn't pass her lips. She flatly refuses to say where the money is now.

She is absurdly unconvincing in her account of why she created the British Virgin Islands corporation used to dump ACLN stock. No one told her to do it and she had no purpose in mind. You just never know when you might need a corporate shell. For what? Nothing. Anything. And the nephew who set up another conduit for insider sales? She can barely remember being related to such a person. She certainly had no idea he was involved with ACLN.

The following day Michael, Charlie, and I are on a train to Monaco. We are to meet with a group of Monegasque officials about the ACLN bank accounts they have blocked—at $15 million the biggest stash other than the Danish accounts—and to wheedle for whatever additional evidence they will give us as to how the money got there. Then Charlie and I will fly to Cyprus to take the testimony of ACLN's "auditors." I also want to talk to the Cypriot authorities about our two resident AremisSoft fugitives, Poyiadjis and Kyprianou.

Heidi stays behind to interview Merhi Ali Abou Merhi. Given the rumors about him, we have chosen as the venue the U.S. embassy in Brussels. It would have been hard to replace Heidi and harder still to explain to our superiors that an SEC attorney is missing and presumed abducted into the white slave trade.

★ ★ ★

Taxis do not seem to frequent the Monaco train station. Even Mike's impeccable French is unavailing in obtaining transportation to our hotel. But after an hour spent at the curb, a woman cabbie—well into middle age and wearing the sort of boldly striped shirt I associate with mimes—pulls up in a geriatric Mercedes. The three of us cram into the back seat, the shotgun seat being reserved for the poodle that hectors us with little yips on the way to our hotel. We assume, because the hotel is not in Monaco but in the French hamlet of Beausoleil, that we are in for a long ride. In actuality, it is two blocks from the station. A five-minute walk, had we known.

The hotel is like a YMCA for dwarves, its Formica-floored lobby the size of a large closet. My room barely accommodates a single bed, with no other furniture except a shelf on the wall for a tiny portable TV. It gets one channel of French-narrated snow. The only window is no larger than a sheet of paper and opens on an airshaft. But it is the best we could do on the per diem, Rich Rosenfeld not being on this case.

If the hotel is in all ways modest, the surrounding city, when we tumble out to look at it, is gloriously the opposite. Monaco rises from its stunningly beautiful harbor—yachts lined up along the marina like rows of perfect white teeth—past clusters of luxury apartment towers and up twisty streets into the coastal hills of France. A fraction the size of Central Park, the principality is a study in compressed affluence. The stores appear plucked from Rodeo Drive and pedestrians from the better Paris neighborhoods. The very air feels costly. And security is extraordinary, particularly near the casino in Monte Carlo. There are video cameras on walls, in bushes, on poles behind palm and carob trees. No undesirable element would make it a single block without setting off alarms. Immaculately groomed and perpetually scrutinized, Monaco is the Disneyland of gamblers and international financial sharks.

The local attorney we've hired to help us maneuver through the Monegasque legal system, James Duffy, lives in one of the apartment towers overlooking the harbor and enjoys a favored status in Monaco, apparently won though many years of civic service. Although not granted citizenship—a privilege normally reserved for the offspring of citizens—he can reside here permanently and own real property. He considers himself very fortunate.

His description of the officials we are to meet is colored with an almost feudal deference to their positions. We are, after all, in a principality. The Monegasque authorities possess wide discretion and can use it to our benefit or not, almost as a matter of whim. He believes that with his assistance, however, we may achieve our goals. Monaco, like the Isle of Man, is looking to exit the international blacklist of financial fraud havens. A show of assistance to a Cub Scout pack of American regulators can't hurt. And it isn't as if Aldo Labiad, once a fixture in a Monaco jail, has any friends here. Still, we must be mindful to do the required bowing and scraping. We are asking for something wholly unprecedented.

The Palais d'Justice sits on a shelf of rock above the Mediterranean, across an open courtyard from the Royal Palace. As we emerge from Duffy's Renault, a black Rolls Royce sweeps rapidly past, bearing the royal person of Prince Rainier III. The local news reports that he is being hospitalized for unspecified medical procedures.

After a quarter-hour spent admiring the architecture of the Palais d'Justice from its lobby, we are led into the chambers of the investigating magistrate. Like many officials in Monaco, he is French rather than Monegasque. We are joined by a prosecutor from the ministry of justice. Both are cordial but seem uncertain what to make of us. With Michael translating and Duffy adding legalistic asides, I rattle on with a semiprepared speech about the prominent nature of the case and our intention to trumpet the assistance of foreign regulators. And then, of course, there's the importance of getting money back to defrauded investors. Widows and orphans every one. Michael adds body language as he translates. The judge and prosecutor appear to find our performance disarming. They smile and bobble their heads.

After listening patiently, and conferring with other officials who flit in and out of the room, they agree to forego bringing a money laundering case against Labiad and Bisschops, which would result in the frozen $15 million being irretrievably forfeited to their government. They will continue the freeze but, there being no treaty in place, need a letter rogatory before they can release the funds. Another favor we will have to ask of DOJ. Moreover, they will provide, in appropriate form, any additional documents we need concerning the bank accounts. Escorting us out, the prosecutor confides that Monaco released Labiad because the Tunisians delayed for too long in processing the paper for his extradition. One small mystery solved.

In the parking lot I feel like high-fiving Mike and Charlie but, still in full view of the Palais d'Justice, deny the impulse. Hot damn! Everyone told us we'd never get money out of Monaco and now it looks like it's in the bag. Duffy seems relieved and eager to depart, as if afraid the judge and prosecutor might come running after us to say they've changed their minds.

On our last day in Monaco, Duffy goes out of his way to be a good host. He takes us to a formal luncheon at a beautiful old wedding cake of a hotel down the coast in Saint-Jean-Cap-Ferrat. The event is for the local American Club. Duffy, we find, is its president and today we are its guests of honor. He introduces us with a speech that alludes repeatedly to the Oliver Stone film *Wall Street* and makes us sound like the Untouchables, except less accommodating to law-breakers. The club consists largely of wealthy retired people, dressed up for the occasion. I sit between two elderly French ladies who married and outlived American husbands. One inquires pleasantly if I am carrying a gun.

A voicemail from Heidi says her meeting with Merhi came off as scheduled and he was a pussycat, at least by the standards of reputed dealers in arms, drugs and human beings. He jumped on ACLN with both feet. Apparently, he took the car bomb personally.

He and his assistant Ivan burst out laughing at many of the representations made by ACLN. ACLN's claim to have shipped around 10,000 new cars to Benin over the past two years, Merhi insisted, were utterly false. It is *he*, Merhi Ali Abou Merhi, who dominates the Benin car market. ACLN has no presence there. If it did, he would know. And the numbers it reported are absurd. He pulled out a letter from the Benin port authority (Conseil National Des Chargeurs du Benin) stating that the total number of cars imported from Korea to Benin in 2000 and 2001 was 58, a number smaller than 10,000. Merhi also confirmed that the *Sea Atef* cost far less than ACLN reported and is half-owned by his company. Moreover, the vessel is in need of repair and never made most of the voyages claimed by ACLN.

Heidi will now fly to Denmark to brief the prosecutors there on the state of our investigation. It's far from certain they will be willing to act as our proxies in obtaining the return of the funds they have frozen. But one must take into consideration the Heidi factor.

★   ★   ★

From the air, Cyprus is a mouse-brown jigsaw puzzle piece dropped on a blue tablecloth. On the flight, Charlie and I get a lesson in history and politics. The Cyprus Airways pilot describes with emotion the 1974 invasion of the northern half of the island by Turkey, resulting, he says, in thousands of casualties with many people still missing, and the deprivation of many Greek Cypriots of their property.

During the 40-minute drive into Nicosia, the elderly cab driver also orates about the transgressions of the nefarious Turks. The passage of 30 years has done little to placate these grievances. We pass the stadium that is home to the island's soccer teams—the rivalries, once political, are now ethnic and geographic. The Cyprus stock exchange occupies a new building that stands exposed in an empty space beside the highway. Our cabbie describes how the market here boomed and then collapsed. It has not come back.

A United Nations buffer zone divides Greek from Turkish Cyprus. It runs through the center of Nicosia, two blocks from the dilapidated Holiday Inn where we will stay. The line is a marked by boarded-up windows and sandbagged doors. Wandering out in the late afternoon, Charlie and I find dusty, sun-blind streets, drowsy cafes, and houses with shuttered, piebald facades, and a pedestrian mall of shoe stores and postcard shops. At one end is barrier patrolled by a soldier. A sign prohibits the taking of pictures.

Even at the far end of the Mediterranean there is no escape from the investing public. An ACLN investor leaves a voice message at the hotel saying he has confirmed we're in Nicosia. He wants to know what we're doing to get his money back.

The Cyprus SEC is on an upscale side street—at least upscale for Nicosia. We meet there the following morning with one of its commissioners, several attorneys, and a representative of the Cyprus Attorney General. The attorneys are young and idealistic, eager to do something about the public perception that their country is a magnet for dirty money and their stock market corrupt. But that perception is largely correct. Cyprus has earned notoriety for sucking in cash from Russian mobsters and former Serbian president Slobodan Milosevic. And the Cyprus stock market has been rocked repeatedly by financial scandals, one of the largest involving Kyprianou. They explain that the government's attempt to prosecute him failed because of an antiquated legal system that makes it nearly impossible to bring complex financial cases. They compare it to that of England's system of a hundred years ago. They also have difficulty obtaining documents from foreign sources. Swiss banking records would be helpful in their case against Kyprianou, but they don't have a treaty with Switzerland. The United States does, which has already paid off in our investigation of AremisSoft. Unfortunately, however, its terms forbid sharing its products with other governments. No matter how much we may want to do so.

We ask about Kyprianou and Poyiadjis. One of the women attorneys, in her late twenties and strikingly beautiful, says they are still on the island. She doesn't think they have made any surreptitious trips abroad, but is certain they will eventually. No one stays in Cyprus forever. It drives people crazy.

Over lunch, I mention the twists and turns in our *other* case involving a rogue Cyprus corporation, ACLN, including the attempted murder in Antwerp. The commissioner laughs and says car-bombing is also popular in Cyprus. Here, however, it is treated as a crime against property because no one ever gets killed. Except, he recalls, for one judge—and that was an accident.

Late in the day, I visit the attorney we hired to assist us on AremisSoft. His office, in a quiet suburban neighborhood, is like something out of Bruno Schultz. A rabbit warren of creaky floors, crooked hallways and towering bookcases crammed with legal tomes. The man is well up in years but quite keen to be of help. To date we have used him only to effect service of process. I wonder, however, if there are other possibilities. Neither we nor the U.S. Attorney's Office have been able to trace the hundreds of millions of dollars Kyprianou made from selling AremisSoft stock. It's been a series of dead ends. Does this guy have any ideas? He says he has contacts at the local banks that might tell him if Kyprianou keeps money in Cyprus.

At this point, anything seems worth a try.

We have arranged to take the testimony of ACLN's auditors at the U.S. Embassy, a plaster-walled fortress with a highly visible Marine presence. The auditors—a father and son team who run the local affiliate of BDO International—surprise us the next morning by showing up. It's not clear we could compel them to speak with us if they declined. But they may not know that.

Questioning accountants from the large international firms is usually a migraine-inducing activity. Every word is parsed by a platoon of defense attorneys. The slightest possible ambiguity means you won't get an answer.

But this isn't a large firm. Quite the opposite. Despite the BDO tag, these guys are strictly local. Looking more than a bit cowed, they come in to throw themselves on our mercy—erroneously assuming we have any. They readily admit they have no understanding of U.S. Generally Accepted Accounting Principles ("GAAP"). So it's hard to fathom how they could sign audit opinions for SEC reports. It quickly becomes apparent, moreover, that they did not so much audit ACLN's financial statements as create them from source documents supplied by company management, many of which we know to be fraudulent. At bottom mere book-keepers, and poor ones at that, they have managed to violate nearly every standard of the profession—including the one forbidding auditors from having any role in creating the financial statements they audit.

They never bothered to authenticate any of the documents provided by ACLN management—including invoices and bank statements—with anyone outside the company. A stunning audit failure. Asked how he verified the accuracy of invoices ACLN received from a related party the younger member of the team seems puzzled by the question. "You just look at them," he says.

★ ★ ★

We now have $45 million or so frozen in ACLN accounts in Monaco, Denmark, Luxembourg, and the Netherlands. Then there's the $200 million or so in AremisSoft money sitting in the Isle of Man—an amount equivalent to 2,000 years of my salary.

I believe at this point—however naively—that the hard part is behind us on both cases. Surely, given the magnitude of the frauds involved, no one can seriously dispute that the proper resolution of ACLN and AremisSoft should include returning as much money as possible to their investors.

Through the summer of 2002, evidence that ACLN was an utter fraud continues to pile up. From Luxembourg we receive copies of ACLN's BNP Paribas statements. Comparing these to the statements furnished by ACLN to its auditors, the father-son duo in Cyprus, reveals the latter to be forgeries. Just looking at them, it seems, wasn't enough. The $117 million in cash reported as an ACLN asset never existed. The account was used solely for hiding the proceeds of stock sales by Bisschops, Labiad, and de Ridder.

Interpol comes through with information that the VIN numbers that ACLN's counsel gave us to document the company's African sales in fact are those of cars that never left Korea, including patrol cars in use by the Seoul police. Also, a letter rogatory submitted to the South Korean government through DOJ elicits the information that Daewoo sold *no* cars to ACLN, directly or through Hwang (either drunk or sober).

In September, we file a fraud action in U.S. district court against ACLN, Labiad, Bisschops, and de Ridder, expecting it will go by default, and a settled action against the BDO Cyprus auditors. They take a bar from ever again auditing any company registered with the SEC and agree to cough up their audit fees from ACLN—a relative slap on the wrist but, given that they're in Cyprus and we're not, more than we could have gotten if they'd just told us to screw off.

ACLN's lawyers make an initial attempt to fight the freezes in Luxembourg and Denmark but give up after hitting some early reversals, perhaps accepting that their clients should never be found anywhere near a courthouse. That leaves us to deal with our real enemy, the vagaries of the international legal system.

A delegation from the Belgian Justice Ministry comes to D.C. to swap information with us. They have traced the funds that went through Belgium and present the results on multicolored charts. When it is time for them to leave, I drive the whole bunch to Dulles Airport, despite the dying transmission in my van, nattering about the glorious goal of fattening the return to defrauded investors, rather than the Belgian treasury. No doubt they regret not springing for a taxi. Privately, I think we should count ourselves lucky if the Belgians keep everything in their country and let us have whatever we find elsewhere.

We learn that the only way to extract the money frozen in the Netherlands is to litigate there. A U.S. judgment will be considered scratch-paper by its courts. Moreover, the Dutch judge who granted the asset freeze imposes a short deadline for us to do *something* there or lose the freeze. The SEC has never before initiated an original action in a foreign country, and it may not have the legal power to do so. After *much* internal debate, however, the Commission goes for it. We sue ACLN and its principals in the Netherlands for violations of the U.S. securities laws.

The hardest trick will be getting the $25 million out of Denmark. The staff of its Justice Ministry, after meeting Heidi on her flying visit in March, was sympathetic but pessimistic. Danish law makes no provision for civil judgments from other countries, even if obtained by a government agency.

Fully understanding the shakiness of our position, attorneys representing the corporation Labiad used to hide money in Denmark challenge the asset freeze.

They win.

We appeal.

We win.

But this only means the freeze stays in place for the time being.

On a sultry Monday night in July, several of us troop over to Main Justice on Pennsylvania Avenue to corner an official of the Danish Justice Ministry in town to negotiate a treaty on behalf of the European Union. Although she had previously advised us, in a phone conversation, not to expect to ever get our institutional paws on the money, she's now guardedly optimistic. Perhaps our recent appellate victory makes her take us more seriously. Two possible approaches strike her as promising, neither previously tried in Denmark: a civil forfeiture action through DOJ and prosecution by the Danish criminal authorities.

★ ★ ★

In ACLN, the problems mainly concern the disconnects between national legal systems. The company's principals are not in a position to fight and, save for the Belgians, no other foreign authorities move to snatch any ACLN assets. All we need to do is figure out a legally acceptable means of pursuing our claims in four different countries. In AremisSoft, by contrast, the amount of money at stake and the legal avenues open to Poyiadjis promise a protracted struggle against a highly-motivated and well-funded opposition.

Anyone who didn't skip the sixth grade remembers the sad story of the fisherman in Hemingway's *The Old Man and the Sea*, who, in his small boat far out at sea, manages to harpoon a giant marlin, only to have its carcass devoured by sharks drawn by the scent of blood. It is an experience with which I will come to identify, although the predators here come with briefcases rather than fins.

The "trough" in the Isle of Man is deep and getting deeper, despite the hemorrhaging of fees to the trustees' attorneys. By early 2003, the balance has swollen from $200 to over $220 million thanks to the trustees, who it turns out were right about getting out of dollars and into Euros. Bless their conniving little hearts.

Meanwhile, the trustees have no complaints about how they're being treated by the courts. On March 5, 2003, the English Deemster delivers her written opinion on their application for funds to pay U.S. lawyers. It's even worse than expected. She clearly regards Poyiadjis and his cohorts as, at worst, enterprising delinquents, while taking a jaundiced view of "the Americans." Without committing anything to writing so blatant as to invite reversal on appeal, she solicitously strokes the trustees' conspiracy theories. She is concerned Poyiadjis has been railroaded by the American legal system, a phrase which in this opinion usually appears in close proximity to the adjective "draconian." Implicit throughout is a harsh view of the American government. It is simply not to be trusted to behave decently.

The practical harm from her opinion goes beyond the additional costs and delays to be expected from opening another legal theater for the trustees' attorneys to preen and posture. It may color the pending determination whether the U.S. default judgment will be honored in the Isle of Man. If the trustees get bounced from the U.S. court—a near certainty—they will yowl that Poyiadjis has been made the victim of frontier justice and it is therefore *not fair* to give the bad Americans his money, however he might have obtained it. Any other Deemster following this one's lead will start out pointed in the wrong direction.

Everyone, including our general counsel's office, is in solid agreement we have no choice but to appeal. We flag to the commission the mounting costs of the case and remind it that, under the "loser pays" rule, we could end up on the hook for the defendants' elephantine legal fees. This has been discussed before many times. But this time the agency's general counsel, dismaying his own staff, has a sudden anxiety attack and complains loudly about the financial risk we are taking on. No matter. The commissioners are willing to accept the hazards inherent in playing in a high stakes game in a foreign country. They approve the appeal.

But how will they feel if, after we double-down with the appeal, we lose? At some point the well of institutional patience will run dry.

We work with Campbell and Justin to draft a brief for the appeal that everyone feels good about. We believe we ought to win—for whatever that's worth. On the day before the filing is due, however, the Manx Attorney General gets cold feet. He expresses doubts about our chances of success and fears a potential cost award. He renews his demand for indemnification. The unlimited access given the Poyiadjis crew to the frozen funds while we remain straitjacketed by budgets not designed for expensive foreign litigation has turned this into a war of financial attrition we could well lose. The A.G. wants to make sure that, if we do, we don't take the Isle of Man treasury down with us. It's not an unreasonable concern, but neither the SEC nor DOJ can take on that sort of open-ended liability.

Kevin Puwaoski, who is now all alone on point for DOJ, pledges to find some means of satisfying him. The AG is sufficiently placated to allow the appeal to be filed.

The sharks are also gathering on our side of the Atlantic.

AremisSoft is in a bankruptcy proceeding in Newark, New Jersey. Kevin and I are notified there will be a hearing before the district court judge and we are expected to attend. We are given the innocent-sounding explanation that the bankruptcy trustee is seeking the court's authorization to support our efforts in the Isle of Man. How nice of him, we think, and walk unsuspecting into an ambush.

As soon as the necessary hands are shaken, we are subjected to a full court press from attorneys for the trustee. They want whatever the government recovers in the Isle of Man to be put into the bankruptcy estate. This would mean the money goes to trade creditors and the trustee's attorneys before investors. And that the law firm of Milberg Weiss, hired on contingency by the trustee to recover assets for the estate, gets 20 percent of the total. That would be around *$40 million* if the funds frozen in the Isle of Man come back. Never mind that Milberg Weiss has done precisely nothing to help recover this money. Moreover, it is no longer counsel to the bankruptcy trustee, so there's no chance it will exert itself productively in the future.

Mel Weiss—king of the securities class action lawyers—is there in person to argue the merits of this proposed atrocity. He is a trollish man in his sixties, looking very pleased with himself, perhaps because he already has more money than the entire population of most zip codes and believes he's about to get more.

What is truly incredible, however, is that the judge is in his corner. Tag-teaming with the trustee's attorneys, he tells us he has issued an order recognizing this claim. He believes this was required under the trustee's deal with Milberg Weiss. Anyway, it would be a big hassle to change the whole plan around at this point. We can't possibly expect that, can we?

Neither Kevin nor I, of course, have the power to agree to anything like what is being proposed. The judge wants to know that we will, at least, recommend his plan to our superiors. I stifle what I am tempted to say, which would have been unwise, and make mushy statements about how we will need time to review the papers and consider. Kevin dishes out similar mush.

This goes on for some time before the judge gives up in exasperation. Weiss, who has been sitting quietly through this exchange, does not seem upset by our resistance. He stares as patiently as a spider contemplating a hopelessly trapped fly.

When I get back to my office in the early evening, there's a voicemail from the judge's secretary demanding that Kevin and I appear in his New Jersey courtroom the next day. There's an undertone of "bring your toothbrush."

When we appear as directed, we get the same arguments from the same people. But this time the judge bears down more forcefully. He accuses us of disrespecting his order. Do we suggest he's shown improper favoritism toward Milberg Weiss? Kevin replies that we have no criticism of his order, but it has nothing to do with the government's case, which is in another venue and based on wholly separate legal claims. This goes on for another hour until we finally think we've convinced the judge we're simply doing our jobs. But no. As we're sidling toward the door, he leaps up and demands to know how *we* would have written the order.

Clearly, this is not over.

On the way back to the train station, Kevin says he's gotten another letter from the Manx A.G. demanding an indemnity. The letter states that the demand is now nonnegotiable.

★   ★   ★

I'd been on the edge of leaving the SEC for a year, perhaps due to having too much time to think while traveling. On a quick stop-over in Athens, Charlie Neal and I checked into a negative-star downtown hotel. The room was like a third-world hospital ward but, when I threw open the window shutters, I found the Acropolis soaring above me—the Parthenon gleaming from the top of the escarpment. Below the window, a hundred-foot drop ended in the courtyard of a Greek Orthodox church. And at the back of the courtyard sat a building with a tile roof smothered in bougainvilleas. Nestled among their vines was a shrunken and discolored soccer ball, long forgotten by the children who used that courtyard for a playground.

For ten years my Saturday afternoons were spent watching my son maneuver a soccer ball across the green fields of northern Virginia. But he was now in high school and that phase of his life a memory. It struck me with rude force, looking down from that hotel window, that it might also be time for me to move on. What had been intended as a brief stint of government employment while I made other plans had somehow become much of my adult life. I wasn't sure I wanted the rest of it to be more of the same, only to end up, finally, as a division dinosaur.

That year did nothing to make anyone feel like hanging at the SEC. The esteem in which the agency had been held for the last decade took a major battering when it was discovered to have been the last to know that mutual funds were letting certain customers trade in opportunistic ways not available to the masses, and that sell-side analysts hadn't truly been in love with all those fly-by-night Internet stocks. On these issues, Eliot Spitzer had eaten the commission's lunch, and with little concern for table manners. It hadn't helped that the chairman during much of that time was Harvey Pitt, a fine securities attorney but a political calamity. Appointed during a contentious period, he had managed to tread a path generously strewn with banana skins without missing a single one.

My group's immediate situation had also deteriorated. For five years we'd been blessed with a front office that rarely thrust itself deeply into case management. The previous regimen of benign neglect, however, had given way to one difficult to keep far enough at bay to limit mistakes, delays, and staff attrition. Nor did my efforts in that direction go unremarked. The Division's latest director gave his verdict: "You are not sufficiently deferential to me," he said, "and you take too much initiative for someone in your position."

Realizing I had not created the best possible impression with our new superior, I'd made a few ill-fated attempts at schmoozing. Learning that he, like me, had gone to high school in Los Angeles, and prepared to recount my own tragic adolescent experiences, I inquired about his alma mater. "I went to a private school for the gifted," he said. At which point further conversation seemed futile.

I repeated this exchange to Heidi, thinking she'd find it amusing. She was incensed. "If he's so fucking *gifted*," she wanted to know, "why does he keep screwing up our cases?"

Yes, well. . . . Save us, I thought, from the gifted.

Every time I remembered the abandoned soccer ball on the Athens rooftop, I thought again of how long I'd left the clock running at the SEC. But how could I, on a daily basis, tell my attorneys they shouldn't even *think* of leaving the SEC, even for a job paying three times as much, when that would mean abandoning cases of great importance, only to then run out the door myself?

By the spring of 2003, however, we had resolved several major cases. And ACLN was under control—the major battles won, if bureaucrats in half a dozen different countries still waited to be fed. It was only

AremisSoft that seemed like a disabled but much-loved child requiring long-term attention.

Until, with a suddenness that surpassed all hope, the tide turned there too.

A raft of nasty motions filed by the Poyiadjis trustees, alleging various forms of bad faith by "the Americans," was given short shrift by the Isle of Man Deemster. He was, at long last, tired of their antics. He scheduled the proceeding to register the U.S. civil forfeiture order for September and wanted to hear nothing else until then. Thus, assuming we won on the pending appeal and kept the trustees from opening a second front in the U.S., Poyiadjis and the trustees would be up against it. They would go into what should be the final hearing facing strong indications that the Isle of Man judiciary wanted to see the last of them. If we won on the appeal, that is. If we lost, we might be forced to conclude that we just didn't have the chips to play at such a high-stakes table.

The suspense was short-lived. The decision on our appeal came down quickly. We won. On everything. The order was a complete rebuke to the trustees. They didn't get a nickel to contest the default judgment in the United States. Our country was not held to be a cultural and political throw-back to the stone age. Best of all, the decision stripped away most of the trustees' potential arguments that it would not be "in the interests of justice" to release the funds to the U.S. government.

Now it seemed a straight road to the September hearing and the end of the Isle of Man saga. That is how we saw it and, as it turned out, Poyiadjis and his advisors shared our view.

★ ★ ★

Six years later . . .

AremisSoft resulted in an unprecedented win for the government in offshore litigation. Kevin and Rich saw the Isle of Man adventure through to the end before going on to other things. The result was not perfect but, under the circumstances, remarkably good. Facing the likelihood he would lose in litigation, Poyiadjis agreed to release $200 million from his frozen accounts to the Department of Justice, which, in turn, kicked it to the SEC to distribute to AremisSoft shareholders. Poyiadjis kept whatever the trustees' ministrations had added to the blocked accounts. Thus he remained a wealthy man, if less so than before, and was no longer a fugitive holed up on Cyprus.

Milberg Weiss got a chunk of the money through the bankruptcy proceeding, if much less than it had originally sought. Mel Weiss's enjoyment of this unearned windfall was interrupted, however, when he was convicted of paying kickbacks to professional plaintiffs in class action suits and sentenced to prison.

Kyprianou remains at large and, so far as I know, still enjoys such nightlife as exists in Cyprus. I assume efforts continue toward recovering his profits from his AremisSoft sales. I hope to hear positive news before I die.

ACLN, frustratingly, is not fully resolved as of this writing, despite the passage of years. The $25 million frozen in Denmark came back to the United States, as did the $2.9 million from the Netherlands. But the $15 million in Monaco and the $3 million in Luxembourg remain, I have been told, stuck in those counties. Apparently their legal systems present more hurdles than expected.

The Belgians prosecuted nearly everyone connected to ACLN for money laundering, and obtained convictions against Bisschops, Labiad, de Ridder, Anny Bormans, and two lawyers who helped them hide their money. If Europe can boast a more evolved civilization than ours, the proof may lie in a greater willingness to put lawyers in jail. The defendants received sentences ranging from two to five years.

Bisschops, however, was convicted in absentia—having vanished at the outset of the criminal investigation. Where he is today, and whether dead or alive, is unknown.

Chapter 7

In the Shadow of Enron

I n the spring of 2004, political campaign spots on San Diego TV rang with ominous sound effects suitable for a program on serial murderers. Primary elections for mayor and city attorney were being played out against allegations of fraud in the city's pension system, irresistible for political exploitation. Law enforcement agencies were elbowing against each other for position, with the U.S. Attorney's Office, the SEC, and the San Diego District Attorney each investigating. The *San Diego Union-Tribune* shouted scandal. And reflecting a sudden national interest in problems long bubbling under the surface in San Diego, the *New York Times* dubbed the city "Enron-by-the-Sea."

The financial markets were, at that time, still recovering from a parade of financial frauds of which Enron was emblematic, but which also included WorldCom, Adelphia, Sunbeam, and Waste Management. Involving large-cap companies—rather than the pink-sheet detritus traditionally caught cooking the books—these accounting scandals had given a queasy feeling to the investing public. Not wanting any more of that, Congress had imposed in the Sarbanes-Oxley Act of 2002 a grab-bag of new rules for public companies, their officers, directors, and auditors. Meanwhile, the SEC and the Department of Justice ramped up their efforts to nail corporate malefactors.

All this sounded a dinner bell for lawyers. Suddenly, law firms saw securities defense as a growth area. I seized the opportunity that arose from being in a hot area to slide from the agency into a position with a large law firm, Vinson & Elkins, confounding a widespread belief that my retirement plan at the SEC consisted of someday dying at my desk.

Among the more meaty engagements for securities lawyers are "independent investigations," self-inflicted anal probes of public companies allowing their directors and executives to get an idea of what's sneaking up on them. And should the government come knocking, a report from an outside firm can sometimes prove handy in deflating its interest. Or not, depending on its contents. That's the risk. While at the SEC, I was the recipient of a number of company-sponsored reports. Some were helpful sources of information. Others were useless. None was an acceptable substitute for a staff investigation.

A few months after my unlikely entry into the world of corporate law, one of my new partners pulled me into one such investigation. The client was the City of San Diego.

My partner had headed the SEC's Office of Municipal Securities until departing for private practice. "Muniland," as he called it, is an odd backwater of the securities industry. Despite the enormous market for municipal bonds, governmental issuers are subject to very limited disclosure requirements. Since cities, unlike private corporations, never go away, rarely go bankrupt, and sell only debt securities, there's little demand that they provide the detailed and up-to-date financial information investors want from public companies.

But San Diego was a special case. In early 2004, it was in turmoil over the funding of its pension system and attracting national media attention because of allegations of illegality. The gestation period for this situation was a full 20 years, its progress nurtured by numerous legislative blunders and much myopic oversight by the city's administrators, auditors, and advisers, not to mention the bond rating agencies. But the flash-point, when it came, caught the city unaware and set in motion a series of events no one would have predicted.

★　★　★

California, like other states, requires that state and local retirement systems be "actuarially sound." Unlike Social Security—a pay-as-you-go scheme that relies on a stream of new contributors to support current retirees—they are supposed to have actual *assets* sufficient to cover their projected liabilities. In short, they are not allowed to follow the federal Ponzi scheme approach.

Pension systems rely on actuaries—an odd breed of number-crunchers in general too nerdy to be accountants—to say how much cash must be ponied up yearly to meet projected long-term costs. Getting to that number, however, requires educated guesses—the actuary's art—about such things as trends in retirement age and life expectancy and the investment returns to be expected from system assets. The better the assets pay, the less fresh money has to be fed into the system to keep it sound.

Of course, no one can predict with confidence what the market will do in future years, so actuaries' estimates are moving numbers, subject to debate and periodic adjustment. Bull markets in particular are likely to invite challenges to an actuary's projected rates of return. When politicians eye their local system's buoyant balance sheet, they think of a multitude of potential uses for the money beyond simply stashing it away to pay obligations not due until after many an election has come and gone. Unfortunately, however, bull markets don't last forever and the excess returns from fat years should be kept to balance the weak or negative returns from lean years. Otherwise the average return is dragged down below what is necessary to keep the system solvent.

This simple truth, however, proved beyond the grasp of San Diego's political leaders. In this they were not alone. Many other cities, counties, and states shorted their pension systems to plug budgetary gaps, even if few did so quite so aggressively. The first diversion of cash from the San Diego City Employees Retirement System (SDCERS) came in 1980 when the city council decreed that half the "surplus earnings" thrown off by the system (anything over the actuary's projected rate of return) would go to retirees in the form of a "13th check" for that year. The hyperinflation of the Carter years had eroded the purchasing power of SDCERS benefits, meager to begin with, and this was seen as a means of aiding pensioners at no cost to the city. By itself, this might have been manageable, but the genie was now out of the bottle. Squeezing "surplus" out of the retirement system became the knee-jerk response to San Diego budgetary problems, the multiplying uses of this supposed perpetual windfall eventually ranked in a provision of the San Diego Municipal Code know metaphorically as "the waterfall."

By the 1990s, electoral changes in San Diego had resulted in the emergence of the municipal unions as major players in city elections. Whenever their contracts came up for renegotiation, thanks to this leverage, their terms of employment improved significantly. This presented a problem for the municipality that a former city manager called "the cheapest big city in the country." San Diego has long been a fervently antitax town. The same mayors and city council members who couldn't say no to the unions also dreaded facing down the voters over higher taxes.

In 1996 contract negotiations, the irresistible political force of the unions met the immovable object of San Diego's antitax populace with lasting results. Union demands for pay increases, which would have quickly ruptured the city's budget, were turned aside only through major concessions on pension benefits. Meanwhile, changing membership demographics were threatening to increase the contributions needed from the city to keep SDCERS actuarially sound. Thus, despite having pushed off onto future taxpayers much of the price of keeping the unions happy, San Diego remained in need of serious budgetary creativity.

Rising to the occasion, the city manager of that era came up with a plan. He noted the pension system was unusually flush after several fat years on Wall Street. Seizing on this fact, he proposed that the city be allowed to drop its contributions below the actuary's number, then ramp up year-by-year until it had resumed paying the full rate in ten years. Like Wimpy in the Popeye cartoons, the city would gladly pay some future Tuesday for a contribution cut today. Otherwise, its officials added, it would have to rethink the unions' benefit improvements. And layoffs could be expected.

The unions didn't kick about the proposed contribution relief. It was the city's problem, not theirs, to find a way to pay the bill when it came due. San Diego is a rich city with many potential revenue sources.

So this was seen as merely a matter of mustering the necessary political resolve some day in the future.

With eight of the thirteen SDCERS trustees being city officials or union members, it might have seemed a foregone conclusion that the proposal would be accepted. The rub, however, was that pension system trustees are not mere representatives of political constituencies. They are fiduciaries expected to defend the soundness of the system they serve, not gamble its solvency to promote measures otherwise beneficial to its membership. So to assure themselves they would not be remiss in their responsibilities if they let San Diego stall on its funding obligations, the SDCERS board looked to its professional advisers: its actuary and legal counsel.

That should have been the end of it. Manager's Proposal I, as it came to be known, was, in substance, a loan from the pension system to the city. SDCERS was not supposed to be in the loan business. It also put the board in the ethically ticklish position of effectively granting or vetoing pension enhancements that would benefit individually those board members who were also city employees. SDCERS was also not supposed to be in the benefit-granting business, in part because of this inherent conflict of interest.

That the proposal cleared these hurdles owed much to the fact that the SDCERS actuary, Rick Roeder, possessed a quality neither common nor particularly desirable in an actuary—creativity. Roeder had been incubating a notion he called "corridor funding" but which might as easily have been called "funding close enough for government work." His brainstorm was that, rather than slavishly follow the fickle dictates of "actuarial science," the city could set its contributions by agreement with the SDCERS board so long as system assets didn't decline below some specified level. When the city promised it would resume paying the full rate should the funding level drop by 10 percent (putting it at 82.3 percent), the actuary was happy. Outside counsel also went along, opining that the board would not be breaching any fiduciary duty so long as it acted with a pure heart, rather than some grubby motive of self-interest. A few trustees grumbled about the way the unions and the city had shaken hands on this deal, and the local press noted that future taxpayers would bear its cost, but otherwise no one seemed perturbed.

And for several years Manager's Proposal I was a big success. When the bull market of the second Clinton term crested in 2000, system funding exceeded 100 percent, despite the city's light contributions and its discovery of additional uses for "surplus earnings." Union members, city officials, and local taxpayers ran in slow motion to embrace one another in a scene back-lit by the Pacific sunset.

But then what was *never* supposed to happen did. The market fell. The Nasdaq bubble burst, the pension system's returns went into free-fall, and no further embracing was to be seen. As a result, SDCERS' assets declined to the point at which the 82.3 percent "trigger" would quite probably be hit. If so, it looked to cost the city a lot of money.

In 2002 negotiations with the unions, San Diego offered another jump in pension benefits in lieu of higher salaries. But this in itself would not solve the city's budget crisis. The recession had tanked its tax revenues. Further, SDCERS investment returns had dried up with the market decline, so now the city would have to pay actual money to cover costs previously satisfied through "surplus earnings."

Tuesday had come at last.

Ignoring the First Law of Holes—"When you're in one, stop digging"—the city begged SDCERS to lower the trigger provision from 82.3 percent to 75 percent. This would have allowed San Diego to fall even further behind on its contributions. But this time it got no takers. The pension system's actuary and outside counsel were (finally) troubled by the city's efforts to shift risk onto the pension system, which the enticement of more benefits only exacerbated. So the board said no.

City administrators decided they could live with anything other than going cold turkey to full actuarial funding. They asked for five years to ramp up to paying what the city should have been paying all along. Otherwise, they said, they might not be able to come through with the new benefits. Also, draconian measures would be necessary to balance the budget, including widespread layoffs. The board looked to its counsel and actuary. They hemmed and hawed but finally swallowed and said "Yeah, why not." After more haggling with the city, the board agreed to accept Manager's Proposal II.

But not everyone was happy. One SDCERS trustee in partic-ular was very unhappy—and her determination to share her views would have far-reaching consequences. It would result in her becom-ing an unlikely protagonist in a political and financial morality play, taken up by the national media, and would change the image of

San Diego from sun-drowsy bastion of coupon-clipping prosperity to fiscal basket case.

★ ★ ★

Diann Shipione was the SDCERS trustee least likely to be asked out for pizza and beer by her board colleagues. She had been appointed to one of the independent seats by mayor Dick Murphy before she and her husband, politically connected lawyer Pat Shea, seriously lost friendship with the mayor. Murphy ascribed this to his refusal to support a project to expand cargo facilities at the San Diego airport promoted by Shea. Shipione in public statements downplayed the rift.

Shipione took her status as an independent board member to heart. She routinely questioned the board on issues big and small, much to the annoyance of her fellow trustees. The city appointees, in particular, treated her with disdain. When the board began its consideration of "Manager's Proposal II," her criticisms took on a sharp focus. She saw the proposal as the latest short-sighted agreement between the city and its unions to temporarily evade budgetary problems by underfunding the pension system. Which it was. When the board passed the proposal anyway, she took the matter to the mayor and city council, whose approval was necessary for its implementation. At a public hearing she described the proposal as "almost corrupt."

Earlier in 2002, a "blue-ribbon committee" appointed by the mayor had delivered a report on city fiscal issues. Though baffled by the pension system's elaborate funding structure, it had recognized that costs were being pushed into the future and warned against this practice. That report, however, seems to have been relegated to the piles of documents public officials hope to someday read. No one else was yelling about any problems. So the mayor and council tossed Shipione's objections to the city bureaucracy, which blew her off with a terse letter.

But any possibility of shrugging off the issues she raised would be short-lived. In January 2003, a class action suit alleged that San Diego had short-changed SDCERS in violation of the San Diego Municipal Code and City Charter and the California Constitution. It would eventually force the city to substantially boost its contributions to the retirement system and effectively result in the recession of Manger's Proposal II.

Nor had the last been heard from Diann Shipione. In late 2003, San Diego announced a bond offering for its wastewater system. Shipione flyspecked the documents and found the section about the pension system to be out-of-date and silent on the blossoming deficit. She took her concerns to the city's bond counsel, Paul Webber, and for the first time found her audience.

Webber was an old-style, somewhat curmudgeonly disclosure lawyer, late in his career. Like the city's outside auditors, rating agencies, and other disclosure counsel, he'd previously seen no reason to plunge into the complexities of the city's pension situation. But now he scrutinized the offering documents through a jeweler's glass. Wherever he looked, he found mistakes, apparently the result of sloppiness but too numerous for comfort. The most troubling error was a statement that the SDCERS's funding shortfall was covered in a reserve. There was indeed a reserve, but it was a mere paper entry that did nothing to backstop the pension system.

His inquiry expanded into a broad examination of the city's financial reporting. The local firm that had not only audited but also drafted much of the city's disclosure[1] had been acquired the previous year by the regional firm of Caporicci & Larson. Together with a squad of in-house accountants, it spent months examining the city's financial documents and uncovered a multitude of errors, most unconnected to the pension system. Some made San Diego look better, others worse, but in each case they were mistakes that should not have been made. The overarching theme was a lack of sophistication on the part of the city's accounting professionals.

City administrators submitted to all this as cheerfully as if subjected to a root canal without anesthetic. San Diego had won awards for the accuracy of its financial disclosure. Suddenly officials who had preened over those awards were being told they'd gotten everything wrong. And worse was to come. Their bickering with Webber over the need for this inquiry gave way to screams of agony when he told them that merely fixing the city's disclosure going forward wouldn't be enough. He wanted it to publicly disclose its past errors.

---

[1] In one of the many ways government issuers are allowed more leeway than public companies, this is permitted within limits. The rationale is that municipalities may not have the in-house expertise to draft their own financial disclosure.

In increasingly acrimonious e-mails to Webber, city officials argued the mistakes weren't material and therefore needn't be disclosed. Materiality is one of the more slippery concepts in the securities field. The crib-sheet version, however, is that information is material if it might affect investor decisions to buy or sell the securities at issue. Caporicci & Larson agreed with the city, pointing out that the errors had only a minor effect on San Diego's financial metrics.

Webber's response was essentially, "Maybe so, but the sheer volume of the screw-ups is material information. Investors should know that the city's internal controls have failed routinely." This theory was not music to the official ear. Webber also insisted that the city disclose certain economic realities facing its pension system, even if not required to do so by any specific rule.

My partner had been hired by the city to advise it about the presentation of investor information on its web page. A small one-off engagement. City officials asked him, as the only other securities lawyer in sight, for a second opinion on Webber's views. He looked at the issue and agreed with Webber.

Without Webber's sign-off, San Diego could not go forward with its bond offering, and he was not going to budge. So City Hall grudgingly resigned itself to what some still considered to be an indulgence of Webber's over-refined sensibilities. An e-mail from one official whimpered, ". . . on to the public flogging."

Among the quirks of the municipal disclosure system is that nothing goes to the SEC. Instead, documents, including annual financial statements, are filed with "the Nationally Recognized Municipal Securities Repositories." San Diego had filed with the "NERMSERS" the statement proposed by Webber and it was ugly. Anyone reading it would see San Diego as a sort of suburban banana republic with performing killer whales.

The press quickly got wind of this unique filing and treated it as a major scandal, perhaps predisposed toward a negative view of city administration. San Diego was at this time embroiled in a particularly tawdry episode. Several council members were accused of trading concessions to local strip-club proprietors for campaign contributions in a matter known as "Strippergate." The *Union-Tribune* jumped aggressively on the SDCERS story, treating it as a scandal equal to the Orange

County financial meltdown of a few years before, visions of Pulitzer Prizes doubtless dancing in editorial noggins.

The attention of the SEC's Los Angeles office was also drawn to San Diego's pension issues. From later discussions with its staff, I believe they found the NERMSER filing mostly confusing. But it sounded bad. So they opened an investigation. The U.S. Attorney's Office in San Diego too learned in short order that the NERMSERS are not, as might be thought, evil beasties that chase Frodo Baggins around Middle Earth. When assistants to the U.S. Attorney called the City Attorney to say they were opening a criminal inquiry, they made clear they weren't about to stand idly by while a pack of out-of-town SECers tromped through their city. Soon the local District Attorney would join in the hunt with her own investigation.

The San Diego press took all this as additional proof the city was rotten to the core. *Surely* all this government firepower wouldn't be pointed at City Hall without good reason.

★   ★   ★

My initial impression was of a city government quite literally in the dark.

It was February 2004 and my flight into San Diego had arrived at dusk. After a short cab ride, I found my V&E colleague in conference with one of the city's in-house attorneys on an upper floor of an office building across a broad concrete plaza from City Hall. In the distance, departing planes traced a path across the rooftops of San Diego with clockwork regularity.

Between the release of the disclosure urged by Webber and the law enforcement pile-on, the city had hired V&E to review the city's pension disclosure in its bond offerings. With charges and countercharges flying wildly, a clearer idea of what had gone wrong was needed. We hoped to provide it through what would be the first major internal review of a municipal issuer. This might also mean redesigning San Diego's disclosure practices in a way that would provide a useful model for other cities.

The immediate challenge, however, was getting out of the building. Although it was only 6:00, the floor was deserted and every light was off. In the windowless corridors between the city lawyer's office and the elevator bay, the darkness was so absolute I found myself groping along the walls, bumping into desks and filing cabinets, as I looked for a means of egress. Coming from a law firm where no one left this early, it seemed like a different world.

At first the wheels turned smoothly. All routine document destruction was halted immediately, despite protests that offices would soon be drowning in paper and the e-mail servers overloaded. The conference room we had been assigned began to fill up with boxes of paper as city employees coughed up everything touching on the pension system. Associates drawn from several firm offices bailed against the rising tide, moving boxes from the unexamined piles into stacks that had been sorted and indexed.

The SEC sent a staff attorney by early on to check out the scene. She eyed the rows of boxes, labeled with the names of the offices of origin, asked for regular progress reports, and left it at that. The SEC's interest in San Diego seemed to be somewhere north of routine and south of major priority. That would change as media attention intensified.

Given its financial situation, the city did not want to hire a separate law firm to go over the same mountains of paper we were examining so that it could handle the document production to the SEC. Asked to do no more than cooperate fully with the agency's inquiry, the firm agreed to represent the city before the SEC. And since the SEC was unlikely to want money from a fiscally stressed municipality that would ultimately come from its taxpayers, and the city would readily agree to the entry of an order not to do again *whatever* the SEC might decide it had done before, this additional role initially seemed limited indeed.

But conducting an independent investigation is different from serving as an advocate for the object of that investigation. Here we could explain that the amount of advocacy involved would be slim to none. Also, the firm had turned down the city's offer to serve as its permanent disclosure counsel—specifically to avoid a potential conflict—and represented no one in the city as individuals. But all that involved far too much explaining. This attempt to save the city legal fees would paint a bull's-eye on the firm's back for anyone inclined to target practice.

★ ★ ★

For help on technical accounting issues, we interviewed a number of CPA firms, finally settling on the San Diego office of KPMG. That its role would soon change from that of mere advisor would have far-reaching consequences.

The city's auditors at that point were Caporicci & Larson. That firm had bought a small local shop with an existing contract to audit the city's annual financials and so thrust itself unwittingly into a blossoming melodrama. After turning the city's financial disclosure upside down at the behest of Paul Webber and finding and correcting a load of errors, it had put its signature on an audit report for 2003. Its work-papers were among the first documents we examined. They suggested it had done an exacting job, unlike what had passed for audits in earlier years. In an interview, the head of the firm was refreshingly blunt about the mistakes made by the previous audit team, even though they now worked for him.

In a phone call to our firm early in the engagement, an SEC administrator cracked, "So when is San Diego going to get a real auditor?" He may have had no idea whether the Caporicci firm was good, bad, or indifferent, but his comment was passed on to members of the city council, who decided they wanted an opinion from a major auditing firm so there could be no possible doubt the city's financials were clean. KPMG was already on site. Its local office agreed to this sudden change in role, apparently happy to add a high-profile client to its roster.

These were nervous days for auditing firms. In 2002 Arthur Andersen—once the gold standard in public accounting—had been convicted of obstruction of justice for shredding documents related to its work for Enron. In 2005 the Supreme Court would reverse that conviction but, by then, Andersen was history. It's demise would cause the remaining firms to experience inklings of mortality, further cranking up the anxiety levels of entities that, as classic deep-pocket defendants, have long been a favorite prey of the nation's plaintiffs' lawyers.

KPMG, moreover, had issues specific to itself. In 2004, when it was hired as San Diego's outside auditor, a Senate committee and the Department of Justice were investigating it for selling potentially abusive tax shelters. The following year, a raft of KPMG partners would be indicted on charges of conspiracy and criminal tax evasion. Meanwhile, KPMG and five of its partners were facing SEC charges that they had facilitated financial fraud by audit client Xerox Corporation. Later in 2004, KPMG would pay $10 million to settle SEC charges it had blown audits of Gemstar-TV Guide, and looming on the horizon were problems with its audit client Fannie Mae, which would eventually sue it for $2 billion. It would survive all of these tribulations but, for KPMG, 2004 was, as the *New York Times* put it, "a year of damage control."

Did any of this matter to San Diego? At first, it seemed not. We were told KPMG would do its audit on a parallel track with our investigation. We would share information along the way, and ultimately reach the finish line more or less in tandem.

It soon became apparent, however, that KPMG was having second, third, and fourth thoughts about taking on what it had come to see as a high-risk engagement. Perhaps its national office had been reading articles about Enron-by-the-Sea. The partner in the San Diego office who had taken on the engagement disappeared and was replaced by someone from the San Francisco office. As the press loudly beat the scandal drum throughout the summer of 2004, the auditors seemed increasingly guarded in their communications with us. KPMG also assigned one of its risk management staff to monitor our investigation—an earnest young man whose background in financial investigations was unclear.

We soon found ourselves to be among the most unpopular people in San Diego.

It became apparent that many in city government worried they would be prosecuted someday by someone for something and feared we were there to facilitate that process, like Aztec priests preparing them for sacrifice. Most everyone we interviewed was afraid. Some attempted to hide their distress. Others did not. Many city employees gave stilted, narrow answers to the simplest questions. The former head of the city's internal audit department declined to be interviewed and fought for months against giving up documents he had kept from his tenure in public service.

Diann Shipione did not respond to our requests to interview her. We were told she viewed us as presumptively lined up with the city. Apparently sides had been drawn early.

Unraveling the history and operations of the city's retirement system proved to be surprisingly complex. Over many years, it had developed into a Rube Goldberg drawing of contingent funding mechanisms and obscure reserves: some held "outside" the system's core assets, others that seemed to serve no purpose whatsoever.

SDCERS's administrator, Larry Grissom, thin and weathered as an aging beat poet, made the best of our bothersome entreaties to explain the arcane mechanics of SDCERS's funding. This was good because he was the only person who had any idea how certain aspects of the system worked or didn't. We also obtained the cooperation of the actuary, Rick Roeder. He had to be cajoled into meeting with us, but then filled in some significant blanks. Still, we had to put most of it together from twenty years of documents.

All the while, the media continued to stoke the fire. The story worked well as a simple matter of city officials enriching themselves at taxpayer expense. And who would step forward to dispute it? Government officials are usually not inclined or, in many cases, allowed to talk to the press.

On September 16, 2004, after nine months of interviews and document review, we delivered our report. It described the history and fiscal follies of the retirement system and cataloged the errors in San Diego's financial reporting. The broad picture was one of political expediency and administrative incompetence trumping sound practice and good sense. It proposed a list of changes to the reporting process to avoid future errors. And it considered the city's potential violations of the securities laws.

The allegations that would frame a case for liability were straightforward. San Diego had done several bond offerings after the funding level of its retirement system had declined significantly, but no one would know that from reading the offering documents. Potentially relevant information was not provided and some statements were inaccurate. Also, some city officials were aware the rating agencies had not picked up on SDCERS's problems and they trod lightly around those sleeping dogs.

Unappealing as this behavior was, however, it was a stretch to say that any among the array of city employees and outside professionals who'd touched its financial disclosure had engaged in securities fraud. The few statements that were flat wrong were arguably both immaterial and the result of confusion or laziness, often on the part of outside professionals, rather than any intention to mislead. And, if the city's public information was often stale and thin, this reflected the loose rules applicable to municipal entities. They report only once a year and narrowly. Much of the negative information that was percolating up through the system—including actuarial adjustments and projections of future funding shortfalls—either hadn't reached the point of being subject to the reporting process or was information that municipalities weren't required to disclose. Thus inaction was, in many cases, all that was required to avoid facing up to a worrisome situation.

There were no obvious heroes in city administration and no awards would be going up on anyone's walls any time soon. But there was little if any evidence of collusion to hide problems. Or that anyone involved in the diffuse and fragmented process of generating the city's financial disclosure had any inkling they might later be accused of violating the securities laws.

With help from consulting actuaries, we quantified the effect of the underfunding from the two Manager's Proposals. They were popularly believed to have caused the entire deficit, then running about $1.5 billion. In truth, it was more like 10 to 12 percent of that amount (although still not chump change). The rest was the result of market losses, changing employee demographics, and increased benefits, some forced by litigation. The second Manager's Proposal, moreover, had added only marginally to the deficit during the year between its adoption and the legal settlement that rescinded it.

The City Attorney's Office—which had been scrupulous about staying clear of our work—praised the report's level of analysis and detail. The city council voted to accept it in fulfillment of our engagement and moved quickly to implement the controls we had proposed and which, I understand, provided fodder for panel discussions throughout Muniland.

Nevertheless, we would not be allowed to ride off into the sunset, waving goodbye to a grateful city, with small children and dogs running behind us to the first bend in the road. Certain elements of the media had apparently assumed any proper investigation would end with heads on pikes. After all, this was a major financial scandal. They'd said so often enough. And here we were leaving town without supplying the blood sport to which the populace was entitled. The *Union-Tribune* quoted Diann Shipione as calling the report a "whitewash." The evening news said she'd changed her mind after reading further, but the damage was done. The "whitewash" comment would stick. The press would also insist we had found "no wrongdoing" by the city, although we'd described rotten internal controls, erroneous disclosure, and gross fiscal irresponsibility in great detail.

This would have been merely vexing but for the fact that the city had thrown out one audit opinion for 2003 and was inveighing KPMG to sign off on another. Without that, the city was out of the capital markets indefinitely. But wherever KPMG was with its audit, it wasn't happy about the city's legal situation, which remained confused and volatile. It had been fretting about whether there were unresolved "illegal acts" in the city's history and announced it wanted an unqualified opinion from V&E on this issue. Not just as to violations of the securities laws by the city itself. *Any* laws—federal, state, municipal—by *anyone* with any connection to San Diego government.

The press took this as confirmation we'd screwed up the investigation by not pointing out which heads should go on pikes. No one thought to ask whether what was now being demanded fell within what we had been hired to do. It didn't. Or whether this kind of representation fits established audit procedures. It doesn't.

Legal issues come up often in audits. Companies sue and get sued and face other legal issues that may affect their balance sheets. In such cases, auditors ask the client's attorneys what to expect. If counsel says a particular result is a near certainty, and here's how the bottom line looks, that number gets thrown into the financial statements. More often, however, the attorney says something like "I have a good feeling about it, but I'm not counting my chickens." Then, under some circumstances, some language goes into a footnote. In any event, the auditor now has gotten as much as it can expect from counsel.

If an auditor happens upon evidence of illegal conduct, for example indications of commercial bribery or price collusion, he can't simply ignore it. He must determine what it means for the client's financial statements and the integrity of its management. But this requirement is not a license to indulge intellectual curiosity or free-floating anxiety. It has never entitled auditors to demand a blanket assurance the client has never violated any rule, regulation, or statute. No responsible law firm would make such a representation. The legal imagination simply can't comprehend every possible form of liability that could face an entity as complex as, say, a major American city, much less determine the merits of each unasserted claim. Often the only answer to such questions is "That's why we have courts."

We had earlier asked the young man from risk management whether there were any guidelines KPMG was following. He said, not really, it's kind of a work in progress, a project the Big Four auditing firms were discussing. We asked if KPMG had examples of the sort of report that would satisfy it. Nothing was forthcoming.

After some back and forth, we complained to the city that KPMG was being impossible. This exchange of correspondence was leaked to the press, like everything else that went to the city council. This, of course, caused us to bond with the auditors even more closely. Eventually, they agreed to refine their demands. They suggested we investigate every story that had appeared in the *Union-Tribune*. Then that we look at every allegation made by Diann Shipione. Since she was sending helpful e-mails to the KPMG audit partner on an ongoing basis, this was something of a moving target. Eventually, we agreed that we would report on 13 separate topics of concern. Some, in fairness, did present potential audit issues involving the application of state and local law to the city's pension system. KPMG also wanted more on the potential liability of individual city employees. Finally, it insisted on an expanded search of the city's e-mail archives. It was conceivable this would turn up something new, but would also cost millions. The city agreed to pay. It had no choice.

Could this deal ever have worked? Possibly. If the scandal story had worn out its legs in the press and KPMG had come to realize there was little prospect of being sued after doing everything required by established auditing standards.

Sadly, however, this was not to be. Indeed, the controversy was merely getting up to full speed.

★ ★ ★

Michael Aguirre was a notable San Diegan before he threw his hat in the ring for the 2004 election for City Attorney. Short and squarish, with tight, tired eyes and slicked-back hair, famously pugnacious in demeanor. Aguirre, had run for local office several times before, always unsuccessfully, and had been written off by many as an unelectable political gadfly. A plaintiff's attorney who had been involved in high-profile cases against the city, and a close friend of Diann Shipione and Pat Shea, he had been an early critic of the city's creative funding of its retirement system. With Shea pushing his campaign, he sought to exploit his credentials as a foe of political corruption to finally win elected office. It worked. Carried along by a wave of public outrage particularly pronounced among subscribers to the *Union-Tribune*, he squeaked past a lackluster opponent to become the San Diego City Attorney. The throw-the-rascals-out populist sentiment, however, was not strong enough to unseat Mayor Murphy, perhaps because his connection to the pension scandal was slim. The election was close enough, however, that a recount was required, putting the mayor's office in a sort of two-month limbo.

Aguirre's victory was not joyfully received within city government. Those officials at the center of the retirement system melee can only have seen his election as a personal abandonment by whatever deities they worshipped. They could assume Aguirre would cast a cold eye in their direction. But the lower ranks were also affected. The frantic reshuffling within the City Attorney's Office was explained to me as an effort by staff attorneys to burrow away into areas unlikely to be frequented by their famously fractious new boss. A walk through that office would inevitably draw requests for career advice. Many employees would leave over the following months as the press reported shouting matches between Aguirre and his staff.

Upon assuming his new position, Aguirre hung a huge banner behind his desk defining the City Attorney as the people's advocate. He knew the role he intended to play: that of a free agent, fighting fraud, corruption, and illegality wherever he found them. Breaking with previous City Attorneys—who viewed themselves as simply the legal arm of city government—he would declare himself accountable only to the people. Aguirre would insist on his ability to initiate suits without council approval, which left open the possibility he could sue other members of city government, up to and including the mayor.

And this was not mere bluster. Those who voted for him in hopes he would shake-up City Hall would not be disappointed. Over his four-year term, he would spread disruption like nothing San Diego had experienced since the rampaging Tyrannosaur in the second *Jurassic Park* film.

You had to admire his balls-to-the-wall willingness to take on all comers. The man knew no fear. He seemed sincere in his crusade, however often it was redefined. And his energy level was daunting. But nuance was an issue. Everything was black or white. Mostly black. And his unshakable belief in the righteousness of his mission—his certitude that San Diego was a putrid, festering sink of political iniquity where you couldn't swing a dead cat without hitting a corrupt official—made him impervious to other viewpoints.

Our relationship with Aguirre became increasingly adversarial as we plugged along with the additional procedures we hoped would satisfy KPMG, and Aguirre, meanwhile, sought ways to clean out every corner of city government with a fire hose. Eventually, he became our competition. Borrowing from our document base, he issued his own reports on the pension system in which he accused the mayor and various members of the city council of various forms of illegal conduct. They were not amused.

Aguirre decided he would resolve the SEC investigation, at least as to the city, by advocating that the SEC charge San Diego with securities fraud. As a negotiation strategy, his proposed capitulation to charges made, so far, only by himself was unusual. The SEC was not likely to seek monetary penalties from San Diego. So the worst potential outcome for the city was what Aguirre was proposing. On the other hand, with San Diego disparaged in the media as Enron-by-the-Sea, it would take considerable political courage for the SEC to walk away without charging the city with something serious. In other words, it wasn't going to happen. Aguirre could therefore say he was merely facing up to the inevitable.

City government was now in a shambles. In May 2004, Mayor Murphy resigned. He was, to all appearances, a decent-enough guy whose one burning desire was to be anything other than the mayor of San Diego. Deciding he couldn't take the battering from the press and Aguirre anymore, he walked. The city's leadership vacuum deepened, with the council squabbling and dithering while initiative flowed to Aguirre. He seemed to hold a press conference every day as the reports bounced out of his office like gumballs from a broken machine.

The same month, the San Diego District Attorney filed criminal charges against six SDCERS trustees. Those who were also city employees, she charged, had violated a state conflict-of-interest statute by voting for Manager's Proposal II, a measure she characterized as a benefits-for-underfunding scam. Although broadly worded, the statute was usually applied to episodes of covert self-dealing by public employees. The defendants here had signed off on a deal—made more or less in public and left unchallenged for years in a city not known for any shortage of lawyers—after being told the alternative was a fiscal melt-down for the city and widespread layoffs of employees. Opinions varied as to whether this would stand up in court but, in any event, it instantly and irrevocably trashed the professional careers of the named defendants.

★ ★ ★

We ground through a series of lengthy memos, backed up with a wall of document binders and interview transcripts, hoping that once we satisfied its list of demands KPMG would finally step off an audit opinion. This hope was dashed when the auditors announced they would not be able to evaluate the adequacy of our work, not being, after all, lawyers. They said that was the responsibility of the city's audit committee. This was a problem because San Diego didn't have an audit committee, a characteristic it shared with every other city in the country. Companies have audit committees; cities don't. They said, moreover, that an audit committee was all the more necessary, thanks to the pronouncements of the City Attorney. In our first report, we'd found insufficient evidence to conclude that San Diego officials had engaged in intentional securities fraud. Aguirre disagreed and had cast the net of responsibility widely. Someone needed to resolve this dispute and that someone was not going to be KPMG. And it should be admitted that, if auditors aren't entitled to blanket representations resolving all the client's legal issues, neither is it their job to choose between conflicting legal opinions should they get them, or their privilege to disregard one from an elected official who also happens to be the client's ranking legal officer.

But where could the city scare up an audit committee? Aguirre had accused most of the city council and many of the city's top administrators of fraud. So they couldn't very well evaluate his work. And, anyway, who in their right mind would want to stick themselves in the middle of the Borgia court on Ecstasy that San Diego was becoming? Aguirre helpfully volunteered to be the tie-breaker between his work and ours but got no takers.

Meanwhile, the press was not taking any sort of breather, with every new aspect of the scandal always good for column inches for at least one news cycle. One day, for example, the *Union-Tribune* reported in outrage that SDCERS had been paying benefits to "dead pensioners." This was literally true. SDCERS made monthly benefit payments to each of its pensioners until notified of the person's death. Sometimes this did not occur right away and SDCERS would have to seek a return of funds transferred electronically into a deceased pensioner's bank account. But the same is true of every other retirement system in the country, including Social Security. There is simply no alternative, at least short of installing an electronic device in each pensioner to signal the cessation of vital signs.

The quandary of who would pass judgment on our efforts was resolved when the city hired former SEC Chairman Arthur Levitt and former Chief Accountant Lynn Turner. They had set up shop together as consultants and initially seemed a solid bet to impose order on this unruly situation. Levitt, although neither a lawyer nor an accountant, had enjoyed a long and well-regarded run at the helm of the SEC during the Clinton years and he and Turner had earned points by being ahead of events in spotting accounting fraud as the next big thing.

Immediately upon taking the engagement, Levitt met with the editorial board of the *Union-Tribune*. Gray-haired and courtly, he managed, in a major feat of diplomacy, to charm that ugly crew into a committed state of almost canine devotion. This was doubtless mortifying for Mike Aguirre. The *Union-Tribune* had previously been a strong supporter of his crusade to shake up the pension system. After Levitt showed up at its offices, however, it turned away from Aguirre as abruptly as a Parisian Apache dancer spurning his heart-broken partner, and from then on would beat on him without mercy whenever he sniped at Levitt.

In their train, Levitt and Turner brought consulting firm Kroll & Associates and law firm Wilkie Farr & Gallagher. We were initially unsure of the need for this entourage, but hoped they would examine our investigative record closely, nod sagely, and tell KPMG to be at peace. When a Wilkie partner scouted out our office, he looked at the many yards of binders and said he'd never seen anyone go to such lengths in documenting an investigation. We never saw him again.

We continued beavering away on the additional tasks on KPMG's list but wondered if merely completing the assigned investigative tasks and rendering our legal opinion would be enough. My impression was that the auditors had an idea of the result they would find appropriate. Since this was such a big scandal, there must culpable individuals deserving to be punished, at least by banishment from the city payroll. Otherwise, how could anyone say San Diego had remedied its problems by cleaning house? That was the denouement KPMG seemed to desire. All evil exposed and banished so that goodness could reign again throughout the land.

The "audit committee"—Levitt, Turner and a Kroll employee—and its helpers must quickly have realized the success or failure of their engagement would ultimately be judged on one fact—whether their efforts had resulted in a signed audit opinion from KPMG. We were advised to approach our role from the same perspective. Moreover, that the press would pay little deference to our views if they conflicted with public sentiment was apparent from the sharp objects it continued to jab into our hindquarters. V&E had, in previous years, been a major provider of legal services to Enron, leading to the firm's inclusion in a class action suit brought by litigation kingpin Bill Lerach. It would later be dismissed from that litigation, but the association was well known. When my partner had accepted this job, he warned the city council that, while he had not personally done legal work for Enron, his firm had, which might make our engagement controversial. This was close enough for some reporters to describe him as a former Enron lawyer.

A bigger source of journalistic grief came from our efforts to examine millions of city e-mails. The city had hired an e-discovery firm to screen the e-mails through keyword searches and upload the results onto a server accessible over the Internet to us, the SEC, Aguirre, and KPMG. Both we and KPMG noticed, however, that in the database e-mails were not linked to their attachments, having been dropped into different files. After complaining without result, we settled down to using keyword searches to find orphaned attachments. When the press got wind of this, and mistakenly concluded that the problem involved a failure to upload a large number of documents, the e-discovery firm sent a letter to the city admitting the problems but claiming V&E had told it not to fix them. This was surprising because we had been nagging it for months to make sure *everything* in the database was uploaded and accessible. The young V&E attorney who'd handled this felt sandbagged.

It would have been nothing more than the sort of glitch that happens in every complex investigation had the letter not been leaked to the *Union-Tribune*. Without speaking with us, it ran a scathing editorial accusing us of undermining the work of the e-discovery firm and being too stupid to realize that the e-mails weren't linked to their attachments.

As we closed in on finishing our additional work, the pressure to put heads on pikes, including threats against the firm from Aguirre, ran up against the fact that no one could make more than an educated guess how the key legal issues would be resolved if put to the test in a courtroom. This was not a case of an employee caught cramming it from the till. Rather, it raised matters of first impression on a host of thorny issues.

A California law firm the city had hired at our request to consult on state law issues concluded that both Manager's Proposals *probably* violated state or municipal requirements that the city cleave closely to the dictates of actuarial science. But the city's liability for underfunding had been largely resolved through legal settlements, so this shouldn't have been much of an audit issue. Whether any officials had run afoul of state conflict of interest laws was a tougher call. Outside professionals had in some fashion vetted the measures. The California firm concluded that some SDCERS trustees probably violated one provision by failing to give notice they were voting on a matter that would affect their own pensions—not that this wasn't widely known—but the incident might be outside the statute of limitations. Its report seemed to us balanced and sensible.

That left our retake on the securities law issues. Assuming anyone had paid sufficient attention to the city's pension issues that it mattered what was in the documents—the legal equivalent of "if a tree falls in a forest . . ."—there were plausible arguments the disclosure was materially wrong, the first hurdle to building a fraud case.[2] The second, and more difficult, is showing that anyone acted with an intent to deceive. It was easy to say city officials had been negligent (like most officials most of the time). But even royal screw-ups are not fraud. While it did not appear that city officials had actually lied about anything, there was a laugh-resistant case some had been "reckless" in signing documents that presented less than a fully enlightening picture of the pension system.

---

[2] An added wrinkle here was that most of the outstanding bonds were insured. Thus investors had little incentive to care what the city did or did not put in its public disclosure as long as the insurers remained solvent.

That was one step down from intentional fraud, but still actionable. Yet each of these people had defenses that, if well-mounted, would have a good chance of prevailing, such as a good-faith belief that the many lawyers who'd pawed through the documents knew what they were doing.

In sum, the government could file a carefully worded fraud case without acting in bad faith; but, if it did, it would take on significant litigation risk and might be well advised to embrace any opportunity for settlement.

In the event, however, our conclusions hardly mattered. When the report was in near-final form, Aguirre demanded to see our draft and found that it rejected various assertions in his reports, citing a certain evidentiary elusiveness. He called a press conference and denounced it as a "whitewash." A few reporters understood we had drawn a line this side of intentional fraud—not provided an apologia for the city's many errors—but others wrote in astonishment that we *still* had found "no wrongdoing" despite everyone and his dog knowing that this was a financial fraud of epic proportions.

Perhaps this was to be expected. After all the front-page perp-walks of the preceding years, the press and public expected no less from any financial reporting matter. They had no other frame of reference.

KPMG was, I believe, looking for a resolution that would mean it wouldn't be stepping into a litigational free-fire zone if it signed off on an audit opinion. It seemed to assume this meant seeing some number of current and former city executives accused of illegal conduct and seriously disciplined. And here we were again being difficult. The audit committee, it could be assumed, would be reluctant to endorse work that was a magnet for abuse and didn't fit KPMG's formula. In any event, KPMG said it had other audit issues to resolve. So there we were—in the dead center of nowhere.

By the end of 2005, we had finished all of the additional tasks assigned to us to the extent the necessary information was obtainable. We had given the SEC everything from our investigation and it seemed anything else it might require could be handled more effectively by a local firm. So we announced our resignation, offering to help any successor firm get up to speed. This left the field open for KPMG and the audit committee to make whatever arrangements they chose, so long as the city would

pay the tab and no one objected to the audit committee being placed in
the position of reviewing work it had a hand in performing.

★ ★ ★

Kroll, in fact, would investigate for another year. For this, it and Wilkie
Farr would charge San Diego $20 million. All the while, KPMG con-
tinued to work on the only audit it would ever do for the city.[3]

The tone of Kroll's written report, when it arrived, was primly
hectoring. Presenting it to the city council in August 2006, Arthur Levitt
read, "The evidence demonstrates not mere negligence, but deliberate
disregard for the law, disregard for fiduciary responsibility and disregard
for the financial welfare of the city's residents over an extended period
of time." Kroll had, in short, embraced the widely promoted view of
the city's pension problems as grounded in illegal conduct by specific
individuals. It had also developed in its investigation allegations of fraud
not related to the pension system.

For some time the city had been aware that, in possible violation
of state and federal regulations, it had provided wastewater service at a
subsidized rate to favored industrial users. This undisclosed issue could
have resulted in very substantial fines but, as it happened, didn't. We'd
passed this matter on to Kroll, which made much of it in its report.
Otherwise, as far as I could see, there was nothing new and surprising.
The history of the pension system was reviewed again through a glass
darkly. In the report's full-throated denunciation of the city as a moral
and legal black hole there were no shades of gray. Political compromises
were always inherently wicked and individual lapses implied vaguely to
be elements of a broad scheme.

KPMG had insisted on thumbs-up or thumbs-down verdicts on all
legal issues. In satisfying this demand, the report concluded the city had
violated the California Constitution, the San Diego City Charter, and
Municipal Code in connection with its pension funding schemes. Some
of this was plausible, if not a legal certainty. It also ticked off a list of

---

[3] After KPMG stated it would not serve as San Diego's auditors going forward, the city hired a regional
firm to do the additional two annual audits that had by then piled up behind KPMG's reaudit of the
2003 financial statements.

former city employees it said had violated the federal securities laws in connection with the pension and wastewater disclosure.[4]

Given all the sulfurous language, one would have thought the city attorney would have been tickled to death by the report. Not a bit of it. Levitt and Aguirre were at each other's throats. Aguirre called the Kroll report "useless" and accused Levitt and his entourage of bilking the city. Levitt derided Aguirre as "irrelevant" and his reports as "result-oriented."

And one would have thought that, once Kroll delivered its report, KPMG would promptly sign off on the 2003 audit. The report supported the sinister view of the city in which the auditors had been so thoroughly marinated. But more important, it had the endorsement of two big names in securities regulation, Levitt and Turner. What more could any accountants ask?

As it happened, lots. The auditors plugged away for another six months before completing their audit, along the way demanding numerous other actions from the city. They eventually found $1.8 billion in adjustments. Mostly this came from the application of a new accounting standard—requiring municipalities to revalue long-lived assets like bridges and street lamps—generally irrelevant to their ability to service their debts. Adjustments related to the pension system were minor.

But at least it was done.

★ ★ ★

In January 2006—a year before the completion of the KPMG audit—the U.S. Attorney indicted three SDCERS trustees and two administrators, including Larry Grissom, for depriving the city and pensioners of their "right to honest services." Like the criminal action brought by the D.A., it did not allege securities law violations, but accused the defendants of short-changing their responsibilities to the system out of self-interest.

The SEC weighed in later that year. In a November 2006 administrative order, it charged the city with securities fraud. No individuals were named. The order tracked our findings in its factual allegations but

---

[4]The city had agreed to indemnify everyone associated with the Kroll report against any legal claims asserted against them as a result of this engagement, including claims for defamation.

adopted Aguirre's legal conclusions. The SEC did not seek monetary penalties from the city, which agreed to the entry of a cease-and-desist order against future violations.

Mike Aguirre claimed vindication from this action but, in fact, it begged the real question: would the SEC charge fraud against anyone who would actually fight? The answer came a year and a half later when it sued five former city officials. The six causes of action in the complaint were equally divided between those alleging negligent conduct and those premised on recklessness. Atypically for an SEC fraud case, there were no allegations of intentional misconduct.

Once the SEC sued the city for fraud, the second shoe was nearly certain to drop. Legal entities like cities and corporations can't directly commit fraud, which requires a particular mental state. Legal entities don't have mental states. They have employees who have mental states. At least sometimes. So when the SEC sues an entity for fraud without naming individuals it is likely to be asked what gives.[5] Particularly in prominent cases that attract press scrutiny.

In deciding whether to litigate a run-of-the-mill case, a government agency will do a cost-benefit analysis, however informal, balancing the importance of the matter against its potential cost and the likelihood of losing at trial. But in high-profile cases in which the agency will be criticized for inaction, the analysis shifts to one of weighing how much grief it will get should it bring the case and lose compared to the amount to be expected should it forego bringing the case at all. And, of course, the pain from an eventual loss at trial will not occur for a few years, so it is given a sort of psychological discounting to present value.

Presumably none of these former San Diego bureaucrats had the financial wherewithal to litigate with a federal agency and, had they been forced to pay their own freight, would have been forced to settle on *any* terms that did not include large fines. That didn't happen. A state court held that the city was on the hook for the defendants' legal

---

[5]This was the situation faced by the SEC in 2009 when it attempted to settle an action against Bank of America for not disclosing mounting losses at Merrill Lynch in connection with its acquisition of Merrill. Bank of America agreed to pay a $33 million penalty to the SEC in an action that named no individuals. The judge whose approval was required, however, rejected the settlement and criticized the SEC for agreeing to a resolution the cost of which would be borne by Bank of American shareholders rather than responsible individuals.

expenses, including any fines they might pay. In effect, therefore, the SEC found itself suing the city's taxpayers.

Its case has not fared well so far. The district court dismissed four of the six causes of action against all the defendants, citing the sketchiness of the SEC's allegations. That left one charge of negligence and one of recklessness against each defendant.

The criminal prosecutions have also proved problematic. The judge drawn by the U.S. Attorney's Office in its "right to honest services" case has displayed little enthusiasm for the government's legal theory. He has suggested that he finds the statute so vague as to be meaningless. The exasperated prosecutors sought his recusal, and lost. District court judges enjoy great power in their courtrooms. If you shoot at one, you'd better not miss. So this smacked of desperation. The case is on hold until the U.S. Supreme Court hears pending matters involving the critical statute—one an appeal of the criminal conviction of former Enron CEO Jeffrey Skilling.

In a December 2009 hearing on one of these matters, members of the Supreme Court shared the concerns voiced by the District Court in the San Diego matter. Justice Breyer suggested that the statute might apply to an employee who complimented the boss on his hat "so the boss will leave the room so that the employee can continue to read the Racing Form." Similarly, it might be wondered whether the SEC supervisor nailed in a recent report by the agency's Inspector General as having racked up 1,800 hits on porn sites over a 17 day period had deprived his employer of its "right to honest services" by surreptitiously squandering his work time in this fashion.

The district attorney's conflict-of-interest action sailed past some initial challenges, the trial and appellate courts both permitting it to go forward over the defendants' objections that the statute didn't reach the sort of benefits at issue here. But the D.A.'s celebration was cut short when the California Supreme Court took the matter on appeal. The proceeding attracted amicus briefs from other California retirement systems and municipalities, as well as labor unions and the California Attorney General, arguing that the lower court opinions criminalize the sort of decisions pension system trustees make routinely. In late January 2010, the California Supreme Court flushed the case completely as to five of the six defendants, finding that the statute under which they were charged did not apply to the conduct alleged against them.

The city attorney also had his share of disappointments. First, he attempted to have himself declared legal counsel to SDCERS. Its trustees resisted feverishly—seeing his proposed incursion into their midst much like European villagers once viewed the approach of Attila the Hun—and defeated his assault. Aguirre brought, then dismissed, suits against various SDCERS trustees and city officials, sticking the city with millions of dollars in legal fees. The centerpiece of his litigational *blitzkrieg*, however, was his attack on the benefits conferred on pensioners at the time of the two Manager's Proposals. This ended badly when a state court held the issue had been mooted by settlements in previous suits.

When judicial reversals started to pile up, the *Union-Tribune* reported: "the complexion of each of the cases has changed, dimming the prospects for resolving the pension mess in the courts and raising the specter that all the legal disputes could be scuttled by this time next year." A San Diego law professor offered the following insights:

> I think the biggest lesson to be learned from all this is it's easy to charge people in a high-profile case, but it's much harder to convict. And it takes very little for the City Attorney to file a lawsuit. But making complicated and novel legal theories stick is a whole other question.

Yes, it helps to have some decent evidence. It's not enough to say "Look here, your honor. Everyone knows these people are guilty as sin. It's right here in the newspapers."

Aguirre also sued a number of firms that had provided services to the city, including V&E. He alleged the firm had been responsible for delaying KPMG's audit by failing to uncover illegal conduct by city officials—that is, by disagreeing with his reports—and by compromising its independence with a dual representation. As this claim was retailed in the press, our work had been rejected by the SEC and KPMG.

My understanding is quite different. The two reports' lengthy factual findings have survived years of scrutiny essentially unscathed and been widely piggy-backed by subsequent investigators, including the SEC staff. Our legal conclusions are also holding up well. We handicapped the possible outcomes of applying various abstract legal standards to novel and complex factual situations, without pretending to the role of ultimate legal arbiter, and subsequent events have shown those conclusions to be at least sensible.

To my knowledge no one "rejected" the V&E reports, except Aguirre himself. The SEC does not accept or reject reports from outside lawyers, it simply makes whatever use of them it chooses. Nor were we in any way hired to provide investigative services to the SEC, although, from reading its filed actions, it seems to have benefited from our efforts. KPMG, for its part, did not do anything quite so absurd as to sit on reservations about our independence for a year and a half and then suddenly find a problem. According to KPMG, once Aguirre had issued reports that conflicted with ours, it had no choice but to kick the dispute to a third party referee.

After Kroll delivered its report in late 2006, Aguirre publicly accused it and Wilkie Farr of conflicts of interest and sued the law firm for allegedly over-billing the city. That suit is ongoing.

San Diego eventually tired of Aguirre's imitation of Yosemite Sam with a hotfoot, shooting wildly in all directions. Murphy's successor as mayor criticized Aguirre's performance as City Attorney, accusing him of delaying the completion of the city's audits by failing to cooperate with KPMG. One of the mayor's spokesman referred to an Aguirre proposal as "the suggestion of demagogues and charlatans." The press was also getting tired of the conflict level he generated. San Diego's free paper, the *City Beat,* archly admonished Aguirre against "using the 'C' word (as in 'corrupt') to describe fellow elected officials unless and until you have enough real evidence to take to trial."

In 2008, Aguirre lost his bid for reelection. By then, I had left V&E and his action against my former firm had been settled. Although the pragmatic result of a litigational cost-benefit analysis, this left unchallenged the story of the great San Diego pension scandal, a tainted narrative that cost the city tens of millions of dollars and branded a slew of people, not noticeably more flawed than the norm, as criminals and fraudsters.

"Enron-by-the-Sea" had proved a most expensive conceit.

★   ★   ★

When I was in my early 20s, my friend Douglas got me a job working with him as a script reader for a struggling Los Angeles film company. Several times a week we would collect an armload of scripts from its office in the Playboy Building on the Sunset Strip. They were always terrible. The head of the company was a Hollywood version of a Hollywood producer, excitable and given to pontification. One day, he summoned us into his office. He said he was tired of depending on agents to bring him material and wanted to originate projects himself. He had an idea he thought was dynamite but didn't have the cash to hire established writers. So he thought of us. The idea, he said, was so great it would write itself.

He wanted to do a story about an American town being torn apart at the seams—reduced to a smoking ruin—by some sort of local conflict. He hadn't yet worked that out what would cause this fracas but had a title he believed would be perfect, a phrase from a magazine he'd read on an airplane. We could call it, he said, *The Sound and the Fury*.

In hopes we could convince the producer to drop this concept and consider others—like more or less anything else—we decided to propose a reason for the demolition of the town so absurd he would see the folly of the whole project. We suggested a high school football rivalry gone berserk. We'd thought about it carefully and this was the very worst idea we could come up with.

And, of course, he loved it.

The film was eventually produced (under a different title). It seems our original script, bad as it was, was not bad enough because by the time it hit the screen it had been thoroughly rewritten to make *certain* it would be among the worst films ever made.

I've often wondered what we could have done to avoid that embarrassing experience. After San Diego, I realized our mistake was in choosing the wrong reason for the conflict that destroyed that unlucky American town. We should have proposed something even more implausible than a football rivalry.

Say a dispute over the local retirement system.

Chapter 8

The Easter Bunny Cometh

A year after leaving the government for private practice, I got a phone call from David Rocker. It seemed Rocker Partners had an SEC issue and he wanted to bring in an attorney who did securities defense all day long, rather than leave it entirely with their all-purpose New Jersey lawyers. A regional office of the SEC was hot to charge Rocker Partners with insider trading for shorting JCPenney stock before one of its subsidiaries was named in a class action suit for bad business practices. The idea was that Rocker Partners had learned the suit was coming and therefore was supposedly required to lay off trading the stock.

I had never met David in person and had spoken with him by phone only a handful of times. But I guess I was the only SEC alum in private practice he knew, and that was a good thing for me. Business was always welcome. Going from the SEC to a firm means building a clientele from a standing start. You begin with no clients and a number of entities that don't like you because at one time or another you sued them, at least if your time at the SEC was well spent. And being on the defense side makes it particularly challenging to keep the billables up because it tends to be a one-shot practice. Clients rarely say: "I so much appreciate the work you did in resolving my previous SEC problem that I plan on getting myself in another jam so we can renew our very enjoyable relationship." Even those who once promised to name their firstborn after you forget you exist once the crisis has passed.

The SEC investigation had been sparked by a *Wall Street Journal* article pointing out increased shorting of JCPenney stock before the filing of a class action suit. The article, unusually poorly sourced, hinted darkly at collusion between short-sellers and class action attorneys. Others have promoted the same theory in other contexts. It has the attraction of combining for maximum opprobrium two independently unpopular groups—like cannibals and congressmen—and wrapping them together in a juicy conspiracy theory. Here the emotional appeal was strong but the evidence weak. While it's always hard to prove the negative, my experience suggests that short-sellers and class action attorneys travel on separate tracks, pursuing different pay-offs, and rarely corroborate.

The grain of truth in this case was that an analyst in the Boston office of Rocker Partners had spoken with a private detective working for a class action firm. They ran into each other while chasing rumors that a chain of drugstores owned by JCPenney over-billed its Medicaid customers. The analyst was looking for a good short and the law firm for a good case. In a mutual hand-washing exercise, they discussed their inquiries and the Rocker analyst gathered that a lawsuit was likely, although he did not treat this as a major reason to short JCPenney. Some months later, the suit was filed but was treated by the company and the market as a nonevent.

To the staff of the Fort Worth office of the SEC, this was enough to make out an insider trading case. Two years after the events described, it opened an investigation and, after establishing the above undisputed facts, told Rocker Partners it was prepared to recommend that the commission sue the firm and its general partners for insider trading. The call constituted a "Wells notice," a commission procedure giving the proposed object of an enforcement action a chance to argue his way out of it. It is supposed to mean the SEC lawyers have carefully weighed the evidence and concluded that it supports an enforcement action. Less scrupulous administrators, whom I believe to be in the minority, can use it to shake the tree in hopes a settled case falls out, which they can then add to their tally for the year. The filing of the action threatened by the staff, whatever the eventual outcome, would have made it difficult for Rocker Partners to continue managing money for institutional investors.

The problem was that the facts simply did not add up to illegal insider trading. Not even close.

The SEC, for many years, pushed the notion that anyone who has information about a company that the great unwashed have yet to learn should not be able to trade the company's stock until the information becomes public. People who are not securities attorneys assume this is in fact the law. It isn't. The Supreme Court firmly rejected that view over twenty years ago. Concerned that, by denying analysts their potential reward for drilling down on public companies, the SEC's approach would lead to a decline in market transparency, the Court held that anyone other than an insider can trade a company's stock from sunrise to sunset, no matter what nonpublic information he has ferreted out, so long as he didn't lie, cheat, or steal to get it. So that there could be no misunderstanding as to who should be paying attention, the Court added: "without legal limitation, market participants are forced to rely on the reasonableness of the SEC's litigation strategy, which can be hazardous. . . ."

Other cracks in the staff's theory were hard to miss. Insider trading requires trading on *material* information—information that can move a stock—not just *anything* nonpublic about the company. The day the suit was announced, JCPenney stock went up. Also, JCPenney stated it did not expect the matter to cost it much.

The Rocker analyst checked with outside counsel before the firm put on its initial short position. He described his contacts with the private detective and was assured the firm could legally trade the stock. This does not sound like the fraudulent intent required for insider trading liability. Finally, Rocker Partners made nothing from its JCPenney trades. So, even had the legal requirements for insider trading been present, there were no profits to give up, a standard remedy in insider trading actions.

All together, these facts add up to a law school exam question testing the students' understanding of what is *not* insider trading.

As mentioned, I'd skipped Securities Law in law school (sounded too technical). So perhaps I should not have felt indignant that, evidently, so had everyone in the SEC's Fort Worth office. Still, after twenty years of federal court decisions, it seemed that some knowledge of the basic elements of insider trading should have made its way to that regulatory outpost.

An attorney from Rocker Partners' New Jersey law firm and I wrote a submission to the staff explaining, without sarcasm, why the staff's case was a howler. We flew to Texas and met with a battery of SEC lawyers. Each seemed more eager than the next to sue our client. At the meeting's conclusion, I was not confident that common sense would prevail. But we never heard another thing on the matter and, five years later, I am cautiously optimistic we never will.

This should have been the end of the SEC's interest in Rocker Partners. In fact, it was only the beginning.

★ ★ ★

Gradient Analytics is a stock market research firm in Scottsdale, Arizona, run by forensic accountant Donn Vickrey. Like several older and larger competitors, it provides fundamentalist analysis of an evolving list of companies. Most of its reports are critical of the covered companies. But then there is little need to dig for positive information. Companies shove it out into the market as fast as they can find it or, sometimes, make it up.

Gradient's reports and related services are pricey and its clientele a mixture of over a hundred hedge funds, mutual funds, and investment banks. Its client roster has included Fidelity Funds and Goldman Sachs, along with many other industry leaders. What these entities hope to get for their money includes promising short plays for those clients who short stock and, on stocks the clients are long, early warnings of potential problems—information generally neglected by sell-side cheerleaders.

Gradient flags companies for scrutiny through computerized "screens" that sift through the companies' financial statements for signs of weakness or business decline. Common examples would be negative trends in cash flow, inventory turns, or receivables aging. After the SEC, in the 1990s, required public companies to file reports electronically, this became a common approach to stock analysis for those with the necessary technology, but with many ways to slice and dice the available information.

After Gradient identifies likely companies through its computerized data-mining, the process turns traditional. Its analysts slog through SEC filings and press reports and whatever else is available. Like other such services, it also gets ideas from its analyst clients.

In mid-2003, Gradient's screens kicked up for scrutiny the Utah-based Internet retailer Overstock.com. The company was unprofitable—not surprising given its short operating history—but, more intriguingly, had a speculative business model, selling closeout merchandise over the Internet, and a CEO who was not only untried at the helm of a public company but also aggressively eccentric.

This was Patrick Byrne.

Byrne was the son of prominent insurance executive, financier, and Warren Buffet associate Jack Byrne and, as a result, was born with a silver spoon, or entire silver tea service, in his mouth. He styled himself a sort of macho-capitalist-Zen-intellectual businessman, and was particularly given to lecturing Wall Street on the errors of its ways. Its capital-raising practices, he said, are rigged to benefit investment bankers over investors, and the numbers reported by public companies are often tarted up to mislead. He vowed to eschew such practices in his stewardship of Overstock.

Byne's biography includes a doctorate in philosophy, mastery of several languages, and various athletic escapades, such as riding a bicycle from coast to coast. He also survived harrowing bouts with cancer while still in his twenties. All of this is impressive. Clearly, Byrne enjoys personal advantages beyond a trust fund. Moreover, his criticisms of Wall Street were (initially) sensible. Where he has become less sympathetic is in his insistence on running Overstock, launched largely with family money, as a public platform for asserting his personal talents and insights—like a junior high-schooler with an ambitious Science Fair project—and his propensity for seeing nefarious doings in any suggestion that his project does not deserve the blue ribbon.

His need for personal significance and his hypersensitivity to criti-cism has led him, with some help from third parties, to a belief that his antagonists are part of a greater threat, a far-reaching conspiracy against the American capital markets that he, Byrne, is uniquely positioned to expose and defeat. Through an open wallet and a willingness to thrust himself into the spotlight, he now stands as the leader of a colorful cult. In his own words, he has declared "jihad" against the shadowy forces undermining our financial system. His movement seeks broad changes to the system used to clear stock transactions, while not neglecting to attack anyone who criticizes Byrne or Overstock for anything whatsoever. The overarching connection—albeit a loose one—is that all of the evildoers he seeks to vanquish engage one way or another in the practice of shorting stocks.

In pursuing his demons, Byrne has shown great resourcefulness, tenacity, and not a little imagination, in addition to a willingness to believe extraordinary things on the basis of slight evidence. It is tempting to wonder what he might have accomplished if his energies had been more fully directed toward, say, making a success of Overstock. Indeed, his father, Jack Byrne, made essentially this comment when he quit the Overstock board of directors. But then history is replete with gifted people with eccentric beliefs. Theosophy, orgone boxes, serial incarnation—whatever. Perhaps the world is simply too colorless for these individuals without added dimensions of mystery and romance.

But, taking a step back...

Gradient wrote up Overstock as a loser in mid-2003, giving it a D rating, which dropped to an F—the lowest possible—by the end of that year. It found much about the company to dislike. It believed Overstock's promotions were not cost-effective for attracting new customers. It harshly questioned certain of the company's accounting policies. It pointed out that Byrne had made numerous unfulfilled promises of future business triumphs. It also mocked Byrne for his New-Age CEO posturing.

Taking up the cudgels against Overstock would prove a costly mistake. It set Gradient on a course that would nearly destroy it. Rocker Partners would later whistle down the same dark alley and receive a similar mugging. The pain both experienced was not the result of Overstock's success in showing up its critics. In coming years it would rack up losses in the hundreds of millions of dollars. Rather, it was because

Gradient and Rocker Partners unwisely ignored the old adage "Never get in a pissing contest with a skunk."

In the course of his jihad, Byrne would assemble a bizarre entourage of legal hired guns, Internet stock touts and freelance conspiracy theorists. Remarkably, he would win the unwitting assistance of the California court system, a committee of the U.S. Senate, and the SEC. His efforts provided a stress-test of the ability of various organs of government to recognize and resist a sophisticated campaign to hijack their procedures for dubious ends—a test that each would fail.

Byrne's initial response to his critics was simple verbal abuse. First up was Gradient Analytics. In an October 2004 earnings call, Byrne referred to Gradient analysts—indulging in the Shakespearean insults he favors—as "lickspittles" and Vickrey as a "jackanapes" and "Chihuahua." After Gradient wrote a negative report on Overstock, Byrne sent Vickrey a furious, all-caps e-mail:

> DONN, YOU MAKE A LIVING TOADYING TO BULLY
> HEDGE FUNDS.... YOU DESERVE TO BE WHIPPED,
> FUCKED AND DRIVEN FROM THE LAND.

By that time Rocker Partners was first among the "bully hedge funds" that had won Byrne's enmity. In February 2004—long after Gradient first flagged Overstock as a company of interest and months after it had bestowed on Overstock its lowest rating—Rocker Partners opened a short position in the stock. It was not yet a Gradient subscriber, and its analysts had not seen Gradient's coverage of Overstock. Given Overstock's continuing losses, cash-flow problems, and repeated failures to meet Byrne's rosy projections, Rocker Partners saw the company as similar to bubble-era Internet start-ups, relying more on aggressive self-promotion than a viable business plan. This made it seem a promising short.

In July 2004, five months into building a short position in Overstock, Rocker Partners took out a basic subscription to Gradient, after being solicited by its sales agent and evaluating sample reports. Its analysts were impressed by the depth of Gradient's analysis and were particularly taken by its detailed work on NovaStar Financial Corporation, a subprime mortgage lender Rocker Partners was short. Moreover, David Rocker and Donn Vickrey soon discovered in each other kindred spirits in their mutual disdain for Patrick Byrne and his company.

Rocker was not shy about expressing his views. At a June 2004 Overstock "road show" (peripatetic presentation to potential investors), Rocker asked Byrne why his company's performance never seemed to match his predictions. He also asked why Overstock kept running to the well of the capital markets despite Byrne's previous claims it would soon be self-sustaining. Citing the refusal of Overstock to take his questions on a conference call, Rocker penned a July 2004 column for the Internet publication *Street Insight* criticizing the company's failure to reduce operating losses despite growing revenues. As a company's sales volume increases, overhead and other costs usually decrease as a percentage of sales, improving operating margins. That was not happening with Overstock, which supported Rocker's belief that the company's business model was flawed.

Rocker vaulted to the top of Byrne's enemies list. In an October 2004 letter to Overstock shareholders, Byrne complained about "a bunch of short-sellers and their sycophants who bad-mouth everything I do or say." He sent an e-mail to Rocker stating:

> What do I have to say to make it clear to you? I don't like you, I don't like people like you. I think you are dishonest and slimy. . . . I don't owe you answers to questions. I have made it clear from the beginning I am going to play this game differently than it has ever been played, and that means, in particular, finding the bullies like you who have gotten away with too much for too long, then tweaking and insulting them. I am not in the closet about it: I don't like you. I am insulting you, I am not wasting time "answering" to you because I don't answer to you. Do whatever you are going to do: you are a bad man, I am insulting you. I will continue to do so. . . .

As the enmity between Rocker and Byrne escalated, Rocker's partner Cohodes fretted about where it might lead. Notwithstanding his own history of mixing it up with companies he thought in need of correction, he repeatedly urged Rocker, "Never argue with a crazy person because people watching won't know who the crazy one is." His advice was ignored. The more Byrne taunted him in public and private, the more Rocker worked to see his views vindicated.

By late 2004, the financial press was treating Overstock and Byrne with skepticism. Byrne assumed it was part of the short-seller-led conspiracy against him and responded by attacking journalists. In a *Red Herring* interview, he referred to them as "condoms," used and discarded by hedge funds. His bile was eventually directed at reporters for every major financial news source, including the *New York Times, Wall Street Journal, Dow Jones Newswire, Reuters, BusinessWeek, Fortune,* and *Forbes.* One of his more vitriolic attacks occurred in an October 2004 e-mail exchange with senior *Fortune* reporter Bethany McLean, famous for her early call on Enron. Angered by her published comments about him, Byrne asked in an e-mail whether she had left the analyst training program at Goldman Sachs because "giving Goldman traders blow jobs didn't work out?" McLean would suffer the lash of Byrne's ire on later occasions as well.

Throughout the history of his jihad, Byrne would demonstrate a propensity for precisely the varieties of conduct he accuses, in outraged tones, others of perpetrating. He makes unsupported charges against those he claims have defamed him. He accuses his antagonists of employing "paid bashers" to damage Overstock's share price while, at the same time, supporting a crew of pseudo-journalists to attack anyone who disputes his theories. *New York Times* columnist Joe Nocera has portrayed Byrne as fundamentally motivated by a desire to make life miserable for anyone who dares criticize him, while purporting to be the oft-abused champion of a high-minded crusade.

Yet it is hard to deny the genuineness of Byrne's belief in his victimhood. He often seems like a man who gets into a fight every Saturday night in the same otherwise placid bar, and wonders, in all sincerity, why that particular establishment attracts so many louts and bullies.

He has shown a particular love of clandestine schemes to punish his supposed persecutors. He funds a "black ops" crew to harass his enemies as described in a later chapter. He once gave $50,000 to a purported private detective for damaging information about Rocker Partners that, as it turned out, didn't exist. The "detective" was criminally prosecuted for fleecing Byrne and others with such false promises. Byrne later purchased the laptop computer of a man who had razzed him on a web thread from the owner's estranged brother. He announced it was a treasure-trove of conspiratorial e-mail messages, then declined to release any of them.

In another incident that lacked only decoder rings and secret messages in lemon juice to be utterly jeujune, Byrne delegated Overstock VP Stormy Simon to contact David Rocker, pretend disillusionment with Overstock, and promise to dish dirt on her employer. Byrne later bragged that Simon met with Rocker in his New Jersey sanctum and "showed him thigh." The plan seems to have been to short out Rocker's critical facilities and induce him to make some improper proposal. To slip him inside information on Overstock? To join him in the hot tub? Who knows.

Rocker found Simon's vague criticisms of Byrne puzzling and told her that if she had evidence Overstock was violating the law, she should speak with the SEC.

All of this might easily have gone the way of other spats between troubled CEOs and their critics. Much huffing and puffing to little effect. This was not to be, however, because Patrick Byrne's agonistes were to be encouraged and exploited by a remarkable rogue's gallery of individuals, who would find in Byrne an ideal patron.

★　★　★

Of the assorted characters swept into Byrne's quixotic crusade, perhaps the strangest is the Internet stock tout who operates behind the *noms-de-blog* "Bob O'Brien," "the Easter Bunny," and, appropriately, "dirty deeds."[1] According to the *New York Post*, O'Brien is a former used medical equipment salesman who lives in Las Vegas. He claims he must remain anonymous to avoid violence at the hands of unspecified enemies.

O'Brien first crossed paths with Rocker Partners while pumping the subprime lender NovaStar Financial. NovaStar enjoys a place of prominence in Rocker Partner's scrapbook of trying experiences, thanks in no small part to O'Brien's success in promoting to retail investors a company that operated much like a pyramid scheme. That hurt those investors who joined the party late and didn't get out in time, and short-sellers, who paid a high price to maintain positions in a stock that for years defied economic reality.

---

[1] Whether his dirty deeds are, like the AC/DC song, "done dirt cheap" is an open question.

Short investments often follow a path of long-term pain followed by sudden jubilation when the short-seller at last "gets paid" for his trouble and patience. Timing, as in stand-up comedy, is everything, and hard to get right. Warren Buffet has said it's easier to pick bad companies than to predict when they will come to grief. They can blow up without warning or their faults can escape notice for longer than anyone who believes in efficient markets would think possible. Even egregious flaws in a company's business model or bald distortions in its public disclosure can remain unrecognized for years. Reasons come readily to mind. The government is slow to catch abusive companies, investigative journalists are few in number and often ignored, and sell-side analysts are limited in their research skills, conflicted in their incentives, and afraid to become targets of issuer retaliation should they prove overly critical. Thus short-sellers often endure years of shelling out interest and dividend payments to support what will eventually prove prescient, if premature, calls. As Cohodes enjoys saying, "Being early is the short-seller's disease."

And so it was with NovaStar.

In the heady years of the subprime lending boom, NovaStar rode that stunning folly of American capitalism as high and wild as a cowboy on a Brahma bull. In this, it was far from unique. Mortgage originators like NovaStar proliferated during the housing bubble and their role in promoting its worst excesses contributed to the current worldwide financial mess. The computer programming adage "garbage in, garbage out (GIGO)" also applies here. NovaStar and its cousins provided the *garbage in* part of the equation, with mortgage loans granted with little or no money down and scant proof of the borrower's ability to pay. Investment banks then shoveled the *garbage out* to the street in the form of "collateralized mortgage obligations" (CMOs), complex interests in pools of mortgage loans. These securities were sold to hedge funds, pension funds, insurance companies, and other institutional investors attracted by their generous and—thanks to what are now seen as rating agency blunders—supposedly safe returns. Thus was financial dross turned into fool's gold through the miracle of "securitization."

CMOs are "structured products" that slice up projected cash flows from pools of mortgages in complex ways that supposedly provide better risk-adjusted returns than competing investment products, at least if you accept a raft of assumptions underlying their valuations. The upper tranches, rated investment grade, stand first in line for the cash thrown off by the mortgages, and pay correspondingly lower rates. Risk and potential yield increase in tandem with every step down the ladder. Even during the boom years, the bottom tranches, known as "toxic waste," were often so risky as to be unmarketable, and so stuck to the balance sheet of the mortgage originator.

This last factor was important for NovaStar. To investors, the company was simply a dividend machine. In the middle years of this decade, its annual dividend often exceeded 16 percent, thus ringing the dinner bell for retirees and other retail investors hungry for income in a low-interest rate environment. This easy credit situation was the product of low federal funds rates maintained by the Federal Reserve Board—its response to the havoc wrecked on the markets by the collapse of the previous asset bubble, the run-up in technology stocks—and the willingness of foreign investors to finance American debt. NovaStar took advantage of this widespread demand for yield to regularly access the capital markets. To pay high dividends while regularly pumping out shares, the company needed to generate and securitize ever-greater numbers of mortgages, and to do so without sacrificing margin. And therein lay the rub.

Finding aspiring homeowners to take the company's money was not difficult. NovaStar merely needed to set its lending standards at the required level of subprimeness. Its commitment to funding loans to anyone physically able to sign an application can be seen from its brash advertisements. One urged mortgage brokers to "Ignore the Rules and Qualify More Buyers with Our Credit Score Override Program!" Another offered mortgages at a 90 percent loan-to-value ratio with no verification of employment. The high incidence of fraud in its portfolio caused its primary insurer to terminate coverage in 2003.

After the 2007 collapse of the subprime mortgage industry, the financial press would dwell in detail on the bacchanalia that had gone before, and NovaStar would feature prominently, having cost any number of investors their life savings. *New York Times* reporter Gretchen Morgenson detailed NovaStar's underwriting outrages, disclosure failures, and violations of HUD rules. Among the company's misdeeds was its failure to inform borrowers that it paid mortgage brokers what were in substance kickbacks to arrange loans with higher than competitive rates. This violated both federal and state law.

To maintain its fat dividend, NovaStar not only had to keep increasing the volume of its loan originations, but also to show at least a *paper* profit from its increasingly risky loans. As a real estate investment trust, NovaStar's dividend was largely determined by its reported taxable income. Critically, this number, in turn, reflected profits the company hoped someday to realize from the "toxic waste" tranches it retained from its securitizations. Accounting rules support this "gain-on-sale" treatment, but the values placed on the retained assets, and hence the profits booked on the deals, are supposed to be realistic. No one can predict with precision how the leftovers from a subprime mortgage securitization will perform over 30 years. That will depend on how many borrowers default on their loans—partly a matter of their creditworthiness, but also influenced by general economic factors—and how will many pay off their mortgages early from a sale or refinancing. Inflation rates, difficult to estimate years in advance, also affect the value of future cash flows. All this comes down to educated guesswork, ever and always an enticing playground for dubious accounting.

By the second half of 2006, 90 percent of NovaStar's pretax earnings came from aggressive gain-on-sale accounting. Those reported earnings supported its dividends and its dividends supported its frequent stock offerings. A break in this expanding cycle, sure to happen sooner or later, would cause the wheels to fall off. Such was the crux of the bear case on NovaStar, and an accurate prediction of the company's fate.

A few short-sellers, including Rocker Partners, saw NovaStar as a Ponzi scheme, dependent on greater and greater infusions of investor capital to stay afloat. Journalist Herb Greenberg also adopted this view. In 2003, the SEC began an investigation of NovaStar's accounting practices, but closed it without result—perhaps daunted by the vagaries of gain-on-sale accounting.

NovaStar insisted that its financial statements were clean, its dividends covered by cash earnings, and its critics a disreputable pack of crooked short-sellers and on-the-take journalists. Hooked on the company's outsized dividends and reassured by its energetic trashing of its critics, investors remained loyal. From 2001 until early 2005, the company's stock price increased ten-fold, then remained relatively stable for two years. Anyone short NovaStar was badly hurt. Herb Greenberg lost reputational capital as his bearish calls were mocked on message boards.

Bob O'Brien, a/k/a the Easter Bunny, was arguably no small factor in insulating the company's investors from reality. By skillfully employing the capacity of the Internet to spread misinformation, he helped NovaStar line up sheep for the shearing while expanding the tools available to companies wishing to silence their critics. What was in it for him is unclear, but his close connections to the company, and his subsequent success at winning the patronage of Patrick Byrne, suggest he was not merely pursuing a hobby.

The Internet has made a great deal of information available to the investing public. This includes everything from SEC filings to the insights of prominent financial pundits. It has also provided a forum for individuals whose opinions might otherwise be confined to the walls of public restrooms, and has given outright crooks access to millions of potential pigeons.

O'Brien used two web sites to promote NovaStar. "NFI-info.net"—named for the company's ticker symbol—was supposedly run by happy NovaStar investors eager to spread the good word about the company, but was plainly a front for O'Brien. NovaStar's generous dividend history was prominently displayed. For the intellectually curious, the site provided a lengthy but muddled explanation of the ability of the company's business model to deliver, apparently in perpetuity, generous returns with no appreciable risk. That a mortgage company in Kansas City could overturn a fundamental principle of market economics was presented as unremarkable. NovaStar cheerleaders, following O'Brien's lead, suggested buying the stock with credit cards. This would allow investors to capture the margin between the interest rates on the cards and the historically higher yield provided by NovaStar stock. It was a good thing for the small investor, they advised, that the big hedge funds had not yet discovered this sure-fire strategy.

Echoed by a coterie of message board trolls, O'Brien bitterly denounced short-sellers and their journalist enablers for attempting to deprive the small investor of the boon that was NovaStar. His bile was sometimes narrowly targeted. In 2005, he put on the Internet Marc Cohodes's home address, with information about his family and a picture of his disabled son. *Barron's* reporter Bill Alpert noted that O'Brien had "threatened a kid in a wheelchair."[2]

O'Brien's other vehicle was his blog "SanityCheck.com." His ambitions with this site extended well beyond hyping one subprime mortgage company. In rambling jeremiads, he presented NovaStar and eventually Overstock as among a multitude of American companies hounded toward oblivion by a conspiracy of market-manipulating "naked" short-sellers, who threaten the very foundations of our economy.

Naked short-selling, which is prohibited under most circumstances by SEC Regulation SHO, involves selling a stock without either owning or borrowing it. This means the trade probably won't settle within the three-day period prescribed by regulation. Not all stock sales clear on time. The number of "fails to deliver" is small in relation to total market transactions, but can pile up for certain issuers. Whether this is caused by administrative glitches, an exception to the three-day delivery rule available to options market-makers,[3] or something nefarious is controversial. A colorful Internet-empowered subculture claims that these "fails" are the root of all stock market evil. The gist of this theory is that short-sellers collude to attack selected stocks through massive naked shorting, often aided by slander campaigns against the targeted companies, then cover at a profit after the stocks tank.

This is a creative variation on the venerable "bear raid" stories that have enjoyed a stubborn popularity for at least a century, rarely accompanied by anything like proof. In his classic 1924 memoir *Reminiscences of a Stock Operator*, Jesse Livermore wrote:

> I have done my share of trading . . . and I can say that I do not recall an instance when a bear raid caused a stock to decline extensively. What was called bear raiding was nothing but selling based on accurate knowledge of real conditions.

A "bear raid" can be detected, by those so inclined, whenever a lot of people short a stock at around the same time. No other evidence is

---

[2]David Rocker also attracted the attention of the crew. A message on the Yahoo! thread for NFI stated: "We need info. on Rocker. Where he lives, telephone numbers, etc. Its [sic] time to get personal with this phucking maggot."

[3]This exception, as provided by Reg. SHO, permitted options market-makers to hedge the exposure they faced from facilitating certain options transactions. It was eliminated by the SEC in 2008. This resulted in a significant decline in fails to deliver, but did not silence the anti–naked shorting crowd.

required. This is unlike the situation in which many traders decide to pile into a stock, which merely shows their confidence in the company. The problem with this theory is that is explains both too much and too little. Bear raid alarums absolve companies of responsibility for declines in their share price—which make them popular with failing companies—while leaving unexplained how bears expect to capture the paper profits that result from the effect of their short sales when they can expect precisely the opposite effect when they buy shares to cover their shorts. This does not mean short-side manipulations never happen. But shorting the stocks of good companies is rarely a profitable tactic. It's hard enough to profit from shorting the most loudly howling dogs on the NASDAQ and AMEX.

Bob O'Brien has anointed himself the prophet of the anti–naked shorting cult. His impassioned pronouncements display the sinewy pseudo-logic of the television evangelist. The works of Satan, as he tells it, are everywhere among us.

> I believe we are the victims of libel, manipulation, related party trading, collusion, naked shorting, fraud, criminal conspiracy and racketeering, money laundering, collusion with class action attorneys and regulators, cover-ups at the exchanges and the [Deposit Trust Clearing Corporation, a private company that administers the securities clearing process], and every violation of [anti-fraud rule] 10(b)5 [sic] in existence.

Despite the overwhelming financial power and down-and-dirty tactics of the opposition, he is confident that his efforts to awaken the populace will succeed: "The small investor has discovered their [sic] voice, and there is now a sense of hope that the system can be fixed, the ship righted, the violators brought to justice."

The image is that of a man back-lit in some public square, wide-shouldered, tie askew, shirt transparent with sweat as he grips the podium, booming out to his rapt audience of salt-of-the-earth folks—like the couple with the pitchfork in *American Gothic*—God's truth about the evils of Wall Street and calling on them to help get the gummint to make things right for the common man, particularly those common men who invest in the stocks O'Brien is pushing. Think of Broderick Crawford in *All the King's Men* before the booze and extra women caught up with him.

For all his absurdities, however, O'Brien is a talented salesman of more than used medical equipment. He writes with great self-assurance and—like Ezra Pound declaiming on monetary policy—his grasp of a technical field is strong enough to make his theories seem plausible to the uneducated. And that makes him dangerous. The world is full of people who feel they have not been given a fair shake and will follow blindly anyone who promises to right the wrongs done against them. They will pay for the privilege.

Thus does populist rhetoric become a tool of predation.

To further his crusade, O'Brien runs a supposedly nonprofit, supposedly public interest organization called the "National Coalition against Naked Shorting (NCANS)." Donations are cheerfully accepted, no amount too small. He once mentioned that he was touched to receive $100 from a grandmother living on Social Security, who "wishes she could send more." "This," he proclaimed, "is grassroots."

Other than the pseudonymous O'Brien, the only name publicly associated with NCANS is that of "executive director" Mary Helburn, a sixty-something woman who lives in northern California. Helburn, like O'Brien, touted NovaStar and is a vocal proponent of short-seller conspiracy stories. She contends that Enron would still be alive and kicking were it not the victim of naked shorting. In a 2005 video produced for an NCANS web site, presumably funded by Patrick Byrne, Helburn claimed that her disabled nephew, Matthew Bailey, "lost half his portfolio due to naked short selling." That does sound terrible. But financial reporter Roddy Body, then with the *New York Post*, contacted Bailey's mother and got a different story. She said, "We haven't lost any money, we live very comfortably." So what was this about? It seems Helburn had told her the video would "help a stock that they owned."

In the opposite corner from O'Brien stand various academics, mainstream financial writers and career regulators who believe that the anti-naked shorting crowd occupies a continuum stretching from the sadly misinformed to the barking mad. One SEC official has dismissed them as "bozos." A particularly passionate adversary of what he calls "the baloney brigade" is blogger and former *BusinessWeek* editor Gary Weiss. Weiss derides NCANS as an "astroturf" (fake grassroots) movement, serving a grubby handful of stock touts and crooked companies. He sees O'Brien as a "crackpot" and "moron" who "managed to suck in a sizable number of rubes to buy this faltering stock [NovaStar] and not sell when things started looking bad." Columnists for the *New York Times*, the *Wall Street Journal*, and *Barron's* have also treated this purported reform movement as a joke.

Without claiming to be an expert on the securities clearing process, I would suggest the skeptics have the better argument. Yes, the system has faults that may present opportunities for abuse. But the dark substratum of the market where naked short-sellers meet to hatch their vile plots seems hard to find outside the cyberspace fever swamp created by O'Brien and his ilk. Rocker Partners was always assured by its prime broker that it had "locates" for its short sales. Other short funds tell me the same holds for them. The SEC—not a friend to short-sellers, either naked or as well-covered as an Eskimo—has so far been able to scrounge up just *one* enforcement case involving naked shorting, and that on a very small scale. The attorney who brought that case is skeptical that illegal naked shorting is a widespread practice; he told me that even Canadian brokerages no longer permit it.[4]

The ethical caliber of the anti–naked shorting crew, moreover, does not inspire confidence. In addition to O'Brien, their ranks have included corporate CEOs whose management techniques eventually led to civil or criminal liability. Companies alleged to be the victims of short-seller conspiracies have a habit of coming to grief as a result of nothing more exotic than their failure to make money. A handy example is NovaStar. As the shorts had predicted, its perpetual-motion machine of dividends begetting stock sales begetting dividends collapsed when it could no longer report earnings sufficient to satisfy legal requirements to support payment of dividends. The end was abrupt and brutal. In February 2007, the company announced that its dividend paying days were over. Its net income had departed and left no forwarding address. Whether NovaStar, with its high leverage and predatory lending practices, was simply an early casualty of the subprime meltdown or, as alleged by the shorts, a Ponzi scheme whose time had come, the result was tragic. The stock fell out of bed, and then, as more bad news emerged, out of

---

[4]A 2007 study of failed trades on Canadian exchanges found that only 6 percent result from short sales and the vast majority of fails-to-deliver settle within a short period.

the window. The retirees and other retail investors who depended on NovaStar for much of their income were devastated and bared their scars on the message boards.

The SEC revived its investigation into NovaStar, the subprime meltdown having made such cases a priority. It soon had company. NovaStar reported that its practices are now under investigation by seven agencies: the SEC, the FBI, the FTC, HUD, the Department of Justice, the New York AG, and the U.S. Department of Labor. One wonders if the Fish and Wildlife Service can be far behind.

Unable to deny having herded lemmings off a cliff, O'Brien proclaimed himself stunned and irate. No one, he said, had told him this could happen. He assured those who had followed his advice to their ruin that he, more to be pitied than blamed, not only felt their pain but also shared it: "I will not be buying anymore [sic] stocks in the U.S. markets, that's for sure. I'm quite done now. The casino has lost its allure." For that one moment, he was unable to blame NovaStar's critics for its problems.

O'Brien would be no more than an interesting example of the genus *conspiratorus Americanus* were it not for the success of his cult in attracting a few high-profile converts. And enjoying pride of place among these is Overstock CEO Patrick Byrne.

★ ★ ★

The story of how O'Brien and Byrne first joined forces, so endearingly bizarre, has been told and retold in the press. It is worth revisiting, however, because its effects continue to reverberate to this day.

The first public sighting of O'Brien as an Overstock supporter occurred during the company's January 2005 earnings call. Phoning in, O'Brien identified himself as a "retired guy" with an investment in Overstock and important information to share with other investors. He and Byrne pretended to be strangers, but Byrne later admitted they had been speaking for several months. After congratulating Byrne on a great quarter, O'Brien offered to explain "why so many people are saying mean things about you."

And so began what Bethany McLean would later describe in *Fortune* as "the first truly weird moment" in Byrne's jihad.

The reason Overstock's share price had faded from its $77 peak, said O'Brien, had nothing to do with its persistent losses or its failure to achieve Byrne's promised performance milestones. No way. The problem was entirely attributable to a short-seller conspiracy. Over the span of 20 minutes, his rambling accusations reached beyond Rocker Partners (with whom O'Brien had previously tangled over NovaStar) to much of the financial press, the DTCC, and the SEC, which had joined together to achieve "a systematic serial killing [of] small-cap companies." NovaStar was still going, so O'Brien could include it among the companies victimized by these dark forces. In closing the call, no longer able to maintain his pose of uncommitted curiosity, Byrne enthusiastically endorsed O'Brien's view of the SEC as a "captured regulator."

In the months that followed, Byrne became O'Brien's most devoted acolyte, like Prince Hal with a stock-hustling Falstaff, or Luke Skywalker with a less syntactically challenged Yoda. That Byrne was evidently a true believer only made him more motivated. As the poet Swinburne (almost) wrote:

> What brought good Patrick's genius nigh perdition?
> Some demon whispered: Patrick, have a mission.

The two men developed their dogma in numerous web postings and in a full-page ad in the *Washington Post*, paid for by Byrne as part of his growing financial support for O'Brien and NCANS. Byrne became the public face of the anti–naked shorting subculture. In a CNBC interview, he pulled out a card with contact information for NCANS and propped it up under his chin for the camera. This stunt appears to have rendered him persona non grata at CNBC. Byrne later charged that CNBC was part of the short-seller conspiracy. He had it on good authority, he said, that a fax machine on its premises was dedicated to receiving the names of stocks that hedge funds wanted slammed. He offered no explanation for why CNBC would agree to such a scheme. A visibly pissed-off CNBC replied that Byrne had now moved from speculation to flat-out lying.

Byrne's blossoming crusade coincided with continuing poor performance metrics from Overstock. Some saw a connection. For example, a departing Overstock employee posted on a web page her view of Byrne as "a brash, disingenuous cad . . . who's been so deluded by the Iagos he surrounds himself with that he has quickly driven his own company to the ground while blaming it on naked-shorting."

O'Brien, for his part, worked overtime smearing Overstock's detractors. For example, he claimed that "a hedge fund guy," whom the reader might easily assume to be David Rocker, had commissioned a murder-for-hire after a department store altercation involving his wife. O'Brien's purported source for this tale was an unnamed journalist who, in turn, heard it in a bar from a stranger with "slicked-back hair."

The most memorable "truly weird moment," however, occurred in an August 2005 Overstock webcast in which Overstock announced it was suing Gradient Analytics and Rocker Partners for supposedly defaming it. Byrne quickly vaulted past that news item, however, to describe his discovery of a conspiracy so vast it defied belief. And, to many, still does. His primary source was Bob "The Easter Bunny" O'Brien. He began by admitting that he had initial doubts about the guy. "He sounded like he lined his hat with tinfoil," said Byrne. "He sounded crazy."

So why did Byrne become a believer? Like Tsarina Alexandra embracing Rasputin, he was converted by the infallibility of the man's predictions. O'Brien had foretold various events concerning Overstock that indeed came to pass. Its stock had been listed on foreign exchanges without the knowledge of the company. Negative articles had been written about it. Other stuff.

Byrne then alleged that "miscreant" hedge funds had conspired with, among others, the detective agency Kroll & Associates and various journalists to destroy Overstock through published hit pieces, circular offshore trades, naked shorting, and other skull-duggery. He accused Kroll of tapping his phone. He described *Wall Street Journal* reporter Jesse Eisinger, instrumental in bringing the Lernout & Hauspie fraud to light, as "running around with banking records that could only have been feloniously obtained and harassing 70-year-old ladies." He attempted to link Jim Carruthers, the Bay Area analyst who had blown the whistle on ACLN, to a man with a similar name Byrne claimed "has a very interesting relationship with a certain lawyer in Detroit who has some very odd practices that maybe we'll have time to get back to." No more was heard of the Detroit lawyer or his odd practices.

Apparently anyone who had ever outed a crooked company was in for it.

Byrne summarized his theories in a diagram titled "The Miscreants' Ball." A cat's cradle of lines and boxes that *Barron's* compared to "the paranoid psychotic diagrams in *A Beautiful Mind*," it includes not only Gradient Analytics, Rocker Partners, and almost every journalist who'd ever dared criticize Overstock, but also the Attorney General of New York, the Department of Justice, the SEC, the long-defunct short-selling firm Feshbach Brothers, and several European stock exchanges. Certain names were selected seemingly at random. Byrne explained that he had included Leon Black in the diagram "just because he's a well-known financier hedge fund guy. Got nothing to say about him." Tom Barton was included although his fund, White Rock Capital, had given up shorting stocks years before. Barton called up Overstock's general counsel and told him to knock it off. The diagram, as it appeared on Overstock's web page, was amended to delete Barton's name.

David Einhorn, president of the hedge fund Greenlight Capital, also found his name on Byrne's diagram. In his book *Fooling Some of the People All of the Time*, Einhorn describes Byrne's attacks on him and his wife, Cheryl Strauss Einhorn. Ms. Einhorn earned Byrne's enmity as a former editor of *Barron's*—"a group of quislings for the hedge funds"—which had published a negative article on Overstock. Byrne admitted Ms. Einhorn was not directly at fault for the offending article, having left *Barron's* some time before its publication, but thought she probably knew its author. Therefore, she could not escape responsibility altogether.

The bottom of Byrne's diagram revealed the ultimate source of the conspiracy. A *Star Wars* fan, Byrne labeled this evil-doer the "Sith Lord." "And here's the funny part," narrated Byrne:

> . . . as this went on I started realizing that there was actually some more orchestration here being provided, by what I'm calling here is the Sith Lord or the mastermind. Now, can I tell you who that designated bottom feeder was who was supposed to end up with our company [at a cheap price]? Can I tell you? I can. But I'm not going to today. The Sith Lord is . . . can I tell you who that is? Well, I could tell you it's a name that everybody on this phone, every single person on the phone would recognize the person's name. He's one of the master criminals from the 1980s and he's back in business. But I'm not going to. I'll just call him the mastermind today.

When pressed by a financial journalist for the identity of this individual, Byrne stated, "The Sith Lord's role is murky to me. If it exists, it seems less about control than about priorities (like Osama bin Laden to al-Qaeda)." However, Bob O'Brien theorized that the Sith Lord is in fact Michael Milken—taking time off from his philanthropic activities to rig the securities markets for the specific purpose of acquiring Overstock at a bargain price. O'Brien reached this conclusion, in part, from the fact that Milken has the same initials as "master mind." Milken, when contacted by the press, said he had "never heard of Overstock.com."

But then, he *would* . . . wouldn't he?

Chapter 9

Mired in Muck

I rarely buy anything online and so had never heard of Overstock.com until late 2005 when, still at Vinson & Elkins, I got a call from David Rocker. He was not a happy man. Rocker Partners had been short Overstock for over a year and was in considerable pain. Despite the company's weak performance, the stock had risen substantially while Rocker Partners built its position. Further, David had gotten into a public pissing contest with Overstock CEO Patrick Byrne and was getting wet.

Byrne was on a tear. He had gone very public with his allegations that Gradient Analytics was a smear sheet for hire, trashing "innocent" companies as instructed by its short-seller clients. In the case of Overstock, of course, that would be Rocker Partners. This seemed to shade into his theories about naked short-selling, although he did not directly accuse Rocker Partners of that practice.[1]

---

[1] In early 2007, Overstock would file suit against a long list of prime brokerage firms, including Morgan Stanley, Bear Stearns, Citigroup, Merrill Lynch, and Bank of New York, claiming they had engaged in

Overstock had filed a defamation suit against Gradient and Rocker Partners in state court in Marin Country, California. The gist of its complaint was that Gradient, Rocker Partners, and elements of the financial press had conspired to manipulate down the price of its stock for the benefit of Rocker Partners. Rather than plead the case as a market manipulation and litigate in a federal court with experience in securities cases, Overstock had chosen as its venue a local court more experienced in landlord-tenant and employment disputes.

Overstock did not immediately serve the complaint on the defendants, so the matter hung in limbo for months while Byrne publicly trumpeted his evidence of the alleged conspiracy. This consisted of declarations from several former Gradient employees critical of Gradient. Byrne hung these documents out for public inspection on the Overstock web site. He and people on his payroll cited them triumphantly on message boards. And Overstock peddled them to the San Francisco office of the SEC, arguing that they proved a market manipulation scheme, and convinced the staff to open an investigation.[2] That was where I came in.

At first reading—or, for that matter, second or third—they sounded damning. Only one declaration targeted Rocker Partners, but the others set the scene in lurid colors. They claimed that Gradient made a practice of publishing "custom reports" on public companies at the behest of its short-seller subscribers. The reports included client-generated material, suggested to be invariably negative and accepted by Gradient without question. Further, the reports would be released when it suited the client, allowing it to "get its position on" before the report came out and ruptured the stock. According to one former employee, Gradient kept a tally of "blow ups" in stocks to which it had assigned low grades. He implied that Gradient claimed responsibility for these events. The same declarant laid Gradient's harsh coverage of Overstock squarely on the doorstep of Rocker Partners.

The language of the declarations tended toward the conclusionary. Names, dates. and other details were scarce. And they cited no actual

---

a "massive stick manipulation scheme," involving naked short-selling. That action, filed in a state court in San Francisco, is ongoing.

[2] Overstock obtained declarations from four former Gradient employees. One of these, however, was so brief and tepid that Byrne did not bother posting it on the Overstock web site.

misstatements in any Gradient report. All the same, the overall impression was troubling.

For all Rocker's combativeness and Cohodes' love of hyperbole, I had never seen any indication of sharp practices from either of them. They prided themselves on being among the embattled minority of honest men in the financial world, and seemed to pay the dues to support that self-image. After the JCPenney farce, I had settled into the view that being constantly accused of malfeasance was simply part of the short-seller's job description. Like hard tackles for Premier League wingers. When Rocker asked me to help the hedge fund respond to an SEC subpoena, I assumed this was another government folly that would collapse of its own absurdity.

Then I read the declarations and decided this might not be so easy.

★   ★   ★

Document productions are rarely intellectually challenging. You scoop up whatever exists, dump out anything irrelevant or subject to privilege—usually meaning some lawyer wrote it—and ship it off. There may be some line calls. And a talent for organization helps when dealing with major volume, whether the documents are holding up the roof in a warehouse or eating gigabytes on a server. But the grunt work can usually be done by paralegals on autopilot.

In most cases, the fewer documents the better. A thin record reduces the chances that, if your client screwed up, it left a paper trail memorializing its screw-ups and, if it didn't, opposing counsel will be able to find something to make it look like it did. Vague, cryptic, or technical language and, worst of all, irony provide particular opportunities for adversarial spin.

From that standpoint, Rocker Partners was a nightmare. It used a Bloomberg e-mail system that was antiquated, difficult to search electronically, and—worse—retained every e-mail in perpetuity. *Nothing* was ever deleted. This was particularly worrisome with these guys because they appeared never to have a thought they didn't put in an e-mail. With their New Jersey lawyers, I sorted through tens of thousands of their electronic missives while Rocker indignantly proclaimed this to be

AremisSoft all over again: a slime attack designed to shut him up while Byrne pimped his company free of distraction.

The e-mails allowed anyone so inclined to follow the course of events in real time and granular detail. And a good thing too, as it turned out. My initial trepidation over too much information slowly gave way to something close to elation. There was nothing there to feed a conspiracy theory. Nothing shady or sneaky or miscreantish. Just lots of what analysts do: chatter about public companies in hopes of unpacking them better than the competition. Taken together, the e-mails between Rocker and Vickrey undercut any argument that Gradient had acted as a front for Rocker Partners.

If Gradient had been pointed in the direction of Overstock by one of its clients, that client was not Rocker Partners. Gradient had begun covering at the company in mid-2003 after it was flagged by one of Gradient's screening programs—and became increasingly critical with every report it wrote. At the end of 2003, it gave Overstock its lowest rating. In its view the company would probably never make money, and its accounting and internal controls were a mess. This was without any input from Rocker Partners, which did not become a subscriber and begin communicating with Gradient until a year into Gradient's coverage of Overstock.

By that time, the hedge fund had formed its own views of Overstock. The process was well documented in its internal e-mails. Cohodes picked up on the company after Patrick Byrne began attracting attention to himself through odd public statements. Cohodes kicked it to Rocker, who dug down on its business model and performance metrics, finding little to like in either. Cash flow was a problem. Customer acquisition costs were rising. The company's persistent failures to live up to Byrne's projections made him look amateurish or dishonest. And his claim to be a New Age CEO seemed situational. For example, he made a point of conducting Overstock's IPO through a "Dutch auction," an approach notable for skimping underwriters on fees. He congratulated himself repeatedly for this; then he went to traditional underwritings for secondary offerings. Rocker, being of a suspicious nature, saw a connection between this decision and the positive coverage ladled on Overstock by institutional analysts soon after their firms were included in its underwritings. He also questioned why two analysts for

W.R. Hambrecht, the investment bank most closely connected to Overstock, were terminated after they went negative on the company. The
company seemed to him to use a carrot-and-stick approach to keep
analysts in line.

The indulgence displayed by sell-side analysts caught the attention
of financial writer Edward Chancellor.

> The investment banks' reports on Overstock during this period are
> reminiscent of the analysis of the dot-com era. There are allusions to
> the vast potential market addressed by the company, "network effects,"
> "option value" of the business, of the need for internet retailers to
> spend money to "acquire rooftops" and the potential for a share price
> spike after Byrne appeared on TV. Comparatively little attention was
> paid to the risks faced by this cash-burning internet stock and its
> eccentric CEO.

Rocker Partners signed up for a basic subscription with Gradient
in July 2004. The fund employed no accountants and, impressed with
Gradient's sample reports, concluded Gradient could fill a need. As
a marketing device, Gradient included with its basic subscription the
option of receiving two free reports on companies of the client's choice.
This was not a major selling point to Rocker Partners and it never asked
to receive a "custom report" on any company. Nothing in any of the
e-mails suggested Rocker Partners believed Gradient subscribers could
influence the timing or content of its reports.

Byrne's "hatchet job for hire" thesis also failed the common sense
test. Gradient reports are typically highly detailed and cleanly sourced to
public documents: not shallow rumor sheets that could easily be tricked
up to order. The majority of Gradient clients are hedge funds or mutual
funds with mainly or exclusively long positions. They look to Gradient
to flag potential problems with their stocks, not to churn out hit pieces
that would cause them to lose money on their positions. Its ability to
obtain and keep its clients—which have included major investment banks
and mutual fund families—rests on its reputation for accuracy. A few bad
calls to please short-sellers and that reputation would be gone. This is
aside from the question of how Gradient could help some clients by
fobbing off tainted reports on the rest who, if they too saw Gradient as
"a hatchet job for hire," would hardly be taken in.

The biggest flaw in Byrne's theory, however, was the assumption that the privately distributed reports of a small forensic accounting firm in Arizona could move stocks in whatever direction it chose. Overstock's share price showed little if any reaction to Gradient reports and increased six-fold during the first year of coverage. Further the reasons for the steep decline in the company's stock screamed from the pages of dozens of sell-side reports, including reports from firms that previously had been bullish on the stock.

The OSTK business plan was the basic Internet two-step—swallow negative margins for a few years while you build a dominant position in your market, then figure out some way to make it profitable. OSTK executed well through step one—handily beating revenue expectations every quarter while that remained the metric the Street cared about. But though the end of 2004, the long-promised "inflection point" into sustainable profitability still proved elusive. This was largely due to OSTK's inability to cut back marketing expenses without losing revenue momentum, much as Gradient had predicted. A Hambrecht analyst wrote in April 2005:

> Falling earnings expectations after the Q4 report, along with a bizarre conference call combined to shave 49% off Overstock.com's peak market valuation prior to the Q1 earnings release. The further deferral of full year profitability likely disappointed many investors.

In August, the same analyst wrote "Whatever you want to call it, gross margin was a huge disappointment," and by the following month was flatly skeptical about the company's earnings projections. And this was while he had a *Buy* on the stock. After many reductions in estimates and price target, he finally threw in the towel in December 2005 and downgraded the stock to a Hold. By then, many other firms rated it a Sell. A writer for the *Financial Post* commented that any claim the stock's decline was "engineered by Gradient, when many other analysts were following the stock, [which] trades at 800,000 to one million shares per day on average, is utterly laughable."

Soon after Rocker Partners became a Gradient client, David Rocker and Donn Vickrey began sharing their views on various companies, including Overstock. This is what analysts do. With their faces stuck to Bloomberg screens, they work the telephone, mainly with other analysts, hoping to figure something out before the competition. Analyst services like Gradient are similar to other financial media. They need to provide information not available elsewhere to justify what they charge their subscribers. In Rocker Partners, Vickrey had found a potential source worth cultivating. It had been in money management for decades and could boast a history of spotting bad companies early.

Before Rocker and Vickrey had their first conversation about Overstock, each had concluded the stock was a loser, its price buoyed by gusts of hype from its CEO. Byrne's references to Rocker as "slimy" and Vickrey as a "Chihuahua" who should be "whipped, fucked and driven from the land," seem to have solidified a bond between them. In e-mails to Vickrey, Rocker expounded on the failings of Patrick Byrne as an executive and a human being, much as he enjoyed doing to Byrne directly when given the chance. When Gradient took his suggestion to compare Byrne's projections to the subsequent performance of the company—all a matter of public record—he proudly took credit in an e-mail to his partners.

That's as far as it went. Nothing in Rocker's e-mails was false or suggestive that Gradient would, to make him happy, publish misleading material—or, for that matter, that he would *want* it to do so. In one e-mail, he questioned one of Vickrey's criticisms of Overstock and cautioned him to make certain of its accuracy. There was no indication anyone at Rocker Partners ever, as Overstock claimed, drafted or edited a Gradient report, sought to control the timing of Gradient reports, or so much as asked to be told what was in the pipeline.

So what to make of the inflammatory declarations from the three former Gradient employees?

It would be easy to pass them off as the parting shots of disgruntled employees, none personally involved in drafting Gradient reports and most terminated for cause. But whistleblowers always have an ax to grind. That doesn't mean they're always wrong. If these purported whistleblowers were blowing mostly smoke, knowing why they were willing to put their signatures on these documents was critical.

The declarations were not simply the independent musings of three people who happened to have similar views about the place they used to work. Big chunks of language repeated across all three indicated that the same person had drafted each: apparently a lawyer and presumably a lawyer for Overstock. Who else would invest the effort? There was nothing, in itself, wrong with that, but it raised the possibility their experiences had been shoehorned into someone else's ill-fitting language. More troubling was the artfulness of that language. The conclusions were arrived at too quickly. The three ex-employees skipped over questions of what they knew and how they knew it to lunge straight for the accusation that their former employers were—not to put too fine a point on it—big whores.

From reading these things, anyone who didn't know better would think Gradient was purely in the business of churning out custom reports for shortsellers. In fact, the custom reports were a marketing tool intended to convince prospective customers they would be certain to get coverage of at least one or two companies of specific interest to them. They were thrown in for free with Gradient subscriptions and given a pass by many of its clients, including Rocker Partners. They accounted for about 1 in 20 Gradient reports.

The practice of doing research on companies as requested by individual clients and then (sometimes) disseminating the results to its client base was presented by the ex-employees as an ethical atrocity. But there is nothing improper or even unusual about an analyst firm doing research projects for individual clients. Similarly misplaced was the indignation that clients who requested "custom reports" had existing views about the companies they wanted researched. What else would anyone expect? No one commissions forensic reports on randomly selected companies, or companies in which they have only a casual interest. Only if an analyst has invested major effort on a stock and come up against questions he can't answer does it make sense to hire a specialist. And then there is no reason to keep the specialist in the dark about why his help is wanted.

But what about the fact that the reports wouldn't simply go into the client's research file but might—should Gradient so choose—be sent to its other subscribers? It is easy to see why Gradient, after investing time in a project, would want to exploit the asset it had created by providing it to its subscriber base. Yet it would have been wiser to let that opportunity pass. The optics were treacherous. Add the assumptions that Gradient reports have the power to move stocks and that Gradient will slant its custom reports to the views of the requesting subscribers, and someone so inclined could spin this practice to do major damage to the firm's reputation. As Gradient learned to its dismay.

At bottom, this was the mechanism of these declarations. Sales types, none of the three ex-employees had been involved in researching and drafting reports. They couldn't say any report was inaccurate or any Gradient analyst had been pressured toward a negative take on a company. To fill this gap, they employed subjective and conclusionary phrases like "it was apparent to me" or "it was common knowledge," which both mean "I have no good reason to believe this but choose to do so."

One of the declarants, however, brought more to the party than vague surmise. Or seemed to. Demetrios Anifantis, like one of the other declarants, had been summarily fired. Gradient claimed Anifantis had tried to extort extra commission by holding for ransom a lead on a potential new client and then walked off with proprietary client information when he saw he was about to get the boot. Soon after Gradient fired him, he was on the phone to Overstock, offering to trash his former employer.

In the longest and most detailed of the declarations—which included language boilerplated from the other declarations—Anifantis rolled up his sleeves and swung an ax at Gradient and Rocker Partners. Some of his statements, like those of the other declarants, were banalities phrased to sound shocking. For example, he implied that Gradient tracked the history of the stocks it covered to demonstrate its ability to affect the price of those stocks. In fact, Gradient did so to demonstrate its *predictive* abilities. But other statements, if true, would go a long way toward validating Byrne's thesis about Gradient.[3]

Anifantis portrayed Vickrey as a lackey to his hedge fund clients, jumping at their beck and call, shoveling out whatever dank concoctions served their purposes. Rocker Partners was painted as the worst offender. He claimed that, beginning in 2003, David Rocker dictated the substance of Gradient reports on Overstock, and told Vickrey when to release each one to best serve his trading strategies. Into this steaming stew, Anifantis also threw one of Byrne's most-hated reporters, Herb

---

[3] More than this, Anifantis gave form and depth to Byrne's views. Before his encounter with Anifantis—as fateful in its way as his earlier epiphany with Bob "dirty-deeds" O'Brien—Byrne's thesis was little more than an inchoate mixture of resentment, suspicion, and inference.

Greenberg. "It appeared to me," he stated, "that Rocker, Vickrey and Greenberg were coordinating the content and timing of their various reports to please Rocker."[4] Anifantis claimed to know these things from participating in Vickrey's telephone calls.

The other declarations were troubling. This one was incendiary. It was far more aggressive and specific than the others, even if it, too, could cite no actual false statements in any Gradient report. And there was a kind of chemistry between this declaration and the others. Standing alone, Anifantis could be dismissed as a vindictive loser, settling scores with a company that had drop-kicked him out the door. And without him, the other statements came across as unfocused, not to mention irrelevant to Rocker Partners. Put them all together, however, and the mutual bootstrapping created a compelling story.

But was that story real? Were the declarations accurate and the inferences they invited fair and likely to find support from other quarters? If so, Patrick Byrne, for all his eccentricities, had a right to feel abused.

There was no question that Rocker and Vickrey spoke frequently and disparagingly about Overstock. For them, a day that passed without ragging on Patrick Byrne was a day without sunshine, an attitude many others would come to share. But could anyone—and in particular Anifantis—say it was more than that?

Most fundamentally, did Anifantis really speak from personal knowledge? Not surprisingly, the objects of his accusations said he did not. Vickrey and Rocker insisted Anifantis had never participated in any of their telephone calls. Cohodes said he had never spoken with Vickrey, much less Vickrey and Anifantis together. The only Rocker Partners employee who had any recollection of speaking with Anifantis was an administrative assistant in the California office who'd asked him several times for copies of old reports. This was confirmed by Gradient's system for monitoring client contacts. Anifantis had dutifully entered onto the system those contacts the Rocker Partners employee remembered but *none* of the calls with Vickrey and Rocker or Cohodes in which they supposedly conspired against Overstock. This was, obviously,

---

[4]Anifantis did not explain why Greenberg would involve himself in this enterprise. Greenberg responded that Anifantis' statements were "based on fiction and so far off the mark as to be malicious."

critical. If Anifantis had not participated in any such calls, his claim to speak from personal knowledge about dealings between Gradient and Rocker Partners was false and his other statements were, at best, hearsay.

His account also included obvious misstatements of fact. He claimed Rocker Partners began influencing Gradient reports in 2003, but the hedge fund had no interaction with Gradient until most of the way through the following year. He identified certain passages in Gradient reports as contributed by David Rocker.[5] Again, his timing was off. Some of these reports pre-dated Rocker's first contact with Vickrey. When Vickrey saw this declaration, he fumed in an e-mail to Rocker.

> The only specific [allegation] . . . was that supposedly you, me and Anifantis were on the phone planning the March 16, 2004 report. Supposedly you told me what to write and edited the piece. The trouble is, you were not a client then. I had never met or spoken to you as of then. I had never e-mailed you as of then. Not to mention that Anifantis was never on the phone with you and me, ever. So, there are quite a few problems with that one specific example. . . . I presume that Byrne chose this date based on some idea that you must have first shorted the stock sometime just before that.

Anifantis claimed that Rocker Partners had requested "special reports" on Overstock. Both Gradient and Rocker Partners were adamant it had not, and there was nothing in the documents to suggest otherwise. Anifantis claimed to have been on phone calls in which Rocker asked Vickrey to sit on reports until Rocker Partners could "get its own position on in the stock." Rocker Partners, however, had a short position in Overstock before its first contact with Gradient and the firm's trading records do not indicate that it shorted more Overstock in advance of Gradient reports. Nor does it appear from an extensive e-mail record that Rocker Partners saw Gradient reports before they were released or, for that matter, even asked to be informed about what was in the

---

[5]None of these statements were claimed by Overstock to be false. The inability of Overstock to connect any communication from Rocker Partners to any statement in Gradient reports it alleged to be defamatory was a problem for Overstock in its lawsuit against the hedge fund.

hopper—much less that it edited drafts of Gradient reports, as alleged by Anifantis.

Anifantis, further, had consistency issues. After being fired by Gradient, he applied for unemployment insurance. He was later to claim he had been terminated for asking too many questions about Gradient's relationship with Rocker Partners and other clients; but he did not mention this gem of a claim at any point in the unemployment proceedings, which included two written appeals from the initial denial of benefits.

One of my former law firm partners liked to say: "You gotta believe your clients." By this he meant that you owe it to your clients to see things from their perspective whenever realistically possible. Here it was easy. That the three declarants who provided Overstock's case against Rocker Partners were less than objective, and one simply false, could be accepted without trying.

But, still, they told a great story.

They told *such* a great story, in fact, that they eventually took for a long ride the SEC, a Senate committee, the CBS news program *60 Minutes*, and a series of California judges.

★ ★ ★

This was a case a government lawyer could truly love. It had everything. Heroes and villains. Evidence delivered up front. Potentially broad implications for the securities markets. Indeed, it could be the mirror image of the institutional analyst case in which Eliot Spitzer ate the Commission's lunch. This time with biased analyst reports used to push stocks down rather than up.

And it was easy to understand. Short-seller wants stock to drop. Greases crooked analyst firm to trash stock. Stock goes down. Short-seller cackles with glee as he rolls in filthy lucre.

Yo! Got it.

When Overstock delivered its case, neatly packaged, to the SEC's San Francisco office, it must have seemed a wonderful gift. Later it may have appeared more like a Halloween trick: a flaming bag of dog crap left on the doorstep.

Byrne turned "In the Matter of Gradient Analytics," as the investigation was titled, into another weapon in his arsenal against his critics. Correspondence from the SEC staff to the former Gradient employees promptly appeared on the Overstock web page. Based on his purported communications with the staff, Byrne pontificated publicly that it was investigating not only Gradient and Rocker Partners but also Herb Greenberg.

And when the investigation was ratcheted up to the "formal" level, celebration was heard from the Byrne camp. In a February 2006 web posting, Bob O'Brien—not yet chastened from the implosion of NovaStar—urged Rocker Partners' investors to withdraw their money from the fund, insinuating that the firm would soon be sued by the Commission.

> Well, in the latest update, my sources tell me that the SEC inquiry into our favorite hedge fund and research group has gone formal. . . . Now, for those of you who don't know what this means in real world terms, it's pretty simple: A federal marshal shows up at your door and serves you with a subpoena, and all of a sudden you are in a completely different ballgame. There aren't a lot of reasons the SEC goes formal other than to subpoena. It is an unmistakable signal that you are going to receive the kind of scrutiny that makes an IRS audit seem like a picnic lunch with a Victoria's Secret model. It is also done exclusively because the Commission is looking at either civil or criminal actions.

Much of this was nonsense. SEC subpoenas are not delivered by federal marshals. They come in the mail. And it was most unlikely the Commission was contemplating a criminal action against anyone. As a civil agency it has no criminal enforcement powers. Also, the agency has hundreds of "formal" investigations going at any time and hasn't the resources to launch a full-court press in each one.

Still, no one could claim that for Gradient or Rocker Partners the investigation was a *good* thing.

Nor was it going to go away easily. The stakes were raised for the SEC when, in a bizarre episode of institutional gullibility, the staff subpoenaed various journalists who had criticized Byrne and Overstock. This was a break with SEC policy, which usually treated anything touching on reportorial sources as off-limits. Herb Greenberg, who had twice proclaimed Byrne among the worst CEOs in America, was among the recipients. Before this was public knowledge, Byrne sent him a late-night e-mail, squeezing every possible drop of gloat from the situation.

Dear Herb,

I write in the spirit of our little sideline chats of the past. If you are not open to this, let me know.

I am just sitting here with a glass of wine in my hands, reflecting on what a really bad week you and your friends have had. The last two days in particular will likely prove to have been life-ruining events for certain people. As I take a sip, I find myself curious: do you guys know? Are you sitting somewhere, blithely oblivious, still chuckling about Whacky Patty, and all that? Or do you understand now that this is going to end badly for you?

The signs are that you guys do understand, as some of your cronies are starting to make desperate-seeming mistakes. *Do* you understand what is happening in your world? How do you rationalize it? How do you tell yourselves it will work out? Do you ask yourself if you should have done something differently? I don't suppose you would tell me what it feels like: even were you in a panic, you'd probably write something like, 'Anything you say Patrick!' But you guys cannot be *completely* oblivious about the meetings that are going on, the questions that are being asked, the documents being drafted, the stories that are being told, the people who are listening. Someday people will be asking you what it felt like, to be where you fellows are now, and I am mildly curious to know: I hope you record the thoughts for posterity, if only as a cautionary tale. And if you would care to send me a letter, I would keep it private if you so desire.

Who knows, I might even be in a position to do you a favor someday.

Call anytime.

Patrick

Greenberg called the staff's action a "witch hunt." CNBC's Jim Cramer had made the mistake of telling "Mad Money" viewers to sell Overstock when it was trading near its peak. So he also got a subpoena from the SEC. Later he would complain that "Christopher Cox's SEC was totally motivated to get me and to shut me up about a stock that I thought was going lower." He wrote "bull" on his subpoena and trampled it on camera. Several other reporters let their lawyers handle the situation.

The journalist subpoenas caused a firestorm of protest in the financial press. That respected reporters were being investigated at the behest of a corporate CEO widely referred to as "Wacky Paddy" made the media's blood pressure spike. The *Wall Street Journal* editorialized that "the journalists are suspected of having sources who tells them things that they then share with their readers or listeners. Where we come from this is called reporting." Never known for understatement, the *New York Post* described the SEC's action as "a mission of majestically misguided folly" that advanced the administration's "war of attrition against free speech." *New York Times* columnist Joe Nocera tried to shove the SEC in a more productive direction.

> The most ridiculous part of this whole story is that the S.E.C. has taken the bait, using the allegations in Mr. Byrne's lawsuit to open an investigation into Rocker Partners and Gradient—and has also ensnared Greenberg as a witness of some sort. But the agency is looking in the wrong direction. Last fall, the S.E.C. chairman, Christopher Cox, sent a letter to Senator Ron Wyden, Democrat of Oregon, saying that he was concerned about "issuer retaliation against research analysts." Surely, he ought to be able to see that what is going on here is a form of retaliation.

But this was wishful thinking. Despite his "I'm on it" letter to Senator Wyden, Cox's tenure was marked by a lack of interest in even the most egregious instances of issuer retaliation.

The chairman, however, was not happy to be the object of media opprobrium. Complaining that he had been left out of the loop, he publicly reprimanded his staff for the journalist subpoenas and decreed they should be rescinded.

In March 2006, Canadian drug company Biovail Corporation, copy-catting the Overstock action, sued Gradient and various hedge fund clients, including Connecticut mega-fund SAC Capital, for supposedly saying false things about it. Issuer retaliation though litigation was becoming fashionable. Having never shorted a share of Biovail, Rocker Partners was given a pass on that one. It was, however, named in a later action by Canadian insurance company and major Overstock investor Fairfax Financial Holdings.[6]

Biovail was represented by the New York litigation firm Kasowitz Benson Torres & Friedman and the Los Angeles public relations firm Sitrick and Company. Both were known for hardball tactics. The *New York Post* reported that private investigators working for the Kasowitz firm lifted the trash of a former Bank of America analyst whom Biovail claimed had unfairly criticized it. Biovail said the private eyes were merely making sure the analyst was not "improperly disposing of evidence." Gradient employees also complained they were being followed and intimidated by the Kasowitz firm's in-house detectives. One planted himself in the front yard of a former Gradient analyst, yelling that the man would be committing "professional suicide" if he refused to sign an affidavit against his former employer.

In promoting Biovail's campaign against its critics, its advisers scored an early coup by convincing the CBS program *60 Minutes* to run a segment on the lawsuit. Biovail president Eugene Melnyk indignantly aired his claims of victimhood. "There's a group of people," he said, "that got together and essentially attacked the company by putting out false reports, and we're just fighting back for our shareholders."

It would later become apparent that Biovail shareholders were in need of protection not from short-sellers but from the company itself. In 2008, the SEC sued it for securities fraud. Biovail took an injunction and paid $10 million to settle the action. The same year, Biovail pled guilty and paid a $24.6 million fine to resolve federal kickback and conspiracy charges, and former CEO Melnyk—by then in forced retirement—was sued by the Ontario Securities Commission for insider trading. And in 2009 Melnyk paid the SEC $1 million to settle allegations he had failed to properly report his ownership of stock in the company. The company's outside lawyers, moreover, received a tongue-lashing from a federal court judge for misusing confidential information from another suit to gin up a phony shareholder action that mimicked the Biovail suit.

Looking back on the *60 Minutes* piece in 2008, the *Columbia Journalism Review* noted, "So, *60 Minutes* had it exactly wrong."[7]

---

[6]Fairfax is discussed in Chapter 13. Fortunately for Gradient, it never issued reports on that company.

[7]This matter would be dismissed in August 2009 based on the court's finding that Biovail's attorneys had committed ethical violations in bringing the suit. Biovail's state court action against Gradient and other critics was dismissed later that year.

But that was all in the future. At this point, Biovail—armed as it was with a platoon of lawyers, detectives, press flacks, and, most of all, a good story—was capable of doing damage to its critics.

60 Minutes reporter Leslie Stahl handled the Gradient ex-employee accusations with the wide-eyed credulity of a cable-channel interviewer chatting up purported victims of alien abduction. While she did point out that Biovail had some poor quarters during the period it claimed Gradient and SAC were attacking its stock, she never asked what was false in any Gradient report or how such a crude approach to market manipulation could succeed, not once but on a regular basis.

The financial press, however, wasn't having any. Stahl was seen as having strayed from her proper playground. The *Times'* Nocera put his finger squarely on the misconception she had promoted.

> The silliest idea embedded in both the Biovail lawsuit and the "60 Minutes" segment is that because an analyst, a short seller, a research firm, and even a reporter are talking to one another—and perhaps even collaborating—that they are somehow engaged in a stock manipulation. That is what people do in markets all the time, on the long and short sides. When you have a big position in a stock, you want to persuade others to your point of view. You make your case in phone calls, or at conferences, or over drinks. You try to get reporters to write articles reflecting your views. If you can get others to agree with you, and either buy or sell because they are persuaded by your logic, that is good for both you and the market.

Well, exactly. But try to tell that to the SEC.

In the Gradient investigation, the staff plunged blithely forward. Kicked to the curb over the journalist subpoenas, it tried the backdoor to get the same information. It demanded that Gradient, Rocker Partners, and others cough up their communications with reporters, none of whom had written anything about Overstock anyone could reasonably claim was inaccurate. It gathered up hundreds of thousands of documents and spoke with a parade of witnesses, including David Rocker. He didn't write "bull" on his subpoena and trample it underfoot. To the contrary, he seemed eager to vent to the staff about Byrne, Overstock, and the failure of the SEC to "do its job." The SEC attorneys agreed he could appear in New York, and I flew up from D.C. to prepare him for the session.

This was the second time I had met David. The previous year, while in New York City on some business or other, I went by his midtown digs to pay a courtesy call. It was a small office in an older building near Radio City Music Hall. David was alone except for one harried secretary. We managed to have something like a conversation while he monitored several screens, typed e-mail messages, and barked orders on the phone and at his secretary. He reminded me of a vaudeville performer who could juggle ninepins while spinning plates on poles.

David's house—where the firm's general counsel and I prepared him for his testimony—was quite nice but not opulent by the standards of the hedge-fund world. Located in an exclusive area of New Jersey, it had once been the guesthouse for the mansion up the hill and had taken the pool with it when the division was made. At one end of the pool was a life-sized sculpture of a bear. Inside the house were many smaller ursine objects. David reveled in his role as a market contrarian.

Mrs. Rocker was there, puttering around the house. Here was the woman Bob O'Brien had implied once prevailed upon her husband to have someone rubbed out for no better reason than because he had offended her in a department store altercation. In the flesh, she was an earnest, soft-spoken woman in late middle age whose conversation centered on her children and grandchildren and trips she had taken with them to Israel to stay on a kibbutz. An altogether unlikely candidate for the role of gangster's moll.

The SEC's New York office had been in one of the satellite buildings of the World Trade Center until September 11, 2001. Due to its proximity to the conflagration of the twin towers, it had melted to the ground. Fortunately, everyone had been evacuated with no casualties. After a couple of years in temporary quarters farther uptown, the SEC had settled into the World Financial Center in imposing modern offices overlooking the Hudson River.

A young attorney had been sent from San Francisco to take David's testimony. Two others were plugged in by speakerphone. Given the investment the staff had made in this case, I was afraid the session would turn contentious when David didn't do them the favor of providing fuel for their suspicions. But no, it was a by-the-numbers session, with the obvious questions asked and the obvious documents marked as exhibits and shoved out for explanation. No surprises and no dramatics. David has a tendency to lecture—particularly when he's dealing with people he considers ignorant or stupid. But today he was clear and confident and never lost his temper. Allowed to ask questions at the end, I took him through every major Overstock allegation with the sort of blatantly leading questions you can get away with in administrative testimony. He denied each of them and the SEC attorneys left it at that. There was simply nothing for them to jump on. David had done nothing but short what he thought was a "dicey" stock, as he phrased it in print, and broadcast his views on that stock, which, as it turned out, were on the mark.

And that was it. Quite the anticlimax.

In February 2007, the staff closed the investigation. As is the usual practice, no explanation was provided. Patrick Byrne, upset that the staff had failed to uncover a conspiracy he believed to be of epic proportions, railed that the SEC was a "captured regulator." Bob O'Brien—who had previously described the SEC as "a boot-licking lackey of Wall Street special interests"—proclaimed this result exactly what he would have expected from such a shoddy and compromised operation.

After a lengthy squabble with the SEC over a Freedom of Information Act request, we received the testimony transcripts of the Gradient ex-employees. All pre-dated the Rocker testimony and gave some insight into why the air had gone out of the investigation.

If it is alleged that Joe Blow got up in the morning, had breakfast, read the newspaper, walked the dog, robbed a bank, went home, and took a nap, it makes very little difference, in prosecuting Mr. Blow for bank robbery, how much evidence exists on the dog and the nap. The witnesses went on for hundreds of pages without providing any evidence of law violations.

They testified that Gradient oversold the professional credentials of its employees and secretly ran a small hedge fund on the side. They thought these facts were very important. They weren't. If Gradient engaged in these practices, it shouldn't have, but they were unlikely to violate the securities laws and, of course, had nothing to do with Rocker Partners. The witnesses knew of nothing false or misleading in any Gradient report. Only one instance was recalled of Gradient holding onto a "custom report" at the request of a client. The subject of the report wasn't Overstock and the client wasn't Rocker Partners.

Even Anifantis proved a dud. Hampered by a murky memory, he testified uneventfully despite the urgings of an eager staff attorney who clearly regarded him as a key witness.

Anyone wanting to embarrass me could do worse than get their hands on some of my early testimony transcripts. But I hope I never did anything as weak as this. The rocks and brickbats declaration signed by Anifantis would have provided a natural starting point to structure the testimony. The attorney apparently forgot to bring it. He asked slow-pitch questions and expected Anifantis to be inspired to declaim in well-organized detail on the wrongdoings of Gradient and its clients. Instead, his answers were vague and sometimes revealed that his declaration had been worded to mislead. Anifantis had stated, for example, that Rocker, Vickrey, and Greenberg coordinated "attacks" on Overstock. But his testimony revealed he drew this conclusion from the mere fact that some of Greenberg's blog posts echoed Gradient reports, sometimes even on companies that Anifantis thought Rocker Partners might be short. And his statement that Gradient, "at Rocker's request, wrote several reports on Overstock that graded the company either 'D' or 'F,'" just meant that Rocker and Vickrey discussed Overstock, after which Gradient wrote reports that continued to give the company low grades—not that Rocker had dictated the grades. Nor was it clear why he thought any reports were made at Rocker's request.

There was little attempt by the staff attorney to challenge apparent misstatements of fact, clarify unresponsive utterances, or refine muddled recollections to provide a solid record. He didn't press Anifantis to explain his stealth presence on phone calls between Vickrey and others, or why had neglected to note them on Gradient's records, as he had his other calls. He made nothing of the fact that Anifantis admitted there were, in fact, no "custom" reports on Overstock, although his declaration strongly suggested the opposite. At times, he seemed to nudge the witness toward answers that would have helped make a case. SEC investigations, however, are supposed to be fact-finding exercises, not result-oriented exercises in testimony massage.

But it didn't matter. From the standpoint of building a case against Gradient, Rocker Partners or anyone else, the testimony of Anifantis and the other former Gradient employees was worthless. Beyond that, it cast a harsh light on their declarations.

Stripped of the layers of innuendo, artful misdirection and obfuscation, there was nothing in them that was remotely illegal. Analysts talk to each other. Sometimes they criticize companies. They appropriate each others' ideas. That was pretty much the substance of what they had to offer. Everything else was spin.

It is possible to admire the declarations as skillful exercises in sophistry. That, however, would require a certain insensitivity to the damage they caused. The SEC attorneys who spent hundreds of hours on the matter—only to dump it as a dead loss after having been lambasted by the chairman for stepping on journalists' toes and derided by the financial press for terminal gullibility—may have taken a dimmer view. Gradient and Rocker Partners for their part were outraged at the way the government had been used as the instrument of a private vendetta. Being forced to respond to an SEC investigation is an expensive and stressful process.

And that was far from the end of it. The tactics that had spawned the Gradient investigation would reappear to great effect elsewhere in Overstock's campaign against its critics.

Chapter 10

Our Tax Dollars at Work

In June 2006, while the SEC's Gradient investigation was still kicking, David Rocker was invited to testify before the Senate Judiciary Committee. The committee was conducting hearings on complaints that short-sellers conspired with bent analyst firms to trash stocks. The source of these complaints was easy to guess.

Citing the ongoing Overstock litigation, Rocker declined to testify but, being in D.C. anyway, I trotted over to the hearing to see how much mischief our elected representatives could stir up on this potentially sexy topic. There was no denying that the claims of victimhood by Overstock and Biovail had the ability to inflame the moral passions. This had been demonstrated by the SEC's Gradient investigation and *60 Minutes*. Truly, it was an engaging story. The worry was Rocker Partners would need to prove in yet another forum that it was no more than that.

Any doubt as to what had gotten the senators in an uproar was quickly put to rest. Arlen Specter, playing ringmaster of ceremonies, mentioned that the idea had come from his colleague Orrin Hatch, senator from the great state of Utah and, as Senator Specter did not mention, a major recipient of Byrne family campaign contributions.

I have not made a study of Senator Hatch's political career. For all I know, he is a model public servant. Judged solely by the way he is represented by the Byrne organization, however, it is easy to conclude that he should not be allowed to vote in general elections, much less hold public office. According to an Internet site funded by Byrne, "Deep-Capture.com," the senator is complicit in Byrne's colorful fantasies.

> One day in the Fall of 2006, Senator Orinn [sic] Hatch called Patrick to his home. . . . When Patrick entered the building, the senator pulled him into a corner of the lobby. "I am going to tell you something," he said. "But I cannot tell you more than this. You are up against some really nasty, vicious people. *They will not hesitate to kill you.*"
>
> The senator took a deep breath and continued. "I want you to do something for me. I want you, the next chance you get, to go on TV or radio and say the following. Say that if anything happens to you, Senator Orinn [sic] Hatch says that he's never going to rest until the United States government has gotten the people who did it. Now, I'm not kidding, Patrick, I want you to do that tomorrow if you can. The senator repeated this several times. And he made Patrick repeat it back to him.

According to New York Senator Chuck Schumer—who showed up just to make this point—the Judiciary Committee did not have jurisdiction over the subject matter of the hearing. But that discouraged Senator Hatch not a whit. He was clearly primed for bear, as it were. In his initial remarks, he said he was not against short-selling *per se* and noted that the naked variety was not on the agenda for the hearing. He then brought up the issue repeatedly, demanding to know why Justice and the SEC weren't all over this naked short-selling thing and, at one point, launching into an impassioned tirade on the evils of this practice. Picking up on the Biovail and Overstock suits, he opined that collusive conduct between hedge funds and "corrupt or conspiring" analysts can destroy investor confidence and "discombobulate the market."

The witness panels, however, did not provide much support for the notion that short-sellers—naked or otherwise, alone or aided by analysts—pose a serious threat to our capital markets. Michael Kasowitz, attorney for Biovail and other supposed victim companies, testified in general terms that short-sellers are a sneaky bunch and love to drive down stocks by spreading lies. But his presentation tended toward the conclusionary and seemed geared to plugging his legal practice.

Demetrios Anifantis might have been expected to steal the spotlight as the star witness. But he shrank from the role. He was happy to beat on his former employer as a company "built on corruption." Both his written and oral testimony, however, lacked specifics. He avoided naming names—including Rocker Partners. This was puzzling, and all the more so because his testimony had, it appeared, been prepared by Overstock.[1] Had he decided that testifying before a senate committee was a serious business and he shouldn't say stuff he couldn't back up?

Two other witnesses undercut the antishorting agitators. A representative of a hedge fund lobbying group made the points that short-sellers add liquidity to the market and have a history of spotting bad companies before the sell-side wakes up from its well-compensated slumbers. Marginal companies have whined about the shorts since the lava cooled, he said, but their complaints rarely pan out. This point was seconded by Yale academic Owen Lamont. In a number of papers he had championed short-sellers as "a disadvantaged minority." True, dat. He pointed out that, in an earlier congressional hearing, three companies had claimed they had been destroyed by lying, conniving, colluding short-sellers. Two of the three were later convicted of securities fraud. Professor Lamont did not see this as a statistical anomaly. "A notable feature of the data," he said, "is that many of the firms fighting with short sellers and analysts are subsequently revealed to be fraudulent."

As a show trial, it lacked drama. There was the expected short-bashing, some political grandstanding and private score-settling, and much moral indignation. But nothing new or solid enough to be newsworthy. Senator Specter, a former prosecutor, couldn't have been overwhelmed by the evidence laid out before the panel.

---

[1] Metadata from Anifantis' written submission indicated it had come off the computer of an Overstock lawyer.

Still, it seemed too much to hope that it would just go away. And it didn't. Exactly. Rather, the inquiry took an abrupt turn away from the announced topic of the hearings—the relationship between hedge funds and analysts—and charged off in an entirely different direction.

One of the witnesses—his testimony so loosely related to the rest he seemed to have wandered into the wrong hearing—was a former SEC Enforcement attorney who claimed he had been fired for too aggressively investigating possible insider trading by a big hedge fund. The fund was Pequot Capital Management. He believed it had been tipped by John Mack, at the time of the Senate hearing the CEO of Morgan Stanley, about at least one merger transaction.

The attorney, Gary Aguirre, was—in a bizarre coincidence—the brother of Michael Aguirre, City Attorney of San Diego. Deepening the coincidence, the enforcement group in which Gary Aguirre worked had been under my supervision until I left the SEC, although this was before he was hired and before there was a Pequot investigation.

Gary was Michael's *older* brother and, after many years as a solo practice attorney in San Diego and a period of semiretirement, he had been hired, in his early 60s, as a new SEC attorney. The unprecedented decision to hire someone at such an advanced age into an entry-level position was explained by the fact that, after applying and being rejected 22 times, Aguirre had brought an EEO action against the agency for age discrimination. So it hired him.

I have never met Gary Aguirre and have nothing against him—none of us being our brother's keeper. In fact, I'm grateful to him for distracting the Senate Judiciary Committee from further investigations made at the behest of large contributors into imaginary threats to the capital markets. Nor do I deny the existence of age discrimination in the legal profession, including government practice. To the contrary, it is as unquestioningly accepted as was racial discrimination a few decades back. Unlike racial discrimination, however, it is not based on blind prejudice. There is a practical reason legal recruiters tend to be most welcoming to the young—and it is similar to the reason the military seeks young men barely out of adolescence. They like their cannon fodder eager and malleable.

Legal employers look for a certain commodity in their new hires: conventionally motivated overachievers who do well in highly structured work environments (i.e., ass-kissing grinds). The older the applicant, the more likely it is he or she has picked up independent habits of thought, outside interests or life values not easily subordinated to the desire of his employers to simultaneously maximize partner contentment and billable hours. In government practice, this translates into general quality of life enhancement to supervisors. Exceptions are made, but therein lies the bias faced by older applicants.

When called upon by the Judiciary Committee and, as the matter picked up steam, the press to justify Aguirre's termination, his former supervisors painted him as the ultimate loose cannon: unpredictable, abrasive and insubordinate. He treated his supervisors as a lower life form, they said. He responded to their instructions as if to the droning of insects and alienated coworkers as a daily routine. He expected outside lawyers to hand over their lunch money at the sound of his voice. In short, his stint at the SEC resembled the running of the bulls at Pamplona detoured through a dinnerware outlet. They admitted Aguirre was both smart and diligent. The problem, as they saw it, was that these are positive attributes only when properly directed, by them, not when fielded without restraint by an aging obsessive out to save the world—or at least the capital markets—before his next retirement. His contention that they had caved to political pressure in closing the Pequot case was flatly denied.

But the Senate panel was not so easily put off. Aguirre's claim that both he and his case were dumped in a suspect fashion had some meat on its bones.

As in most insider trading investigations, the evidence was largely circumstantial—but there was a lot of it. Pequot had demonstrated a talent for buying stocks in advance of public announcements that boosted their prices. Seventeen of these plays had caught the attention of the NYSE and NASDAQ. One became particularly significant. In July 2001, the hedge fund made a substantial profit from rushing into the stock of Heller Financial shortly before the announcement of its acquisition by General Electric. Two of the banks involved in the transaction were Morgan Stanley and Credit Suisse First Boston (CSFB). John Mack had been CEO of Morgan Stanley until March 2001 and, during the period the Heller transaction was in the works, was being vetted to become CEO of CSFB. Mack was a close friend of the head of Pequot,

Arthur Samberg. Right about this time, he leaned on that friendship to make highly profitable investments in Pequot funds that were closed to others. He and Samberg were in contact shortly after Mack was interviewed by Credit Suisse senior officials about becoming CEO of CSFB and shortly before Pequot started grabbing up Heller shares.

Was this worth investigating? Sure. And no could say that Aguirre didn't investigate. He sent out nearly 100 subpoenas. When he didn't get documents fast enough he pestered and threatened. He beavered though countless e-mails. He squeezed every relevant document until it begged for mercy. He questioned Samberg twice. Samberg denied being tipped by Mack but didn't have much of a story as to why he had so suddenly and fortuitously fallen in love with Heller Financial.

The next step, as Aguirre saw it, was to drag Mack into the SEC's palatial new headquarters and grill him under oath.[2] At first his supervisors were supportive. Then they weren't. After some dithering, they told him that, before he could question Mack, he must establish that Mack knew about the Heller acquisition before Pequot started buying its shares: not just that he hung with people in the know. Otherwise, see, Mack could tell them whatever he wanted and get away with it.

Aguirre disagreed. He had heard that the standard approach to insider trading cases is to take the major witnesses early and "lock them in" to their stories. They might admit something before they see its true importance or lie in a way that could later be proved, thus destroying their credibility. This is true but the "testimony by ambush" approach tends to be less effective when, as here, the witness has had several years warning that the staff is coming and is advised by half the lawyers in New York.

On the other hand, it is not the case that taking the testimony of someone in Mack's position sooner rather than later must be an exercise in futility. Insider trading cases often turn on a few simple facts, not all of which are in dispute. A government attorney who goes into testimony in an accounting case without fully digesting yards of documents will probably achieve nothing but a reduced sense of self-worth. But in an insider trading case, many of the issues will be in plain sight. Did you

---

[2]One of C. Northcott Parkinson's "laws" of institutional behavior posits that government agencies typically enter a period of decline soon after they obtain impressive quarters.

know about the merger, or the drug test, or the earnings number before it was public? How did you find out? Who did you have contact with that week? Many witnesses testify honestly. And no sophisticated witness will lie lightly about facts the government may be able to prove down the road. So, by bringing in witnesses early, the staff can sometimes avoid spending time establishing facts no one denies. Assuming, hypothetically, John Mack was aware of the Heller acquisition before it was made public and knew that evidence of his knowledge could fall into the SEC's hands, he might well have admitted that fact for purely tactical reasons. This in itself would not have meant he broke the law, but it would have moved the investigation along significantly.

Aguirre concluded Morgan Stanley had pulled strings to impede his investigation. He saw many indications of this. In response to Aguirre's demands to take Mack's testimony, his immediate supervisor had begun counseling caution. They were dealing, he said, with people who had enough "juice" to go over their heads in the agency. In fact, they had already done so. Mary Jo White, a former U.S. Attorney for Manhattan and now with a law firm that represented Morgan Stanley, had called the head of Enforcement, Linda Thomsen. She had a problem, she said. Morgan Stanley wanted to hire John Mack as its CEO but the SEC investigation was a wrench in the works. They couldn't very well hire the guy if there was a chance he would get charged with insider trading. How would that look? Perhaps she added: I know you have to do your job, Linda, but do you have to do it so damn slow? The trades your people are looking at took place four years ago!

Thomsen looked at documents White sent directly to her, bypassing her staff, and responded that she saw in them some smoke "but surely no fire." One of her immediate underlings also gifted Morgan Stanley's lawyers with some vague reassurances.[3] The message conveyed was: we don't have anything yet but, hey, that could change tomorrow.

While far from a free pass, this did raise the question whether the same solicitude would have been shown to counsel representing, say, Acme Slingshots, Anvils, and Rockets. It also played into a traditional gripe of the Enforcement rank-and-file; the upper tranche of the defense

---

[3] That the same administrator joined White's law firm the following year was not seen by the Senate committee as a good fact for the SEC.

bar sometimes seems to have better access to the division's front office than do SEC staff attorneys, and may use it to backstab their cases.

Aguirre complained. He accused his supervisors of being gutless wimps, seemingly unaware that criticizing government officials for being hypercautious is like knocking Sumo wrestlers for being plump. He got no satisfaction. He threatened to quit. He did quit. He changed his mind and withdrew his resignation. He complained more. As he put it, he "informed every link in the chain of command from [his] branch chief to the SEC Chairman in over thirty written communication of the special and favored treatment my supervisors were giving the suspected tipper." This did not have the desired effect. He went off on vacation and—shortly before the end of his probationary year with the agency—was summarily fired. Linda Thomsen wrote a termination memo all but saying he was too much of a pain in the ass to be tolerated further. No way would she be bullied and blackmailed into running her shop to suit a first-year attorney, even if he was her elder by some years. Some negative adjustments to Aguirre's evaluations were made retroactively by his supervisors.[4]

If Aguirre's superiors though this would be the end of it, they were deluding themselves. Someone who will apply for employment with the same federal agency *22* times, then file an EEO complaint when not successful, who will crank out *100* subpoenas in one investigation, and who, when he thinks he is not getting his props, will carpet bomb the bureaucracy with *30* memos and e-mails, is not someone who will go down without a fight.

How Aguirre came to the attention of the Senate Judiciary Committee, I don't know. My guess is Patrick Byrne saw in Aguirre support for his view of the SEC as a "captured regulator" and hooked him up the committee. In any event, Aguirre found in that body a sympathetic ear. Several months after his initial appearance, and after much behind-the-scenes poking around by its staff, the Judiciary Committee held a hearing devoted specifically to his story. With the attitude of DC cops rounding up an Anacostia drug crew, it hauled in a busload of SEC officials—including Aguirre's entire chain of command and the agency's Inspector General—and badgered and berated them for hours.

---

[4]This, too, proved hard to explain to the Senate committee.

It was ugly. Senators Specter and Grassley in particular were convinced Aguirre had been canned for blowing the whistle on cozy dealings between the SEC and white shoe law firms. They also concluded that the IG—who had conducted an internal investigation that purported to exonerate Aguirre's supervisors—couldn't find his sock with his foot. No explanations were credited or excuses entertained. Much pain was inflicted and careers damaged.

The press found this controversy irresistible. The *New York Times* cried scandal, while the *Wall Street Journal* dismissed it as a personnel molehill blown up into a political mountain. The blogosphere generally supported the scandal theory. Eventually two senate committees issued a joint "interim" report slamming the Commission and a final report that, if more measured in tone, left little doubt its authors thought the agency had screwed up royally. Any member of the public who followed the matter would probably conclude the SEC's process had been badly compromised by outside influences.

And why not? Don't we all believe, deep down, that most government officials are out to screw us, or at least to take advantage of their positions to make a quick buck?

Nevertheless, anyone with a few years before the mast at the SEC might feel some skepticism about the crude melodrama presented to the public eye. Yes, some members of the East Coast legal elite enjoy better access to SEC honchos than everyone else and exploit it to get in extra licks for their clients. There are various reasons for this. They may have personal relationships with SEC officials from their own period of employment with the agency. They may be in a postion to make trouble with the press, politicians of members of the Commission if they don't get a high-level hearing on their issues. Also, some are in fact quite good lawyers and, when they insist on going on about something, may actually have good reason.

But the notion that big players can call up Enforcement officials and say "please can this investigation because it's causing problems for my wealthy client" and get the response "and would you like fries with that?" is as silly as Patrick Byrne's claim that CNBC has dedicated a fax machine to collecting orders from short-sellers. Even those SEC managers whose ambition is to jump from government into a law firm partnership—far from all—know they won't get there by compromising investigations. Their economic value to a firm will depend in large part on how far they make it up the SEC ladder and what kind of reputation they take with them when they leave. Both of these things depend on getting results—bringing in big cases—not doing favors for defense counsel that make big cases go away.

Does this mean Aguirre simply imagined a connection between the pestering of the front office by lawyers for Pequot and Morgan Stanley and the ensuing epidemic of cold feet among his supervisors? Not at all. Just that there were more moving parts than he may have realized.

A more realistic scenario than the one he embraced comes easily to mind. Linda Thomsen gets a call from Mary Jo White about one of the thousand-odd investigations percolating up through the building. She doesn't blow her off because anything involving a potential Morgan Stanley CEO is likely to end up in the press. Should that happen in a way likely to cause her pain, Thomsen would like to be forewarned. So she calls down the ladder far enough to find someone who might actually know something. She hears the details and wants to throw up.

A certain now-retired SEC supervisor had a favorite expression to indicate that a matter submitted for his approval was a risky proposition. He would peer over his glasses, offending memo dangling between thumb and forefinger, and say: "Do you know how many ways I could get my dick caught in my zipper on this one?" Ms. Thomsen would probably not have expressed herself with the same anatomical metaphor, but the basic concept would have come to mind.

The Pequot matter, quite simply, had trouble written all over it. Anyone with experience in insider trading cases and not a congenital optimist would look at it and think: they may well have done it but it will be damn hard to prove, and we could blow thousands of staff hours trying. Unlike accounting cases, which can often be made almost entirely on documents, winnable insider trading cases require either critical admissions or very strong circumstantial evidence. Sophisticated players like Pequot are rarely so considerate as to provide either. This may explain why a surprising proportion of SEC insider trading cases are brought against people who live in mobile homes or their parents' basements.

The Pequot case was then at the point many insider trading investigations reach just before they stall. Trades timed so well someone just *had* to know something. A marbles-in-the-mouth explanation from the trader. A plausible source of the tip. But suspicious as all this sounds, more is needed. When the SEC goes into court without more, it usually loses.

There are lots of things that can take a case over the line. The trader lied to the staff and got caught. He "lent" money to the suspected tipper, then forgot to ask for it back. He rarely touches options but this time made a big play in short-term, way-out-of-the-money calls. But there has to be *something* more than suspicious trading and contact with an insider. Unlike with horseshoes and hand grenades, close counts for nothing.

Even had the staff made the next big leap and proved John Mack knew about the Heller deal in time to tip Pequot, any decent defense lawyer could have made it go away. "Mack and Samberg talk all the time," counsel would point out in exasperation. "They *like* each other. So they spoke on that particular day like they did on a hundred others. What law does that violate? Pequot is an arbitrage fund. It makes bets on likely acquisition targets. It wins some; it loses some. So it got it right on Heller. Big whoop. Here's a list of twenty other stocks where it got it wrong. You put a couple of nothing facts together and think you have something that lets you ruin people's lives! Is the concept of *coincidence* beyond you people in the government?"

But, you might ask, can the "concept of coincidence" be stretched to cover 17 incidents of suspicious trading?

Probably not if there's one potential source tying the trades together. If a hypothetical John Mack, for example, had access to inside information relevant to a bunch of Pequot hits, that would be a pattern with potential. Without that, it's not a pattern—it's 17 separate insider trading cases.

The hungry zipper factor in this matter was heightened by two other concerns; first, this was not a case that would settle without *much* better evidence and, second, not one the Commission could cheerfully lose. For major players in the financial sector, agreeing to an injunction in an SEC insider trading case, even without admitting guilt, is career suicide. Had the SEC charged Mack and Samberg with insider trading they would have fought long and hard. The SEC, however, has the resources to litigate only a small fraction of the six hundred or so cases it brings each year. So it thinks intensely before suing anyone who will go to the mat. This creates a bias toward jumping on people who can't fight back. If this seems unfair, remember that we live in a world where levels of privilege begin with prenatal care.

Moreover, given the people and entities involved, the case would have attracted much media attention, some of it skeptical. That raised the stakes further and would have made the agency even more skittish about pulling the trigger.

And then there was the age of the case. By the time Aguirre and his supervisors faced off over whether to question Mack, it already had four years on the clock from the date of the conduct and was nowhere near done. This is a very sensitive matter. Generations of commissioners have pounded on the staff for taking too long to bring cases. They know this is important because the press carps about anything over, say, two years old. Few commissioners have much insight into how cases are made, but I haven't met one yet who couldn't count.

To sum up...the enforcement director is informed that Pequot is a low-percentage, increasingly long-in-the-tooth, resource-intensive investigation, run by a staff attorney whose supervisors describe him as unstable. She has already gotten calls about how he is pissing on the shoes of securities bar heavies. She is under pressure because the case is holding up a change of top management at a major investment bank. She may hear from the chairman on that and he won't be happy. It has little settlement potential, if litigated will be well defended and, if taken to judgment and lost, will attract major criticism to the Commission.

Thomsen may have had some harsh words for her underlings about how it had gotten to this point. But recriminations are futile and a decision had to be made. The decision seems to have been to clue Morgan Stanley that Mack was nowhere close to being charged and make sure no one—including one "no one" in particular—escalated things by dragging Mack in for testimony, unless and until they had more on him. And, if they got too much blowback, remove the source before he passed his one-year anniversary and got the union involved.

Was this the best they could have done under the circumstances? Probably not. Bringing Mack in would have been the better course. If nothing else, it would have reduced any appearance of favoritism. The possibility Mack would have provided evidence of insider trading was not *completely* negligible. And at least the staff would have gotten his story and could stop wasting time guessing what it might be. From the transcript, Morgan Stanley's attorneys would be able to glean more about how much or little the staff had on their prospective CEO than from vague mutterings about smoke and fire. This would have permitted a more informed decision on hiring him.

After Aguirre was out, the staff finally questioned Mack, albeit in grudging response to congressional pressure. He said he didn't know about the Heller transaction, much less tip anybody about it. So the staff said thanks for your time and closed the investigation. Two years later, it began looking at possible insider trading by Pequot in situations that did not involve John Mack, subsequently informing Samberg of its preliminary determination to sue him and his fund over one of these situations. In May 2009, Samberg announced he was closing the fund: he said because of the damage done to it by the publicity attending the SEC investigation.

As someone once said, never assume there's a conspiracy behind events that can be explained by simple incompetence. The Pequot case did not represent the SEC at the top of its game—it handled the case poorly at every level—but neither did it prove the agency to be "a captured regulator." However much we may want to think otherwise, the favoritism that occurred was of the sort that leaks into many aspect of government on a daily basis. The modest but sometimes telling bias that people hope to obtain when they hire lobbyists or lawyers or make political contributions. Indeed, it might be said that the Senate committee demonstrated greater favoritism when it called a hearing that targeted the critics of a major political donor.

Too bad that's not news.

Chapter 11

Warming the Bench

In the Spring of 2006, Marc Cohodes called me at my law firm with what seemed an oddball proposition. David Rocker was retiring at the end of the year, leaving Marc as the sole managing partner of the hedge fund. He was interested in beefing up its body count, including by adding a general counsel. He asked if I would be interested.

I told him to look for someone with more experience in representing investment companies. Maybe someone who had worked in the Investment Management Division at the SEC, rather than Enforcement. It was a technical area outside my core practice. Anyway, I liked the people I worked with at V&E and had no desire to leave the firm.

After the name change to Copper River, Marc hired as the fund's general counsel a young lawyer with the skill set to take care of the legal problems of a money management firm. I expected that would be the end of my involvement with Copper River—at least until someone ginned up another SEC investigation into its propensity to express accurate opinions about bad companies.

That summer, however, Marc was on tour of the fund's East Coast investors and swung by for lunch. He had, as it turned out, an agenda. Although the fund was now lawyered-up, he still wanted me to join. His thought was that I could winnow though a backlog of short prospects and advise on which companies had potential problems. My dozen years chasing accounting frauds for the SEC, as he saw it, was close to what he and his colleagues did all day long: taking apart the financial disclosure of public companies to find the nasty little secrets. So I would fit in as an analyst as well as additional legal counsel.

It was intriguing in the same way as might be a proposal to take up hang gliding. But this time I avoided being abrupt and said I'd think about it. I assumed this was a spur of the moment thing, quickly forgotten. Marc surprised me by calling daily to see if I had thought about his idea. After a few weeks of this, I concluded he was serious. He backed it up with an offer that meant I wouldn't be losing anything for a few years and if the fund did well, so would I.

All the same, I would have let it pass with a "thanks for the thought" were it not for the fund's location. My father's family is from the Bay Area and I spent my kid summers and the occasional Christmas at my grandparents' house in Berkeley. With its morning fogs, eucalyptus- and redwood-shaded pathways, funky architecture, and San Francisco Bay views, I'd never found anywhere I liked better. And my parents lived in Los Angeles, which is a lot closer to the Bay Area than to Arlington. Both were in their 80s and my father was blind. As their sole offspring, the prospect of reducing the mileage between them and me sounded great. Finally, our son—who had been an infant when we moved to Arlington for what was supposed to be a year or two—was now in college on the West Coast. We wouldn't be extracting him from his childhood home. He had already left it behind.

My wife Eileen was game. She thought we'd been in one place long enough. There were Montessori schools in the Bay Area. She was hopeful one would hire her.

So, as they say, it seemed like a good idea at the time.

★ ★ ★

The Copper River office was in a small cedar-shingled complex looking down on the terminal of the Larkspur Ferry, which shuttles commuters and stray tourists from Marin County past Angel Island and Alcatraz to San Francisco and back again. The office was comfortably unpretentious. Carpeting that had long ago given full value. An enormous poster of a long-dead magician draped one wall; a multicolored scattering of Crocs littered the floor; and on Marc's desk sat a framed photo of former Lernout & Hauspie CEO Gaston Bastiens in handcuffs with FBI agents escorting him to jail. The picture enjoyed the pride of place a more traditional office might have afforded a wedding or graduation photo.

A bank of windows looked out over Highway 101 and the Marin estuary. Marc, Monty Montgomery, and a third analyst, Russell Lynde, lined up along it, most of the time studying their Bloomberg screens and nattering about each new item that affected a portfolio name or offered entertainment value. Monty was a slightly grizzled 50 years old, former-athlete stocky, with a relentlessly sunny outlook rare in smart people. His knowledge of the financial markets and command of sports trivia were both remarkable. I never saw Monty in anything but shorts and sandals, no matter the temperature. No one was better prepared for the onset of global warming. Russell, married with an infant daughter and another on the way, was Marc's young protegee. A Wharton grad with an open personality and ingrained work ethic, his passing resemblance to Brad Pitt subjected him to occasional barbs from Marc and Monty, neither of whom would ever be mistaken for that actor. Behind them, routing phone calls, filing documents, and laying off the occasional sports bet was the office administrator, Navid Niakan, who could be described as a study in the applied art of mellow. Later, Marc would add to the ensemble a particularly stolid Basset hound his daughter had rescued from the pound.

Such was the crew some proclaimed to be a fearsome threat to the capital markets.

For six months I commuted between Virginia and California while my wife and I arranged the move. Marc lived five minutes from the office and let me crash at his house whenever I was in town. He had come a long way from his single-parent childhood in Chicago. His house—designed in large part by his wife Leslie—combined modern blocky shapes with a Japanese spatial openness and was snugly integrated into the land-scape. It was all on one level to permit maximum mobility for their son Max, a warmly gregarious young man with an appetite for exotic foods and travel, always with Marc, and a keen mind stuck in a body that served him badly. Leslie also ran the family's horse farm in Sonoma County. The place began on a small scale as a show of encouragement for their daughter Emily, who quietly collects equestrian trophies (as well as academic honors) like I do parking tickets. Mother and daughter, however, had turned it into a successful business—boarding and training horses—while Emily was still in high school.

Marc was fiercely proud and protective of his family and still seethed over Bob O'Brien's trashy spotlighting of Max. People's families should not be fair game.

Things tend to prey on Marc's mind. His favorite topic—which he worried like a sore tooth—was the failure of the SEC to jump on crappy companies, particularly those Copper River was short. No matter how clear the evidence, nothing ever seemed to move the government to action. He viewed this phenomenon with perpetual bewilderment. "How is this allowed to happen?" "How can this go on?" These phrases were never far from his lips.

He infected both Monty and Russell with this bug. Responding to their choruses of "Why doesn't the SEC get its head out of its ass?" I found myself of two minds. I couldn't deny they were *kind of* right. Whatever ability the SEC once had to be proactive on accounting cases seemed to have gone by the boards. It does far fewer such cases than it used to and these days it seems content to scrape up the road-kill of the financial highways and nail it to the wall as a trophy. On the other hand, not all of the dodgy conduct that analysts think must violate some law really does. And I understood the limitations of the agency—its thin manpower, haphazard training, and procedural atherosclerosis—and didn't want to encourage false hopes.

Marc also had difficulty accepting the unfolding absurdity of the Gradient litigation. David Rocker, in retirement, was now completely out of the picture, but Marc still fumed regularly about the folly of "arguing with a crazy person."

★ ★ ★

The Overstock suit against Gradient and Rocker Partners was handled by two Texas firms who were carving out a niche practice representing companies who claim to have been harmed by naked short-selling.

One firm was the subject of a *New York Post* article alleging it took, as compensation for legal services, shares of a penny stock company it represented in a naked shorting suit, then dumped the stock "after the publicity surrounding the legal battle goosed the stock price."

The other firm was run by John O'Quinn, a larger-than-life figure in the Texas tort bar who made a fortune from silicone breast implant cases, now widely viewed as based on junk science. The firm made headlines when it was reprimanded by a federal judge in Texas for bringing thousands of silicosis (cancer) cases based on bogus medical diagnoses. In a scathing opinion, the court found "These diagnoses were driven by neither health nor justice. They were manufactured for money." The O'Quinn firm's role in about 2,000 such cases, the judge concluded, showed a "reckless disregard of a duty owed to the court." O'Quinn—who would die in an October 2009 car crash—also had a history of running afoul of state bar rules against improper solicitation (ambulance chasing).

According to *Forbes.com*, O'Quinn hoped naked shorting cases "w[ould] be his next multibillion dollar jackpot." He sued various brokers, market-makers and others seeking hundreds of millions in damages. Most of these actions have now been thrown out of court. In September 2004, for example, a U.S. District Court in Texas dismissed a complaint filed by an O'Quinn client, JAG Media Holdings, against approximately 100 financial services firms for allegedly facilitating abusive short-sales. After giving JAG several chances to state a coherent legal theory, the court reached the end of its patience: "The only conclusion that the court can come to . . . is that Plaintiffs do not have a viable claim."

The U.S. District Court in Manhattan took the extraordinary action of booting one such case brought by an O'Quinn client to punish its lawyers for violating discovery orders and misrepresenting those orders to another court. O'Quinn was sufficiently implicated in this misconduct that another judge of the Southern District denied his application to appear in his courtroom.

There was reason to hope that the Gradient suit would also be dismissed well before trial. California has attempted to discourage punitive suits against people who seek to exercise their right of free speech even to the point of criticizing that most advantaged category in American society—the over-lawyered and terminally litigious. Its "Strategic

Lawsuit Against Public Participation" (or "anti-SLAPP") statute re-quires the plaintiff in an action raising free speech issues to demonstrate a "reasonable probability" he will prevail in his suit. Merely making allegations that, if true, could entitle him to a judgment is not enough.

Unfortunately, the reach of the statute was limited when a California appellate court decided "reasonable probability of success" really means something more like "a remote possibility of success" on at least one of the plaintiff's claims. The California courts are widely noted for their ability to reform the poor draftsmanship of the state legislature to more clearly reflect what that body presumably intended.

Still, the Gradient suit seemed to exemplify the sort of abusive litiga-tion the statute was intended to squelch. It had a strongly punitive thrust. By early 2006, the opinions of Gradient and David Rocker about flaws in Overstock's business model had been adopted by sell-side analysts and were reflected in the company's share price. Nevertheless, Patrick Byrne was not going home without his pound of flesh. His attorneys made that clear. That is not to say Byrne didn't hold fast to his initial convictions about Gradient. Just that the only evidence Overstock could muster was artfully-worded declarations from several terminated Gradient salespeo-ple. Only one of these guys had anything to say about Rocker Partners, his allegations found no support elsewhere, and both the hedge fund and Gradient were adamant he was a flagrant liar.

Whether his attorneys actually set any store by Byrne's conspiracy theories is known only to them, but the matter was shaping up along lines sadly common in civil litigation. Find a category of defendant in-trinsically unpopular with juries but also deep of pocket (i.e., hedge funds or, worse, short-selling hedge funds). Make inflammatory allega-tions in the complaint to promote prejudice against the defendants. Use the filed complaint, which can't be used as the basis for a defamation suit, to beat on them in every available public forum. Lastly, extract cash in exchange for ending the pain.

In early 2006, Gradient and Rocker Partners filed a motion under the California anti-SLAPP statute seeking dismissal of the suit. Still in private practice at this point but not involved in the litigation, I followed the matter for its curiosity value. To Gradient the statute was a potential lifesaver. The firm had limited cash and its modest liability policy was being tapped out to defend against the Biovail suit, this being before various law enforcement agencies jumped on Biovail. If it had to go to trial or even far down the discovery road in either of these matters the costs would swamp it financially and push it into bankruptcy. The merits of the cases would ultimately make no difference. Thus does our judicial system act as the weapon of those capable of bearing its costs better than their opponents. For anyone willing to spend a million dollars to make an adversary do the same, the courts are always open for business.

If Gradient could win an early exit from the Overstock suit, however, its chances of survival increased dramatically. Obviously, dismissal would also be cause for celebration for Rocker Partners.

To defeat the motion to dismiss, Overstock had to provide at least *some* evidence the Gradient reports contained false statements about Overstock and that Rocker Partners was somehow responsible for those statements. Also that Rocker Partners knew the reports were not straight. Overstock had to rope Rocker Partners in with Gradient. Otherwise the case against Gradient would collapse from an inability to prove it published the reports from a bad motive—to help a short-seller stomp on a stock—rather than because, rightly or wrongly, it believed what it wrote. The First Amendment demands no less in its requirement that the defendants acted out of "malice."

Overstock submitted a declaration from its head of finance, David Chidester, disputing various of Gradient's contentions about Overstock's accounting. That was all the proof it needed on that issue.[1] However, the guy couldn't say any of the challenged statements came from Rocker Partners. Overstock could only point to assertions from Anifantis that Gradient accommodated requests from David Rocker for negative coverage of Overstock and hope the court would leap to the conclusion that *everything* Gradient published on Overstock, at least after Rocker Partners became a subscriber, was at the behest of Rocker Partners. This would be quite a leap. Gradient began publishing its views on Overstock over a year before it started talking to Rocker Partners. There was no reason to think it did so for any reason other than because it believed what it wrote. That it continued to express opinions in the same vein after Rocker Partners became a subscriber hardly shouts conspiracy.

---

[1] Chidester was fired by Overstock in January 2010 after evidence mounted that the company's internal controls were deficient and its financial reports misstated during his tenure as CFO.

Assuming Rocker Partners somehow caused Gradient to write inaccurate reports, moreover, there was no evidence it believed the reports to be inaccurate, at least putting aside the Anifantis declaration. And that dealt mostly in innuendo. If you put together various statements from Anifantis, interpreted them in a certain way, filled in gaps through inference, then extrapolated about possible motives, you could get there. But no one would go to the effort unless he had unreservedly bought into Overstock's portrayal of Gradient as a "hatchet job for hire." From the defendants' perspective, Overstock was disguising a well-orchestrated smear job as a legal case.

Gradient made little effort to challenge directly the veracity of its former employees, even Anifantis. Under the anti-SLAPP statute—as watered down by previous court decisions—any factual showing from the plaintiffs, no matter how dubious, would trump anything offered by the defendants. So why argue about facts? Better to stick to the legal issues. The risk, however, was that by not standing up to the smearing, Gradient could be seen as conceding the substance of Overstock's campaign of corporate character assassination.

The trial judge bought Overstock's story without hesitation or notable analysis. In his comments from the bench he seemed confused by the evidence. He took a statement from Anifantis disclaiming knowledge of the truth or falsity of Gradient reports, for example, to mean that he had written the reports and didn't check on their accuracy. In fact, none of the ex-employees Overstock had rounded up had been involved in generating reports on any company and none could say whether the reports contained untrue statements. But however he understood the story, the judge found it compelling. The central legal holding in his opinion took up one short paragraph. The company needed nothing more than the Anifantis declaration to get past the anti-SLAAP statute and proceed to discovery.

This decision was a disaster for Gradient, threatening to pitch it into years of litigation it could not afford. But its lawyers were optimistic they could pull things out on appeal. This was based on their unsupported claim that the appellate judges would be of a higher order than the local guy. More sophisticated. Less likely to be taken in by rhetorical smoke and mirrors.

The appeal by Gradient and Rocker Partners was supported by the CFA Institute, the trade association for financial analysts, and Reporters for Freedom of the Press. They expressed concern that suits like this could "chill" analysts and journalists from doing their jobs, which once in a while involves saying negative things about public companies. They could have saved themselves the effort.

The hearing before a three-judge panel took place in April 2007 at the state courthouse in San Francisco. Now employed by Copper River, I tagged along behind our litigation counsel to get up to speed on the case. The whole thing took an hour and any hope the panel would reverse the lower court's decision was dashed within the first few minutes. The judges aggressively grilled counsel for the defendants while treating Overstock's attorney with a solicitude that came close to coaching. The panel's lack of familiarity with the financial markets was starkly evident. One judge was disturbed that Gradient would be so rude as to question whether Overstock's revenue recognition policies squared with GAAP. She thought this amounted to a bald accusation of financial fraud. In fact, companies and their auditors—not to mention outside analysts—regularly question the propriety of specific corporate accounting policies, which can turn on complicated standards and subjective judgments. Sometimes companies get it wrong, and this may violate certain provisions of the securities law, but doesn't constitute fraud unless done with an intent to deceive. Indeed, Overstock has now amended its financial statements twice, covering a multiyear period. Under applicable accounting rules, a restatement is permissible only to remedy material errors. Thus Overstock has admitted significantly misstating its financial results in SEC filings. This does not, however, mean it has committed fraud.

The only potentially unwelcome question to Overstock's counsel was phrased more as a matter of intellectual curiosity than skepticism. A panel member ventured to ask how Rocker Partners could have been responsible for Gradient reports published well before it became a Gradient subscriber, as Overstock appeared to contend. An excellent question. A truthful answer—it couldn't have been and indeed it wasn't—would have led to another excellent question: So what does that do to the whole idea that Gradient targeted Overstock to benefit Rocker Partners?

Overstock's counsel vaguely alluded to evidence in the record that the two entities were in contact before a subscription fee changed hands. I have no idea what he meant by this unless he was referring to a single reference in the Anifantis declaration to contacts between the two firms in "2003 and 2004." Everything else in the record contradicted this assertion. The judge nodded and dropped the matter.

It was obvious the judges weren't merely *accepting* Overstock's purported evidence for the limited purposes of the motion. They were embracing the company's whole tale, down to the last drop of melodrama, and to the point where counterarguments were simply dismissed out of hand as the predictable dodges of bad characters caught in the act. Clearly, the panel believed that no public company would go to the trouble of bringing a case like this out of mere spite. And the declarations from the former Gradient employees dovetailed so nicely with each other and the company's allegations they simply *must* be true. The panel likely assumed they were just the tip of the iceberg. Who knew how many more would come out in discovery? And swallowing all this—hook, line, and sinker—they were deeply offended by the nefarious scheme they concluded had occurred.

It reminded me of coasting through FTC applications for asset freeze orders from judges who viewed boiler-room operators as a lower life form and therefore guilty until proven innocent. Now, however, I found myself allied with those judicially assigned to a bottom rung of the evolutionary ladder. It also brought back memories of the AremisSoft case and the SEC's rough treatment by the Deemster from Hell.

We harbored no illusions the panel would, upon further reflection, come around to our position. The courtroom had rung with the unmistakable sound of three judicial minds slamming shut. Still, we were not prepared for the beating we got. If short-sellers were a legally protected minority, the opinion would constitute a hate crime. The first paragraph left no doubt how the panel would rule.

A company that produces and publishes subscriber-based analytic reports on public companies, regularly collaborating with the principals of hedge funds and other institutional investors to produce custom, negative reports on targeted companies, stepped over the line into defamation and other torts with respect to the flurry and timing of reports on an online closeout retailer. The hedge fund principals took short positions in the stock and worked closely with the publisher to put out reports that were anything but the purported unbiased and objective assessment promised to subscribers, So says the targeted company in its complaint and so aver various declarants. . . .

I've read many hundreds of legal opinions but don't remember seeing one that so directly goes for the throat of one side to a lawsuit. Surely not at such an early stage of a proceeding. To refer to Overstock as "the targeted company" is to endorse its pose as victim. More troubling is the suggestion that a chorus of witnesses "aver" to the purported facts in the court's introductory roasting of the defendants. But the court itself recognized that the key points hinged almost entirely on the statements of one former Gradient employee.

After some throat-clearing it got down to business. "Demitrios Anifantis . . . ," it stated, "submitted a declaration revealing [not *alleging*, mind you, but *revealing*] the following." The opinion then repeated the substance of that declaration as deferentially as if it had been discovered in a burning bush. Assertions of dubious validity—such as that a certain fact was "common knowledge"—were accepted without question. Implications were treated as evidence. In short, at every point the court was invited down the garden path it showed a passion for botanizing.

The court accepted that, if the company and its auditors disagreed with Gradient on an accounting issue, Gradient must be wrong and could only have been acting in bad faith to continue with its blandishments. By this token, all those who raised doubts about Enron should have been sued for defamation.

Nor did the court doubt that the work of a small analyst firm in Arizona could, all by itself, depress the price of Overstock shares for months or years. Overstock claimed that its share price had dropped from \$70 to \$30 thanks to the scheming of the defendants.[2] In securities cases such damage claims are typically supported by expert analysis of the response of the stock price to the relevant publications. This is called an "event study." Overstock had provided no such evidence and was

---

[2] As of this writing, several years after Gradient published its final report on the company, the stock is trading around \$13 per share. The company has compiled losses of approximately \$260 million and currently has a negative book value.

unlikely to do so because its share price never reacted significantly to Gradient reports and the actual reasons for its decline were, to borrow a phrase, "common knowledge."

No matter. The court, after remarking derisively that the defendants had "trot[ted] out a string of federal cases" on this issue, found that for present purposes Overstock had done enough by showing that "its stock price had been on a steady rise for several years; appellants began frequently publishing defamatory reports staring in late 2004 . . . ," and then the stock went down. *Post hoc ergo propter hoc.* An awkward conclusion considering that everywhere else in the opinion the nefarious collaboration between Rocker and Vickrey is said to begin a year earlier. Also, many of the statements the court found to be defamatory popped up in Gradient reports dated well before the fall of 2004. But consistency here would have meant considering why it took more than a year for these supposedly toxic reports to have any effect on the share price, and then suddenly—bang!—a wild stampede out of Overstock.

Patrick Byrne crowed in a press release that the "blackguard defendants" had gotten their just deserts. So that no one would miss the importance of this score, he noted that "this case is about criminal activities that are undermining American capital markets." Little had Rocker and Vickrey suspected that merely by sharing their views on a Utah internet company they could imperil the American financial system.

The court's documented hostility toward the defendants was the more surprising because unnecessary. It did not need to take sides on the ultimate merits of the case to find that Overstock had met the minimal burden required to defeat an anti-SLAPP motion. Nevertheless, the panel chose to write a screed denouncing the defendants as presumptive wrongdoers. This was not only legally gratuitous but could be predicted to bias and prolong the subsequent proceedings. With its harsh language, the panel signaled to the lower court that nothing short of victory at trial should entitle the defendants to extricate themselves from this proceeding, in its view a remote prospect. All of this based, remember, on the unsupported and disputed statements of a former Gradient sales representative dismissed for misconduct.

So how to explain this exuberant exercise in judicial sophistry? Most obviously, the panel had been thrust into an area utterly outside its experience. Congress has mandated that securities cases—which, at bottom, was the nature of this case—should be decided in federal court. By framing its suit as a state law defamation case rather than as a stock market manipulation, however, Overstock avoided the jaundiced eye of the federal bench and invited the sort of judicial on-the-job training Congress had sought to avoid. A court experienced in financial cases might have reacted more skeptically to a legal theory so often employed by penny stock firms to stall for time while their pump and dump schemes ripen. This was a smart move, as it turned out. The panel showed no awareness that the claim "Short-sellers screwed my company" is the financial world equivalent of "Would you like to buy a bridge?" It swallowed whole the company's theory of damages, attributing Sith Lordesque powers to two relatively minor figures in the capital markets. And—ignoring amicus briefs on this point from national analyst and press organizations—it failed to grasp the potential harm to the financial markets that results from indulging episodes of "issuer retaliation" through litigation.

Another factor was the complexity of the case. The court had gotten quite a lot thrown at it, legally and factually. Faced with a confusing mass of detail and wildly conflicting claims—some going to technical areas of financial analysis—the appellate panel followed human nature and grabbed onto the explanation that seemed to address everything in the simplest fashion.

Short-seller wants stock to drop. Greases crooked analyst firm to trash stock. Stock goes down. Short-seller cackles with glee as he rolls in filthy lucre.

Yo! Got it.

This is closely related to the concept of "first mover advantage." Whoever tells their story first occupies the high ground and enjoys a significant psychological edge. A person trying to make sense of a contested fact situation, particularly if it is complicated, is likely to take as his template the first explanation he hears and then try to work every new bit of information into it, while presumptively rejecting things that don't fit. Here the template had been provided by Overstock.

The adage "where there's smoke there's fire" has great intuitive appeal—to ermine-collared judges as well as the average schlemiel. A good plaintiffs' lawyer, however, is a human smoke machine. Overstock had spun an emotionally compelling story, rich in detail, that, if true, meant something bad had occurred that should not go unpunished. Under those circumstances, it would have been a hard call to deny the plaintiffs the chance to prove up a potentially serious case just because their evidence had a hole or five coming in the door.

Finally, there is the factor that might be called "the romance of the whistleblower." There is a tendency to accept at face value the statements of anyone eager to rat out a supervisor or employer. The appellate panel clearly did so here. It treated the statements of Anifantis and the other former Gradient employees as almost conclusively reliable. This was naïve. Whistleblowers *can be* crucial witnesses to wrongdoing. They can also be biased, dishonest, confused, or inclined to howl at full moons. Whether the Overstock declarants were some or all of these things or, instead, the real article was still far from clear.

It is ironic that the court's warm reception of these purported informants was at the expense of the two species of genuine whistleblowers most important to the integrity of the stock market. The contributions of short-sellers to airing the dirty laundry of corporate America is belabored above. As for independent analysts, the SEC has recognized them as a vital but fragile part of the financial ecology. It and the New York AG required the big sell-side firms caught promoting the dot-com dogpound to help fund the operations of independent analyst firms for a period of years.

The virulent tone of the appellate panel decision, as much as its holding, drastically changed the likely outcome of the litigation. Not only would Gradient and Copper River have to pay millions in attorneys' fees to take the matter through discovery, but it was now much less likely the lower court would resolve the matter in the defendants' favor through summary judgment, thus eliminating the cost of a trial. Not after the appellate panel had branded the defendants with a scarlet "M" for "miscreant." And court-ordered mediation sessions would be exercises in futility. The mediators, having read the appellate decision, would assume Gradient and Copper River were toast. The only question remaining would be how many zeroes to put on the check. Thus had a California statute intended to short-circuit retaliatory litigation against whistleblowers and gadflies become an implement of pay-back and intimidation against exactly such elements.

The appellate court, in sum, had handed Overstock a gun to place at Gradient's head. I saw Donn Vickrey at two hearings six months apart. He looked like he'd lost twenty pounds in the interim. Eventually,

Gradient buckled and paid Overstock to settle the matter. There was an undisclosed payment to Overstock, presumably within the limits of Gradient's liability coverage, and a rather tepid apology. In an October 2008 press release, Gradient said it "now believes that, to the best of its knowledge, Overstock's stated accounting policies did in fact conform to Generally Accepted Accounting Principles and regrets any prior statements to the contrary."

Patrick Byrne, never one for understatement, proclaimed: "We were suing [Copper River] and Gradient together. If this were World War II, Germany has now been liberated and now we can focus on Japan."

The press, however, was dismissive. Roddy Boyd, in *Fortune*, noted that Gradient simply lacked the funds to continue the fight. "It is a small company and its insurance coverage was running out," he wrote, and "much of its free cash flow had to go to defending itself in this case as well as another suit filed against it in February 2006 by Canadian pharmaceutical company Biovail." In other words, Overstock had successfully played to game of "I will spend ten dollars to make you spend ten dollars unless you pay me five dollars to go away." The *Times*'s Joe Nocera parsed the language of the Gradient mea culpa and found it light on contrition.

> On the one hand, it does have the tone of an apology, which I'm sure Mr. Byrne likes. But like so much else when it comes to Mr. Byrne and Overstock, it is all smoke and mirrors. Read it again closely, and you'll realize that in four carefully worded paragraphs, Gradient has admitted . . . nothing! And Mr. Byrne has accepted the firm's admission of nothing.

But clearly Byrne intended no such dispensation when it came to what was now Copper River. In a phone call to Marc Cohodes, he said that if Copper River didn't settle the matter on his terms, its fate and that of its principals would be certain financial ruin. In a touching moment of generosity, however, he offered to support Marc's disabled son, after he drove Marc into bankruptcy.

If he did not in fact ruin anyone financially, after the events described in the remainder of this book Byrne did extract a settlement from Copper River. In late 2009, facing mounting litigation costs and prevented from distributing funds to its investors while the Gradient litigation was ongoing, Copper River paid Overstock $5 million to end the matter. This was a small fraction of what Overstock had demanded previously or what the case would have been worth had it been supported by evidence that anyone at Copper River had ever said anything about Overstock, in private or in public, that was remotely inaccurate. Byrne, of course, claimed victory, not only as to Copper River but also, in a perfervid press release, as to all those he believed had conspired against him and his company, including prominent journalists and other people not named in the suit.

It was in his view a great victory for the truth and justice. "The good guys," he opined, "won."

Chapter 12

The Overstock Flame Wars

After an early honeymoon period during which his New Age CEO posture played itself out, Patrick Byrne severely blew his welcome with the "old" financial media. He had overpromised and disappointed and, when he drew criticism, attacked a number of prominent financial reporters in a very personal way. This made him no friends.

Innovating around his setbacks with the financial press, he developed the possibilities of "new media" to take the battle to his expanding list of critics. The result provides a cautionary tale of a digital domain with a virtual troll under every bridge.

The Internet is the ultimate populist medium, available to everyone with a laptop, an ISP account, and fingers. Should one's object be to discredit or annoy selected others, the Google Corporation provides a product that can be greatly empowering. Internet search engines allow completely false allegations that a certain individual, say, cheats on his taxes, is a closet Dolly Parton impersonator, or runs an illegal mink ranch in his basement to be seen by thousands, perhaps millions. Nothing is screened for accuracy.

Remedies available to the alleged mink-rancher, should he feel libeled, are often illusory. Some online hit-men hide behind aliases, such as Bob "the Easter Bunny" O'Brien, and dare their targets to find them. Abusers of message boards are sometimes ejected by the host organization—for example Yahoo!—only to reappear under new user names. Even when the slime-artist can be identified, the victim's only remedy lies within the legal system, whose dubious virtues are celebrated in the previous chapter.

People in certain professions are automatic losers when they become involved in controversy. Reporters, in particular, have little recourse when attacked. Their role is to write stories, not wander into them. Any mention of their names other than in the form of a byline is a blow to perceived objectivity—their primary stock-in-trade. Government administrators, the more honorable tranches of the legal profession, and many financial professionals are also vulnerable to tactics that damage their public reputations and have little effective remedy when defamed.

In the early days of his campaign against naked short-selling and related evils, Byrne was a tireless poster on message boards. Typically, he used a pseudonym. This became an issue after a different company's CEO, hiding behind a username, got in hot water for slamming a competitor's products. But, in fairness, Byrne did not try to fool anyone about who he was. Indeed, he wanted the world to know and praise his opinions. The problem was that the world did not cooperate. When he posted on forums he could not control, the great unwashed had free rein to engage in mockery and general disputatious conduct. A dedicated group of naked-short-conspiracy deniers and Byrne satirists dogged him with disparaging comments.

On the other hand, he did make some converts. One devoted poster expressed himself in the following curdled prose.

Dr. Byrne has asked me to lay down my life for his cause, and I have done so! I love the good work this beautiful human, Dr. Patrick

Michael Byrne, has done. Each day I breath [sic] the clean air of corrected living, I bless his parents for bringing such a kind and devoted man to my rescue. You may be a better person today for all that we have done. Yes . . . we. It is a hard war fought by sturdy and brave men. If I could ask one thing to change in this unfair world it would be the view of our heroic leader. He is a man among boys. He teaches us and holds us close. He protects us from the evil of the miscreants. He is our light, our life.

Presumably to escape the hectoring on better-established sites, Byrne decamped to InvestorVillage.com, noted both for penny-stock promotions and for obediently bouncing skeptics from its Overstock thread. This, however, was of limited utility. Who, other than the already converted, would see anything there? To spread the gospel, more effective channels were required. So Byrne and associates set up not one but two web sites. To his supporters, they remain beacons of insight and integrity shining through the murk of our corrupted financial system.[1] To his detractors, they are conspiracy-obsessed smear sites, spewing forth incoherent rants, cracked attempts at journalism and crude libels.

The first of these sites, Anitsocialmedia.net (ASM), is run by former Salt Lake City traffic reporter Judd Bagley, whose background also includes opposition research for Florida Republican politicos. The latter experience informs the work he does for Byrne. ASM indulges in the sort of personal attacks that can turn American elections into mud-baths. Recall the Swift Boat Veterans' trashing of John Kerry in 2004 (which Byrne supported with cash). ASM, with its "guerilla business strategies," follows a similar no-holds-barred approach.

Bagley is also something of an Internet sleuth. He brags about monitoring the online activities of selected miscreants: in particular "phantom shares" skeptic Gary Weiss. He did this, he says, by implanting "spyware" on InvestorVillage to harvest the "Internet protocol addresses" of visitors to the site, infiltrate their computers and keep track of the other

---

[1] As one student of conspiracy theories notes: "belief in the conspiracy makes you part of a genuinely heroic anti-elite elite group who can see past an official version propagated for the benefit of the lazy or inert mass of people by the powers that be." David Aaronovitch, "A Conspiracy-Theory Theory: How to Fend Off the People Who Insist They Know the 'Real Story' Behind Everything" (*Wall Street Journal*, December 19, 2009). See also *Voodoo Histories: the Role of Conspiracy Theories in Shaping Modern History* (Riverhead), from the same author.

sites they visit. Bagley's spat with Weiss crystallized around his allegations that Weiss had improperly rigged entries on Wikipedia—which Byrne has called "an instrument of mass mind control"—to disrespect Patrick Byrne and his *jihad*. Weiss replied in kind. He derided Bagley a "nauseating Internet stalker" and cited attempts by Bagley to edit Wikipedia items through a host of "sock-puppet" user names.

Bagley has also, in a recent misadventure, used "pretexting" to infiltrate non-public information in the Facebook accounts of people on Byrne's enemies list (as well as their family members) and learn the names of their Facebook "friends." He then published the results of his deception on the Internet. Apparently, the intent was to show that various people shared "friend" status on Facebook and therefore must be joined in a conspiracy against Patrick Byrne. As a result of public furor over this episode, Bagley was barred from Facebook.

ASM, however, was a mere warm-up for Byrne's most ambitious foray into capturing the eyeballs of prospective conspiracy hounds. In 2008, he unveiled "DeepCapture.com." According to its web site, Deep Capture is the work of "citizen journalists" devoted to unmasking the plots of miscreant hedge funds, corrupt journalists, and shadowy gangland figures to profit from the destruction of public companies through naked shorting and other misconduct.

Its centerpiece is a lengthy diatribe by citizen journalist Mark Mitchell entitled "The Story of Deep Capture." Whatever else one may think of this work, it can claim a certain originality of style. If Hunter Thompson, by blurring the line between reporting and fictionalized memoir, created "gonzo journalism," Mitchell practices what might be called "bozo journalism." He departs so completely from established professional standards in his efforts to promote outlandish conspiracy theories as to mate journalism with a cyberpunk novel. William Gibson with an ax to grind. As financial writer Lee Webb puts it: "The incredible 40,000-word screed has been described as Joycean, though some readers have found the style less stream-of-consciousness than manifestation-of-apophenia, making spurious connections among unrelated matters and then drawing or inviting specious conclusions."

The site seeks to project an us-against-the-world camaraderie with self-congratulatory references to "rock stars" Byrne, Saunders, and other anti-naked-shorting notables. Its basic tone, however, is one of smug condescension and, in its relentless sneering and smearing, it raises defamation to the level of a cottage industry.

Mitchell is a former editor of the *Columbia Journalism Review*, a highly respected media watchdog organization that, among other things, awards Pulitzer Prizes. How he came to leave the *CJR* and join Deep Capture is subject to dispute. Some have claimed he was given the bum's rush by *CJR*. Mitchell has countered that he left the publication because it accepted a donation from short-selling hedge fund Kingsford Capital. A miscreant hedge fund could have no motive for such largesse, he concluded, except to stifle his pending investigation into, yes, *naked short-selling*. This deduction caused him to "snap" and walk from the publication.

I know one Kingsford Capital partner slightly. In general persona he is almost as menacing as Mrs. Rocker. But even if every partner of the fund had horns and a tail, it would be hard to understand why it would go to such lengths to silence Mitchell. In "The Story of Deep Capture," Mitchell comes up with nothing on Kingsford beyond its alleged role in his employment history. Thus if, as Mitchell contends, Kingsford paid hush money to *CJR*, it might consider requesting a refund.

My guess is that Mitchell's stress level spiked into the red from his efforts to piece together the disparate elements of anti-naked-shorting doctrine with the ancillary phobias and antagonisms supplied by Patrick Byrne, while simultaneously confronting a dearth of empirical evidence. This would have been like trying to gift-wrap a live ostrich. It could make anyone snap. The enormous difficulties he faced are apparent in the following extracts from "The Story of Deep Capture," summing up earlier chapters.

In 2005, Patrick Byrne, the CEO of Overstock.com and future Deep Capture investigative reporter, began a public crusade against illegal naked short selling (hedge funds and brokers creating phantom stock to manipulate stock prices down). He said, over and over, that the crime was destroying public companies and had the potential to trigger a systemic meltdown of our financial markets . . .

So much was indisputable. He does not mention, however, that the source of this insight was an Internet stock tout operating under the pseudonym "The Easter Bunny."

Soon after, I began to investigate a network of short sellers, journalists, and miscreants. I concluded that many of the people in this network were connected to two famous criminals—"junk bond king" Michael Milken and his associate, Ivan Boesky. I also began taking a close look at the Mafia's involvement in naked short selling.

In my last installment, I described some of the strange occurrences that attended this investigation. Where the story left off, I'd recently been threatened in a bookstore, and then ambushed by three thugs who told me to stay away from this story. My unwitting employer had been bribed by short sellers, Patrick had been told by a U.S. Senator that his life was in danger,[2] and a Russian matryoshka doll had appeared on the desk of an offshore businessman. Inside this matryoshka doll was a slip of paper marked with the letter "F" . . .

Obviously, Dan Brown and Robert Ludlum have much to answer for.

Soon after receiving the matryoshka doll, the offshore businessman invited Patrick Byrne to a greasy spoon diner in Long Island. Over the previous year, the businessman had provided Patrick with some information about the naked short selling scam, and the hope was that he might have something more to say.

But that day at the diner, all he had was a message.

"I'll make this quick," the businessman said, with two other witnesses present. "I have a message for you from Russia. The message is, 'We are about to kill you. We are about to kill you.' Patrick, they are going to kill you. If you do not stop this crusade [against naked short selling], they will kill you. Normally they'd have already hurt someone close to you as a warning, but you're so weird, they don't know how you'd react."

In a later conversation with a colleague of Patrick's the businessman said [verbatim]: "These things don't happen to me anymore. I mean, I've been out of that world [the world of Mafia stock manipulation] for a dozen years or more. These . . . there are defined signals here that

---

[2]This was the alleged encounter in the lobby of Senator Hatch's apartment building.

lead me to believe that they [the Mafia] have been disturbed. The only way they coulda been disturbed is if they own Rocker or if he is using them for leverage."

Rocker [he concluded]. That's David Rocker.

But Mitchell overpromises. Nowhere does he meaningfully link Boesky or Milken to a short-seller conspiracy. There is nothing to advance the Easter Bunny's thesis that Milken is the "Sith Lord," scheming to drive down Overstock's share price so he can acquire the company on the cheap. And, considering that the stock has been as low as six bucks and change, nothing to explain why—if that is indeed Milken's plan—he has yet to make his move. Also, Mitchell fails to come up with anything to connect David Rocker, the Russian mafia, and naked short-selling.

Mafia thugs wander through "The Story of Deep Capture" occasionally, but as almost spectral presences, like Banquo's ghost. They float in, read their lines, and disappear. At one point, Mitchell attempts to tie together the Mafia, Ivan Boesky, and the hedge fund SAC Capital. But the results are mystifying.

> That's when three guys in Armani suits saddled [sic] up to me in a quiet bar. . . .[3] [O]ne of the Armanis introduced himself to me as a former Boesky employee, and told me a story about a fellow who got his brains blown out after "peeking" into the ladies underwear department at Saks Fifth Avenue. Steve Cohen's SAC Capital is known colloquially as "Sak." I do not know for certain that Armani was telling me I shouldn't be "peeking" at Cohen's dirty underwear. It was a strange encounter, to say the least.[4]

A strange encounter for sure. Particularly if Mitchell was really all by himself when it took place.

Armani suits are, to him, a sort of Mafia uniform. Whenever an Armani suit appears, threats are made and the plot thickens. But then nothing ever happens. No one gets bumped off or finds a horse-head where his Snoopy doll should be. Mitchell's gangsters are chronic underachievers.

---

[3]I first read this sentence to mean Mitchell had been in a Western bar or perhaps a leather-themed establishment. But I believe he meant to convey that this person "sidled" up to him.

[4]This may be a mutation of the earlier story from Bob O'Brien in which the evil hedge fund manager was implied to be David Rocker.

The touching or pathetic thing about the Internet, depending on your perspective, is that, like a computer dating service, it promises to find a hook-up for anyone, no matter how off the chart he or she may be. Even Deep Capture seems to have found a like-minded audience. One reader, for example, contributed the following insights to its web site, with helpful emphasis in caps:

> Mark,
>
> As I read your story, I could feel the fear those goons tried to permanently embed within your mind. Thankfully for America, you finally stood up to these fear tactics and let the world know about this. I think some readers above have missed the point of the stories told by those goons. The point of the stories told to you was NOT to tell the truth—their purpose was to instill fear in your mind so that you would not reveal what you knew. The fact that there may be no truth in the story told you about a person being killed at SACs, I mean in Saks Fifth Avenue, WAS NOT THE POINT. The POINT of the story(s) was to instill fear in your mind, just as the punch was meant to instill fear. And of course their attempts to be "nice" was also a lie.
>
> Thank your Mark to pushing through that palpable fear to let us know what happened.

"The Story of Deep Capture" serves up every sort of logical fallacy and rhetorical dodge ever used to win public office or sell a bad product. Every adversary or disbeliever is subject to an ad hominem attack ("Roddy Boyd has his head in a garbage can"). Each such target sports a deprecatory label such as "notorious," "crooked," "financial flimflammer," or the all-purpose epithet "miscreant." Weasel words are used to dress up rank speculation as deduction ("there is every reason to suspect ..."). Technical language is combined with conclusionary assertions to suggest that any doubters must either be pathetic amateurs or in league with the miscreants. Correlation *always* implies causation. Whenever financial reporters and short-sellers focus on the same company, for example, the reporters must be acting at the direction of the short-sellers. *Why* they would feel so solicitous toward short-sellers is never explained. And red herrings abound. Take, for example, the distracting statement "Wikipedia takes the unprecedented step of blocking the [Internet Protocol] addresses of Overstock and 1,000 homes in Judd

[Bagley]'s neighborhood in Traverse Mountain, Utah. It is impossible to underestimate [sic][5] the significance of this."

Cataloging such abuses, however, misses the point. The overall effect of the piece is not so much to trick the reader with specious arguments as to wear him down through obfuscation and misdirection until he suffers what might be called "illogic fatigue." Take a hodgepodge of purported "facts"—a few verifiable to provide a patina of reality—then make connections in every possible direction and repeat and repeat until it all turns into a "booming, budding confusion," impossible to refute. The following passage, for example, spins off like a reeling top from an accusation that Gary Weiss exploited some improper "in" with Wikipedia editor Linda Mack to sabotage entries about the threat of naked short-selling.

> John Cooley, a former correspondent for ABC news, wrote a public letter describing how Linda Mack had once worked as a research assistant for ABC. His former boss, Pierre Salinger, fired [Mack] when he began to suspect that she was spying on ABC for MI5, the British intelligence agency. Soon after Cooley sent this letter, I interviewed a man named Edwin Boiller, who was once accused of supplying the suitcase bomb that blew up Pan Am flight 103 over Lockerbie, Scotland, in 1988. [Mack]'s boyfriend was on that plane, so that could explain her interest. But Boiller says that [Mack] once showed up in his office and identified herself as an agent of M15.

After many pages of such stuff, the reader may simply reach the end of his mental endurance. Like a drowning man thrown a life preserver, he will grab onto the author's proffered explanation for the engulfing wave of allegation, accusation, and speculation—or at least concede there must be *something* there. Hey, these guys can't have made up the *whole thing*, right? I mean, nobody's that crazy.

And the "something" the Deep Capture crew seems most intent on persuading its readers to swallow is the notion that certain individuals do not deserve to occupy even a smidgen of this planet. This seems more the purpose of the piece than convincing the reader of the evils of naked short-selling, which gets relatively little ink.

---

[5]I assume the author meant "overestimate" although the sentence is probably correct as written.

All the usual suspects are rounded up on Deep Capture. Gary Weiss is slammed as a "liar, message board maniac, Wikipedia hijacker,[6] forger, fraud and friend of crooks." He will never be forgiven for his skepticism about short-seller cabals, his disparaging references to "Wacky Paddy" and his ability to hold a thought from the beginning of a sentence past a few dependent clauses to its end. Jim Cramer is a "sociopath." Reporter Roddy Boyd, in a recent post written by Byrne, is described as having less dignity than "a crackhead living off $2 dollar hand-jobs at the bus station." David Rocker is evil incarnate. Bethany McLean, with her "Midwestern looks" and "red velvet voice," is portrayed as the scarlet woman of the captured New York financial media. Deep Capture suggests she once put the moves on Byrne, hard as it is to imagine any set of circumstances that could bring her to such a desperate pass.

Nor do I escape unscathed.

Shortly before I left the law firm for Copper River, I wrote an opinion piece for the *New York Times*. The theme—familiar to anyone who has read this far—was that efforts to police the stock market might be improved if the SEC would develop better outreach to people who actually know something about the market, including even short-sellers. That article and the fact that I joined the hedge fund previously run by bull-goose miscreant David Rocker put me squarely on Byrne's radar.

Deep Capture suggests that, resembling the fax machine at CNBC, my role at the SEC was to take orders from short-sellers about which spotlessly innocent companies to persecute, only to close the investigations in the dead of night after the short-sellers had made their corrupt profits. None of the victim companies are named. Nor did any such misbegotten and ill-fated investigations ever take place. Short-seller tips were a factor in a relatively small number of the cases I worked, all of which proved well-founded. This illustrates a form of reasoning frequently practiced by members of the Byrne organization. From the fact they have no evidence something happened even once, they deduce it must have happened repeatedly. If there is no proof that naked shorting ever took down an otherwise viable company, then it must have happened hundreds—"perhaps as many as a thousand"—times. If no false statement about Overstock can be attributed to anyone at Rocker

---

[6]Call me anything but please, *please* not a "Wikipedia hijacker."

Partners, then Rocker Partners must have been guilty of a pervasive campaign of defamation.

Beyond all this, the scenario of a rogue SEC attorney routinely carrying water for hedge funds would not be credited by anyone with any notion of how the agency works. Decisions about which companies to investigate are reviewed by numerous people up and down the bureaucracy. The Commission itself has to sign off on every matter in which subpoenas are issued. Individual administrators are not without influence, but no one can subject a company to SEC scrutiny on his or her personal say-so.

I would like to look at this as one of those bizarre adventures that make for good dinner-table anecdotes. But in an era in which *google* has become a widely used verb, the rantings of Deep Capture can reach a big audience. Old friends have checked up on my activities and found its charges littering the Internet . They are, of course, curious how I became the object of such vitriol. It is a challenge to explain that a somewhat *unusual* but very rich dude who runs a troubled Internet business in Utah has decided that I am part of a broad conspiracy, operating much like a secret society, against the financial markets in general and him in particular and (pause for breath) finances two squirrely online smear sites that purport to detail my role in said conspiracy.

★ ★ ★

Bloomberg offers an award for best business blog of the year. While the contest is in progress, anyone who cares to can vote once each day. Deep Capture was nominated by someone last year and Overstock urged fans of the site's unique style of journalism to vote early and often.

It won.

★ ★ ★

For every action a reaction. While the mainstream financial press has become less inclined to tangle with Byrne, apparently letting Overstock's wilted share price speak for itself, various bloggers regularly weigh in on the company and its management. Among the most committed is Gary Weiss, who, notes the *New York Times*, "has made a second career out of ridiculing Mr. Byrne on his blog." Every odd utterance from Byrne or disappointing earnings announcement from his company receives its due. Weiss illustrates his posts with a picture in which Byrne appears to suffer from elephantitis of the head and another that displays him in what appears to be an advanced stage of inebriation.

Yet, for all the passion and imagination he has put into ridiculing Byrne and his minions, Weiss is a staid and traditional figure compared to another dedicated Byrne detractor: self-identified reformed felon Sam E. Antar.

Antar is a man with a past. He provided the accounting expertise behind one of the most notorious financial scams of the 1980s: East Coast electronics retailer Crazy Eddie, Inc. ("His prices are insaaaane!"). Indeed, Crazy Eddie's audacious revenue and inventory fraud escaped detection for most of a decade thanks to Antar's slick machinations. Antar then avoided jail time by flipping for the government against a cousin and other felonious relatives.

But that was twenty years ago. The often-disputed F. Scott Fitzgerald quote about the absence of second acts in American lives should be finally laid to rest by the second coming of Sam Antar. In our declining social order, the line between notoriety and fame is imprecise. If you possess either, you are not just some ordinary everyday run-of-the-mill doofus. You are someone special. A celebrity. There is always a way to exploit that status, whether by endorsing quack products, running for public office, or selling home-made sex tapes. Sam, a diminutive baldish man well into middle-age, did not produce a sex tape. Rather, he decided to do something of social value. He began proselytizing against the very pastime he once so skillfully pursued—accounting fraud. His web page provides the following credo:

> I believe that former criminals like me must do more than just express regret for our crimes and pay whatever punishment society imposes on us. I believe that it is our obligation and responsibility to educate society, so that society can avoid future perils caused by new generations of criminals.

Very compelling. To his celebrity criminal status he thus adds the heart-strings appeal of the reformed sinner.

He might nevertheless be of little note were it not for the fact that Sam is, truly, no ordinary doofus. He is financially sophisticated, smart as hell, and energized as a meth-head at the start of a three-day run. He has a knack, also, for selling his primary product: Sam E. Antar. In web postings and lectures to corporations, business schools, and law enforcement agencies, he has branded himself as a uniquely qualified expert on the art of financial fraud. It is a good story and he sells it with flair. For a magazine profile, he was photographed with a parrot on his shoulder and an enormous cigar thrust pugnaciously from his mouth.[7]

To Sam's credit, he does not claim to have been a victim of anyone else's misconduct or to have ascended the morality ladder through a convenient spiritual conversion. He cheerfully told one reporter: "My fear of serving a long prison term was my primary motivation and no sense of morality was involved in my decision to cooperate with the government." There is in many of his statements a lingering pride in his past accomplishments in crime. In person (I met him once), he projects an anxious intelligence and the I-am-what-I-am insouciance Danny Devito does so well on screen.

Sam has made himself a thorn in Overstock's side by writing a series of blog posts using the company as a case study in financial manipulation. "My research on Overstock.com," he explains," is a freebie for society to help me try to get into heaven for past sins, though I doubt I can ever make up for my past evil acts at Crazy Eddie."

Given his criminal past, he might have been easily ignored by Overstock, except that he has drawn blood by repeatedly exposing significant problems with its disclosure. Among these is its inept use of "pro forma" (non-GAAP) accounting measures.

The most common such measure is "EBITDA" (earnings before interest, taxes, depreciation and amortization). This is close to pre-tax net income with a couple of accruals backed out to take it a step closer to cash accounting. Its proponents argue that it gives a better idea of a company's recurring income stream than GAAP net income. The alternative view is that it air-brushes out of a company's reported numbers certain real economic costs the company would prefer didn't exist. The SEC allows

---

[7] The parrot was an unfortunate casualty of his divorce. He told me that his ex-wife, who had temporary custody of the parrot, let it die through neglect. He has handled the divorce with equanimity, but the loss of the parrot still rankles.

companies to use EBITDA and other pro forma numbers as a supplement to GAAP disclosure. Any company following this route, however, must reconcile these numbers to the most closely analogous GAAP measures.

Patrick Byrne once disdained companies that report their financial results under metrics other than GAAP. "I don't believe in EBITDA," he said in a 2004 interview. "If somebody talks about EBITDA, put your hand on your wallet; they're a crook."

Except, apparently, when he does it.

In 2007, Overstock began emphasizing EBITDA numbers in its earnings releases and analyst calls. There was initially no more explanation for this than for the company's earlier decision to forego the Dutch Auction method for Overstock's securities offerings. The company was entitled to change its mind so long as it followed applicable regulations, but that was the problem. Rather than using plain vanilla EBITDA, it customized that metric by backing out expenses for stock-based compensation (primarily option grants to executives). Again, the company could properly do this as long as it didn't call what it was doing EBITDA and it reconciled its pro forma number to the most directly comparable GAAP measure. It did neither.

Antar was all over this. In detailed blog posts, he pointed out that nowhere in EBITDA does one find the letters "SBC" for stock-based compensation and that Overstock had reconciled its pro forma earnings number to "operating loss" when, under SEC guidance, "net loss" is the right item. The company initially derided Antar as grossly misinformed, then quietly conceded his point by amending its disclosure exactly as he suggested.

As securities law violations go, this is not a big deal. All the same, it was an embarrassment to company management when former criminal Antar, who is not an attorney, could school Overstock on compliance with SEC regulations.

Overstock compounded the embarrassment when it took a feeble swing at explaining why it had gone the low road of pro forma disclosure. In its earnings release for the third quarter of 2008, it contended: "because our current capital expenditures are lower than our depreciation levels, discussing EBITDA at this stage of our business is useful to us and investors because it approximates cash used or cash generated by the operations of the business." The idea is that if a company is capitalizing new costs at about the same rate it is depreciating or amortizing (thus expensing) previously capitalized costs, the result is a stable situation close to cash accounting. On other hand, if, like Overstock, its business practices have changed so that it is deferring by capitalizing fewer costs, the drag on GAAP earnings from previously capitalized costs can give a falsely negative view of the company's current situation. Hence EBITDA makes sense.[8]

The problem this time was that Overstock's facts did not support its explanation. Pouncing again, Antar pointed out that, for its last reported quarter, Overstock's new capital expenditures substantially exceeded total depreciation and amortization.

So far, this may seem merely a game of one-up-manship on a technical accounting issue. But Antar has cut close to the heart of the company's operations by also bringing into question its inventory accounting, a very significant item for a retailer. Antar can claim the perfect resume for making such judgments, having hidden from Crazy Eddie's auditors as much as $20 million in unsold inventory in a single year. When a company reports sales at a certain level, it would naturally be supposed that its inventory is turning at a corresponding rate. If the sales are fake—as they were with Crazy Eddie—the company must find a way to conceal the resulting inventory glut. Antar rose to this challenge with great skill.

With Overstock, however, the inventory issues were more banal. In the same way companies are required to evaluate the collectibility of their receivables and write-down or reserve against those that are unlikely to be paid, they must also true up the values they assign to their inventory. A reduction in inventory valuation will cascade through a company's financial statements, increasing its cost of goods sold and reducing income.

Antar concluded that Overstock had overvalued its inventory at least through 2006. In this, he received some surprising support from Patrick Byrne.

---

[8] Or you could simply look at the company's GAAP statement of cash flows and quickly reach the same conclusion.

In an early 2007 conference call, Byrne reminisced over the "game plan" he had devised in early 2006 to reduce the level of crap inventory in Overstock's warehouses. He said he "knew that things were going to get very ugly" and "the company was going to have take medicine but that we could come out of it a far better company, and that medicine was going to be in the form of some expenses, it was going to be in the form of dumping a bunch of inventory." This was, in fact, the story of Overstock in 2006. It worked down its inventory levels drastically through substantial mark-downs. This resulted in disappointing margins for several quarters. Despite now having much lower inventory levels, Overstock then *increased* its reserves at year-end.

This caused Antar to ask: If management knew the company was sitting on a pile of bad inventory it would have to take a big hit to shovel out the door, why didn't it write the stuff down when it first had that revelation, and maybe even disclose Byrne's "game plan"? That would seem to be what accounting standards and SEC regulations demand. Antar fingered the year-end increase in reserves as particularly curious. If all the junk was really gone, then presumably Overstock's reserves should have been much lighter. Indeed, if the original reserve level (as a percentage of inventory) had been appropriate, the flushing out of the company's warehouses should have brought a major reduction in reserves, even absent any improvement in average inventory quality.

Instead of admitting the problem, however, management made reassuring noises through most of 2006. In earnings calls, it presented the problem as something dwindling in its rear-view mirror. After the first quarter, Byrne told listeners: ". . . we've come out of it now, but we did mark things down in order to flush things through. So that hurt our margins a bit." The next quarter, company president Jason Lindsey acknowledged that the process of dumping bad inventory was not complete, but assured analysts "We are more than adequately reserved." And in the third quarter conference call, Byrne said the company was "clearing a whole bunch of stuff out," which, he acknowledged, would hurt the company's margins for the fourth quarter.

The last quarter of 2006 was indeed dreadful. By discounting aggressively, the company shrank its inventory from $73 million to $27 million. At the same time, it increased its reserves from $4.5 million to

$6.6 million. Margins slumped predictably. Overstock president Lindsey explained:

> We took all that to heart in the fourth quarter and although the fourth quarter results are very bad, and I admit they are very bad, they were bad on purpose. In other words, we used the fourth quarter to get rid of all the slow-moving inventory. I am quite pleased with the inventory balances we have now.

Fair enough, but, again, if management saw a serious problem a year earlier, as Byrne has said, how could it avoid disclosing it back then and making the appropriate adjustments to its financial statements? Antar asked this question in blog postings the company ignored. Patrick Byrne has seemed at a loss as to how to deal with the pesky Antar. Byrne's associates, however, have taken some shots. Judd Bagley has implied that Antar's divorce proceeding will yield some good dirt. And Deep Capture delivered up the following gem:

> Sam Antar is a convicted felon, but he never went to prison because he testified against his cousin, Eddie Antar, in return for house arrest. Now he is paid by short sellers with ties to David Rocker and associates of Michael Milken. The assignment to which he devotes the majority of his time is to use the Internet to harass and smear the reputations of Deep Capture founder Patrick Byrne and his colleagues.[9]

But this approach is obviously ineffective against someone who signs his letters "Sam E. Antar, convicted felon." And when Byrne, in conference calls, refers to "Sam Antar the crook" the derision lacks bite and sounds merely petulant.

Antar has experienced his own frustrations. He has made frequent entreaties to the SEC to jump on Overstock for a variety of possible securities law violations. The agency's Salt Lake City office opened an investigation of the company before Antar came on the scene but closed it without enforcement action, This led to a disillusionment with the agency that once caused Antar so much grief. Interviewed by *StockWatch* columnist Lee Webb, he fumed, "I used to respect them. Even as a

---

[9] The allegation that Antar is paid by "short sellers with ties to David Rocker" is pure fantasy. David Rocker has been retired for years and Copper River has never paid a nickle to Sam Antar or any of Overstock's other critics, unless one includes its Gradient subscription fees. It's a safe bet the same can be said for Milken.

criminal, I respected them because they were smart. They're not like that anymore. . . . They're fucking morons!"

Yet eventually Antar's persistence paid off. As a result of dysfunctional internal controls, Overstock underbilled or overpaid certain of its "fulfillment partners" in 2007 and 2008. After discovering these errors, it declined to revise its books for the affected periods, rather opting to recognize new revenue in whatever periods it received cash to settle up the underbillings. This may seem like no big thing. Overstock's total revenue, after all, came out the same at the end of the day. But a basic premise of accrual accounting (as embodied in GAAP) is that revenue is normally recognized when "earned," not when payment is received. Thus we have the concept of the "account receivable." The amounts involved here were not huge, but Overstock's decision to adopt what was arguably non-GAAP "cash accounting" on one selected item improved the company's apparent earnings trends and flipped a loss in the last quarter of 2008 to a rare profit.

Antar wrote a series of lengthy and precisely-considered blog posts accusing the company of creating a revenue "cookie jar" that it accessed over several quarters to tart up its reported results. Patrick Byrne scoffed that Antar was spouting "gibberish" that no real accountant would take seriously.

Oh well.

In a highly unusual about-face, the SEC reopened its investigation of Overstock, demanding information about a variety of issues including the practices targeted by Antar. Nor was that the extent of it. Overstock's auditors through 2008, PriceWaterhouseCoopers, had apparently bought off on at least some aspects of the company's approach. Failing to leave well enough alone, however, Overstock decided to change auditors for 2009, replacing PWC with Grant Thornton. In reviewing the company's SEC filing for the third quarter of 2009, Grant Thornton concluded it couldn't stomach Overstock's accounting for its underbillings and overpayments and insisted it restate its financials going back into 2008.

In November 2009, Overstock responded by firing Grant Thornton, replacing it with KPMG. In an SEC filing, Overstock and its CEO accused Grant Thornton of reversing itself after previously supporting the company's accounting. Grant Thornton replied, in effect, that Byrne was making things up. Byrne shot back that he was *not* making things up—Grant Thornton was making things up when it said *he* was making things up.

It could only be that the auditors were at fault because, as the *Financial Times* observed, "Patrick Byrne cannot blame this one on the Sith Lord.

This dispute did not end happily for Byrne. KPMG sided with ex-felon Antar. In early February 2010, Overstock announced that its financial statements for the periods at issue should no longer be relied upon by anyone who might otherwise have considered doing so, pending their restatement. The result is that the company will now have restated at least once for every fiscal period since becoming a public company."

Chapter 13

The Bird in the Bush

F airfax Financial Holdings, a multinational insurance conglomerate headquartered in Toronto, has been accused by some of its more impassioned critics of employing the most devious accounting since Enron. Less committed critics have been troubled by its complex corporate structure and opaque financial disclosure. The Fitch agency, in a 2004 report, complained about "the myriad of evolving intercompany transactions and ownership relationships, both on- and off-shore, as well as a lack of adequate disclosures regarding certain entities and transactions that could affect parent company liquidity." As Bethany McLean summed up these concerns in *Fortune*, the company's operations "involve financial machinations so complex that obfuscation seemed to be a business strategy, and the question isn't only whether the machinations are legal but whether anyone can even figure them out."

Insurance companies, like other financial entities, can pose major valuation challenges. Their assets are largely intangible and their primary liabilities—future payouts to policyholders—calculated through actuarial analyses of future costs. In other words, educated guesses. Nevertheless, they are supposed to be conservative investment vehicles, their assets providing solid assurance to insurance regulators of their ability to stand behind their policies. Yet Fairfax seems in some respects to operate more like a hedge fund than a traditional insurance company. And its elaborate structure, with much activity through subsidiary companies in far-flung jurisdictions, has made it difficult to assess the credibility of the numbers that fall out of the bottom of the financial consolidation process.

Fairfax has been a long-term favorite of short-sellers, who for years predicted its imminent collapse. And at times they seemed on the very verge of "getting paid." Fairfax has experienced severe liquidity crises, has extensively restated its financial results, and was under SEC investigation for several years, although this ended uneventfully in 2009. It is the subject of a class action suit alleging securities fraud. In 2007, a rumor circulated that Prem Watsa, the company's Indian-born CEO, was preparing to flee to his country of origin to avoid arrest.

In the face of all of this, however, Fairfax has survived and prospered. Since allegations about the company's practices reached a crescendo several years ago, its share price has gone mostly up. In 2008 Fairfax was the most profitable company in Canada, having reaped enormous gains from investments in credit default swaps and other derivatives. It has silenced its most vocal antagonists with a lawsuit. No government enforcement action has been taken against it or appears to be contemplated. And Mr. Watsa—of late widely lauded in the press for his investment acumen—does not appear to be going anywhere.

Does this mean the system has worked as it should? Has a good company triumphed over its false critics and rewarded its true believers? Or, to the contrary, does this mean that the forces of truth and justice have been, as so often before, overmatched?

Perhaps the market, through its ineffable workings, will someday answer these questions. But probably not. The facile hope that "time will tell" is clearly inapposite to Fairfax. So far, the passage of time has done nothing but add to the questions surrounding this company. Time, in fact, has been one of the most important pieces in the complex and ever-changing puzzle that is Fairfax Financial Holdings.

★ ★ ★

The Fairfax story is inspiring or enraging, depending on one's position in its securities. It is the brain-child of Vivian Prem Watsa, a former door-to-door air conditioner salesman who, over twenty years ago, went into the money management field with an approach consciously imitating that of Warren Buffet. First, find a pool of cash to invest. Insurance companies are likely prospects because policyholder premiums provide enormous investable "float." Many insurance companies make their money—when they do—not from the policies themselves but from making more on their investments than they lose from their underwriting operations. Also in the Buffet mode, Watsa styles himself a value investor, looking to the long-term prospects of companies rather than hoping for quick pops from fad stocks. His biggest scores, however, have come from aggressive plays on derivatives and directional bets on interest rates, not long-term investments in Coca Cola or Dairy Queen.

For every criticism of Fairfax, there is a defense, which, in turn, sparks a counterargument. In the early 1990s, Fairfax, on an acquisition binge, bought some seriously troubled insurance companies in the United States, Canada, and Europe. It was seen as the final foster home for companies no one else would take, including one British company with huge asbestos-related liabilities. Some of these companies are now in "run-off"—writing no new policies and hoping claims on the old ones don't exceed the entity's remaining assets. Its critics claim that the continuing losses from these acquisitions led Fairfax to resort to dubious accounting for reserves and asset valuations to avoid regulatory takeovers. Fairfax bulls reply that the company has been open about the problems of its insurance subs and has made great progress in stanching the losses. And, anyway, who cares as long as the company makes enough money on the investment side to more than cover policy losses? It's the bottom line that counts.

But what about the bewildering complexity of the Fairfax organization, a cat's cradle of public and private entities spanning the globe and connected through a maze of cross-ownership and financial guarantees? One analyst created a chart of the Fairfax organization. It took up most of a wall. The reply, of course is, So what? Many companies have complicated structures. Fairfax is hardly unique in that. It's not illegal to be complex. Tough luck if you aren't smart enough to understand the intricacies of its business.

In early 2003, the bears appeared to be winning. The company's results had been poor for several years, it stock was in decline, and some observers believed its problems were deep and intractable. Reporter Peter Eavis, then with *The Street.com*, suspected Fairfax was cooking its books. He noted that the company's offshore reinsurer—whose balance sheet was critical to the overall health of the Fairfax organization—provided no meaningful financial disclosure. The company was, in essence, telling the market to "Just take our word for it." Fairfax moved assets around foreign subsidiaries so relentlessly that Eavis wondered if "liquidity is swirling in a circle." Citing recent downgrades and the company's history of reserve deficiencies, he asked: "Has Fairfax fallen into a deep hole it can't climb out of?" On the other hand, he had to admit Watsa had made some "spectacularly clever derivative bets on the S&P 500 and U.S. Treasuries."

In January 2003, the brokerage firm Morgan Keegan initiated coverage on Fairfax with an "underperform" rating. Analyst John Gwynn—known for exposing fraudulent practices at insurance company Conseco—wrote a blistering 54-page report concluding that the company was underreserved to the tune of $5 billion. The stock fell by 28 percent that day. Shortly after, Gwynn revised his shortfall calculation downward to $3 billion. This did not engender confidence in his methodology but the spotlight he had focused on the company remained in place.[1]

Rocker Partners took its initial short position in Fairfax shortly after the Gwynn report was released. It had followed the company for some months and, when it saw the stock slump in response to the report, jumped. Fairfax was on its prospects list thanks to Tom Hanson,[2] a brilliant mid-career analyst with a big Australian fund and former official of the Australian and New Zealand governments. Hanson knew Rocker analyst Monty Montgomery from years before when, like Gwynn, both Hanson and Montgomery had been ahead of the Street in

---

[1] As a result of discovery in litigation, it appears Gwynn provided this report to several clients in advance of a more general distribution. This was in conflict with Morgan Keegan policies and resulted in his dismissal. Gwynn died shortly after leaving that firm.

[2] For privacy reasons, I have used a pseudonym.

spotting accounting problems at Conseco, and they talked about financial companies regularly.

The intricacies and nuances of insurance accounting were and remain a specialty of Hanson's and he treated Fairfax, with its convoluted dealings and foggy disclosure, as a challenge. He looked into some of the company's Asian investments, held through a Mauritius subsidiary, and came away skeptical about their reported valuations. This was another black box, with no identification of the investments it held and so no way to confirm their value. Hanson's primary concern, however, was the possibility the company's insurance operations were badly underreserved. He agreed with Gwynn that the hole was around $3 billion. He concluded this deficiency had been concealed by Fairfax in part through the extensive use of "financial reinsurance."

Reinsurance is a common risk-spreading mechanism in the insurance industry. An insurer has bitten off more risk from writing policies than it cares to swallow and lays off some of it to another company along with part of the premium stream. By reducing its policy liability, it also reduces the reserves it must carry to satisfy regulatory requirements.

There are, however, an infinite number of ways of dividing up the risks and rewards from a portfolio of policies. For example, the company to which the policies are "ceded" can agree to cover losses only up to a certain dollar amount. This is called "finite reinsurance." The more complicated the arrangement, the more difficult it becomes to determine how much risk is actually being shifted and, therefore, how much the "ceding company" can reduce its reserves and still remain in compliance with regulatory requirements. The incentives to reduce reserves can be compelling. Because accounted for as liabilities, their reduction increases corporate earnings. Under insurance regulations, moreover, dropping reserves can allow an operating subsidiary to dividend up additional cash to its public company parent—important if the parent is having liquidity problems. Great ingenuity has been shown in devising deals in which the ceding company reduces the liability it must recognize for a group of policies without similarly reducing the economic benefits it hopes to obtain. Many of these deals are, in substance, more like loans from the ceding company to the purported reinsurer than true insurance contracts. When the primary purpose of a contract is the cosmetic improvement to an insurer's balance sheet, this is called "financial reinsurance."

The accounting standards in this area leave much room for abuse. For a contract to be treated as a legitimate reinsurance transaction rather than a financing agreement, it is necessary to show merely that the reinsurer is exposed to *some* possibility of loss. The SEC has defined this to mean, rather arbitrarily, a 10 percent chance the reinsurer will take a 10 percent loss, however that might be calculated. Usually by some computer model. During the 1990s the invitation for devious financial engineering offered by this rule was accepted by many stressed insurance companies and rarely challenged. When the SEC sued insurance companies for accounting abuses, it usually stayed out of the deep end of the pool, labeled "financial reinsurance."

Fairfax made heavy use of such reinsurance, raising the question of whether it had violated even the permissive accounting standards applied to these products. The numbers were big. A contract with reinsurer Swiss Re, for example, allowed Fairfax to drop its liabilities by a billion dollars and book a paper gain of $300 million.

Hanson peppered the company with letters asking about a variety of things that intrigued him. He believed he'd found disconnects between the balance sheets of subsidiaries and their consolidation into the parent company's financial statements. He had questions about reinsurance treaties. He got one blow-off letter and was otherwise ignored.

Later, he would regard being ignored by Fairfax as a blessing.

What Fairfax could not ignore was a major new law enforcement initiative from the New York Attorney General. In May 2005, Eliot Spitzer brought suit against American International Group (AIG) for allegedly padding its financials with phony financial reinsurance. His attack on AIG resulted in the forced resignation of its long-serving and autocratic CEO, Hank Greenberg.[3] The SEC was in those days stumbling along in Spitzer's train, having taken press bashings over being scooped by him on spotting systemic problems with sell-side analysts

---

[3]Greenberg has argued that the AG's harsh treatment of AIG set in motion a train of events that eventually led to its takeover, at enormous taxpayer expense, by the federal government. This view requires assumptions about what AIG's investment practices would have been had Greenberg not been deposed as its CEO, particularly with respect to company's assumption of massive amounts of risk on credit default swaps.

and mutual funds. When he decided to focus next on the insurance industry, the SEC promptly joined the posse and launched a spate of investigations. One targeted Fairfax.

Fairfax conducted an internal inquiry—apparently sparked by the SEC investigation—that turned up big chunks of bad financial reinsurance. The contracts were complex but, when all the countervailing provisions were netted out, the economics fairly simple. Fairfax gave cash to another company that would come back in the future with interest at a specified rate. The "reinsurer's" losses on ceded policies would track the "premiums" (cash) shifted from Fairfax. No apparent transfer of risk anywhere. Thus, these contracts operated more like loans than insurance. In early 2006, Fairfax subsidiary Odyssey Re restated its financials to remedy improper accounting for finite reinsurance. The issues were technical and the total hit to shareholders' equity was a relatively small $35.6 million. Prem Watsa assured investors there would be no more restatements. Then in July 2006 Fairfax announced it would restate four years of financials to fix bad financial reinsurance at the parent company. It would later close out the Swiss Re treaty—taking a $300 million loss that cancelled out its earlier gain—without amending previous financial statements.

Other troubling issues were surfacing for Fairfax. Ubiquitous *New York Post* reporter Roddy Boyd questioned why most of its winning investments were through private offshore entities whose results were unverifiable, while its investments in publicly traded stocks tended to do poorly. One of the losers was the Italian accounting fraud Parmalat. Another was Overstock, which Fairfax and a fund run by one of its directors had generously supported with debt and equity buys when Overstock was running low on cash. Boyd also questioned a convoluted transaction with a Cayman Islands entity, obliquely mentioned in the company's SEC filings, that allowed Fairfax to avoid as much as $300 million in tax liabilities. For this story, the *Post* dug up a picture of Watsa gaping at the camera with a caught-stealing-the-silverware expression. Morgan Keegan also raised a red flag about this deal.

All of this might suggest a company on its last legs. Its critics, after nipping at its heels for years, had finally sunk their teeth into something vital. But not bit of it. Rather than the beginning of the end for Fairfax, this episode was merely a discordant prelude to its period of greatest success.

★   ★   ★

Prominent among the odd cast of characters populating the Fairfax story is New Orleans "stock detective" Spyro Contogouris. After dabbling in various other fields and getting embroiled in litigation with a Greek family whose assets he was managing, Contogouris set up a small company that generated research for a stable of hedge fund clients, including SAC Capital and Jim Chanos's short fund, Kynikos Capital. Fairfax seems to have been of particular interest to his clients. Over many months Contogouris sifted through its public disclosure with a diligence greatly exceeding that of sell-side analysts, looking for inconsistencies, inadvertent admissions, suspicious transactions—whatever would support his growing conviction that Fairfax was a financial house of cards.

His activities allegedly went beyond digging up information and reporting it to his clients. Once he settled into the conclusion that Fairfax had much to hide, he began rattling the company's cage by sending letters to its officers and outside auditors accusing it of financial improprieties. According to a suit later filed by Fairfax, he went so far as to bring his accusations to the attention of the minister of Prem Watsa's church. Fairfax also accused him of making crank phone calls and other shenanigans as part of a campaign of "psychological warfare."

For his part, Contogouris would claim that Fairfax used the Kasowitz and Sitrick firms to harass and intimidate him through conduct much like that alleged against them in the Biovail matter. He said they filed false police reports against him and, using fake identities to pose as prospective clients, attempted to obtain through fraud the results of his research.

The controversy went public in July 2006 when Fairfax filed suit in a New Jersey court against Contogouris, Morgan Keegan, Gwynn, a Fitch analyst who had complained about the company's impenetrable disclosure, and numerous hedge funds, including SAC Capital, Kynikos, and Rocker Partners. Claiming damages of $5 billion, the complaint alleged the hedge funds had employed Contogouris as part of a conspiracy to drive down Fairfax stock. Bob O'Brien crowed on his blog,

"Fairfax is suing the whole gang of SAC-cartel hedge funds, including our favorite, Rocker Partners."

All of this came as news to Rocker Partners. No one there had been aware of the existence of anyone named Spyro Contogouris before being accused of entering into a conspiracy with him. Nor did Rocker Partners have any relationship with SAC, which its people saw as a predatory hot money fund best given a wide berth. Other alleged coconspirators were known to Rocker Partners only as names in the financial press. Nevertheless, in increasing detail through various iterations of the complaint, Fairfax portrayed David Rocker as the evil mastermind behind the "Fairfax Project," a entity that I strongly suspect exists nowhere outside the four corners of the Fairfax complaint.

The suit came as a further surprise since Watsa had previously disclaimed any inclination to sue short-sellers and had a history of shunning personal publicity. But one possible explanation for the decision to take up the cudgels against the shorts and related annoyances is supplied by the timing of the suit. It was filed the day before the company announced its multiyear restatement. Thus, one day before the company gave its skeptics a measure of vindication, it sued the most prominent among them, claiming their carping amounted to racketeering under New Jersey law.

If diverting attention from bad news was the goal, the tactic worked. Any negative effect on the company's stock price from the announced restatements was muted by the press coverage attending the suit. Indeed, the stock began a long upward move that would cause it to double within a few months. Prem Watsa contended the lawsuit had released downward pressure on the stock previously caused by the "dirty tricks" of the Fairfax Project conspirators.

The matter threatened to cost Rocker Partners years of aggravation and millions in legal fees. New Jersey, unlike California, does not require that people who sue others for mouthing off about them make any kind of initial showing that their critics are wrong. Fairfax, with its deep pockets, could therefore inflict years of costly litigation on anyone it chose before it had to prove up anything whatsoever. Because court filings cannot be used as a basis for defamation claims, moreover, it could trumpet the lurid allegations in its complaint without risking liability.

In an early hearing, the judge commented that the allegations, if accurate, would be quite troubling. "Everyone loves this story," one of the defense attorneys observed in dismay. Evil short-sellers, crooked analysts and bent detectives—what's not to like? Hollywood should be calling for the movie rights. In fact, a number of recent movies and TV shows have used short-sellers as villains, even a James Bond film. Should this trend continue, short-sellers may someday be required to register with the police whenever they change residence.

The filing had the effect of silencing most criticism of Fairfax. Morgan Keegan dropped coverage. Its press release said it had yielded to a "litigation strategy designed by Fairfax to silence negative research." Other defendants, on advice of counsel, adopted a bunker mentality and went silent. And the company had more bullets in its gun. When ICP Capital, a fixed income shop with a bear bet on Fairfax subsidiary Odyssey Re, became obstreperous—asking too many questions and talking to the media—it found itself retroactively included in "the Fairfax Project" and named as a defendant in the New Jersey litigation. An ICP spokesman told Bloomberg: "Anyone who questions the company gets sued."

While most of his codefendants opted for discretion, however, Contogouris fought back. In November 2006, he filed a complaint against certain Fairfax entities and officers, as well as auditors Pricewaterhouse-Coopers (Canada), in federal district court in New Orleans. He posted it on his web page, complete with exhibits. Although clearly not the work of a federal court litigator—some of its assertions of law are facially wrong—it is nevertheless a fascinating document. Contogouris had turned over every rock he could find on Fairfax and found some interesting items. In a hundred page document of 264 numbered paragraphs, illustrated with flow charts and quoting heavily from the company's filings, he portrayed Fairfax as a huge shell game, shifting assets around so quickly they appear to be in several places at once, and hiding billions of dollars in liabilities in a mind-numbingly complex structure of foreign entities, many located in jurisdictions where accurate financial disclosure is considered bad manners. As he summed up his views: "Fairfax is the greatest known insurance fraud of the 21st century."

In this he echoed other Fairfax skeptics. What distinguished his effort was not the bare assertion that Fairfax was cooking its books, but the amount of detail he marshaled to support that view. And if his efforts were not conclusive, they set the table with a banquet of issues for government investigators to tuck into, assuming they still have an appetite for complex international financial cases.

Contogouris laboriously traced a host of Fairfax transactions not described in its public filings. His thesis was complex but came down to a few key allegations. Finding itself in a major liquidity bind, he alleged, Fairfax freed up assets of its California insurance subsidiary by conning slow-witted insurance regulators into believing Fairfax was otherwise standing behind the sub's ability to pay claims when, in truth, that security was illusory. Meanwhile, the assets in question—mainly stock in the Fairfax subsidiary OdysseyRe—were run through a maze of European companies and used to support new Fairfax borrowings and thus stave off a cash crunch at the parent level. So well were competing claims against these assets hidden through transactional sleights-of-hand, the company could pledge them as collateral for loans not once but twice:

> Defendants and Fairfax illegally removed and then placed United States policyholder assets in "secret" structures that enabled them to underwrite securitization of these assets and convert funds for other corporate uses. In effect, Defendants and Fairfax "double pledged" United States policyholder assets in order to secure letters of credit to support, among other things, their own insurance subsidiaries deficient operations and to "inflate" their publicly traded company shares.

The intent, according to Contogouris, was to prop up the company's financial statements to "buy time" for its managers to "try to invest their way out of massive reserve deficiencies." This, of course, was a variation on the old bear case against Fairfax: that it was, in essence, a hedge fund using the float from a bunch of loser insurance companies to gamble on risky investments, always just one big bet away from destruction. Contogouris also fingered "bogus offshore finite reinsurance contracts" as a means used by Fairfax to inflate its financial results—by this time an easy call—and accused its Irish subsidiary, nSpire Re, of double-counting assets to give a false appearance of solvency.

Fairfax heatedly disputed the arrangements posited by Contogouris. And, in fairness, his fusillade raised more questions than it answered, and answered none conclusively. Some pieces didn't fit together. The evidence of the "double pledge" of assets supposedly locked up in the vault of a Fairfax insurance sub was sketchy at best. No one could reasonably look at this document and say "That's *it*—this guy's got the company dead to rights."

In any event, whatever effect Contogouris would otherwise have had was undercut by the announcement, exactly one week after he filed his suit, of his arrest. He was charged by federal prosecutors in New York with embezzling money from the Greek nationals he was fighting in a civil suit. The charges, described in a declaration from FBI agent B.J. Kang, were straightforward. Contogouris, while administering a U.S. business for its Greek owners, said he'd paid state and federal taxes on their behalf. According to the FBI agent, however, they owed no such liabilities and Contogouris had simply pocketed the money provided for the payments. Fairfax made the most of this development. Attorney Kasowitz told the press that the charges "don't surprise us, given Fairfax's own claims against Mr. Contogouris and others for being engaged in a racketeering conspiracy."

Contogouris denied the charges, which were unrelated to his Fairfax jeremiad. And his lawyers said the prosecutors had gone off half-cocked in filing criminal charges. But, of course, that's their job. Defense lawyers, that is—not prosecutors. It didn't matter. The man's credibility was shot. *Fortune* quoted an A.M. Best analyst: "I think people didn't believe what was in the [Fairfax] lawsuit until Spyro got arrested," he said. "Then everyone said, 'Wow. This is true.'" Fairfax stock jumped 10 percent that day.

The Contogouris arrest had its unusual aspects. The news was announced by Fairfax days before the prosecutors got around to it. And it seemed odd that a U.S. Attorney's office get involved with something that was already the subject of messy civil litigation. If Contogouris had really jacked money from his Greek associates, they were not without a remedy. The FBI agent who had made the collar on Contogouris, B.J. Kang, had handled a previous matter relating to Fairfax. The private detective who had taken Overstock for $50,000 by promising negative stuff on miscreants hedge funds had also touched Fairfax for bogus intelligence on its enemies. Kang signed the declaration supporting the arrest.

And his interest in Fairfax did not end there. According to *Fortune*, when an ICP partner later complained to an FBI agent of his acquaintance that someone working for Fairfax was stalking ICP's employees, the result what not what he expected:

> He gets a call from the agent asking him to come in. When he arrives, an agent he's never met, B.J. Kang, greets him with some abrupt questions. "What hedge funds do you work with?" he asks. And then: "Why is Marc Kasowitz interested in ICP's employees?"

The obvious speculation—supported by a *New York Times* report that Fairfax "shared information" with the FBI—was that Fairfax lawyers knew Kang from the earlier matter and somehow convinced him to pursue criminal charges against Contogouris.

To add a further dash of weirdness, over a month prior to Contogouris's arrest by the FBI, the *New York Post* (Roddy Boyd again) reported that the Greek investigator had been working undercover for the agency in its investigation of Fairfax. If so, Contogouris had a remarkably abrupt and serious falling out with the FBI. Perhaps blabbing to the *Post* about your "undercover" activities will do that.

Whatever was behind the man's arrest, it came to nothing. In an embarrassing moment for the U.S. Attorney's Office, it dismissed all changes against Contogouris in July 2009 "in the interests of justice." Meaning he hadn't done what the prosecutors had accused him of doing. His dispute with the Greek nationals also fell out his way. They paid him for his trouble and apologized for suing him.

The Fairfax litigation against him and others, however, is ongoing.

★ ★ ★

Between the filing of the Fairfax complaint and the arrest of Contogouris, I moved from the law firm to Copper River. Fairfax was then a major sore point at the fund because of the New Jersey litigation. So it seemed worth the effort to get a handle on what was behind all the charges and countercharges. But that would prove no easy task. The company's filings were voluminous. They included not only the thick tomes filed with the SEC but also filings made with foreign regulators by the company's offshore operations and the "statutory filings" of its domestic insurance subsidiaries with state insurance commissions.

Of course, it was also quite possible that immense haystack would contain not a single needle. It happens. Short-sellers, reporters and even government investigators have been known to bark up the occasional wrong tree. Other than the company's admitted misuse of financial reinsurance—which had been treated as a very serious matter when other companies did it—there was no clear evidence of bad accounting.

But if there was nothing more there, why the mystery? Why not end the guessing game and provide disclosure that informs rather than confuses? Why treat every question as an accusation, every skeptic as a blood enemy, and every rule as something to be finessed? Any decent securities attorney would insist such an approach does nothing but paint a kick-me sign on your corporate posterior.

Unless you have something to hide and are playing for time while you reach into the hat for another rabbit.

Monty's Australian buddy Hanson was good for background. He had a head start on Fairfax and much technical knowledge of the insurance industry. At the SEC, I'd worked insurance cases but, alongside Fairfax, the issues were child's play. Hanson knew what resources an insurance company needs to stay afloat and was adamant that parts of the Fairfax structure didn't make it and were dragging down the rest. The company's projections of claims liabilities, he said, showed a history of blind optimism. And by comparing the company's financial results as reported under U.S. rules to those as reported under Canadian standards, Hanson concluded that Fairfax had more financial reinsurance propping up its balance sheet. I wasn't sure he was right, but it was quite an impressive exercise.

Also intriguing was the transaction with a Cayman Islands entity, questioned by the *New York Post* and Morgan Keegan, that had provided Fairfax with a tax avoidance windfall. Like other Fairfax deals, it seemed designed at least in part to confound the understanding of outside observers.

In March 2003, Fairfax reported that it had purchased an additional 4.3 million shares of its majority-owned subsidiary Odyssey Reinsurance. The seller was NMS Services, a Cayman Islands subsidiary of Bank of America Securities. This pushed Fairfax's interest in Odyssey over

80 percent, the threshold for consolidating parent and subsidiary for tax purposes. And a good thing for Fairfax this was. Odyssey was profitable and therefore subject to significant tax liabilities. Fairfax, on the other hand, carried on its balance sheet a $1 billion tax asset (reflecting accumulated losses). Consolidating Odyssey with its parent would result in its tax liabilities being offset against its parent's tax asset. In effect, Odyssey would pay taxes to Fairfax rather than the IRS. From 2003 through 2005, this resulted in tax savings of around $300 million.

So far the transaction made perfect sense and raised no obvious legal issues.

But nothing with Fairfax is ever simple. The transaction was not structured as a straightforward purchase by Fairfax of Odyssey shares. Instead—presumably because Fairfax did not have the cash to buy the Odyssey stock outright—it financed the deal with two Fairfax notes in the total amount of $78 million. One of the notes covered the cost of 1.4 million shares, the other of 2.9 million shares.

Still no problem. Nothing says Fairfax couldn't buy the shares on credit, so long as it accounted for the transaction properly.

The next layer of complexity came from the fact that the seller, NMS, did not own the shares it sold to Fairfax, at least prior to this transaction. Fairfax's selective disclosure of the deal documents, indicates that the transaction was structured around a short sale. The contract protected NMS from "equity risk" and compensated it for any extraordinary dividends declared by the company. It also allowed NMS to call back the shares at certain times. These deal points suggest NMS was acting as a middleman to permit Fairfax to buy shorted stock that might eventually have to be returned to its source.

Again, this was not necessarily improper. A short sale transfers ownership every bit as much as a long sale. And the papers suggest that Fairfax was assuming at least some part of the economic risks of holding the stock. Whether this permitted Fairfax to properly assert ownership of the stock for tax purposes is impossible to say without more information and much technical knowledge of tax law.

But a few pieces didn't fit. Total short interest figures reported by the NYSE during that period never reflected a 4.3 million share increase in that interest or a market-wide short interest in Odyssey of more than 3.5 million shares. And where could NMS have borrowed 4.3 million

Odyssey shares for it to loan, in turn, to Fairfax? That was 25 percent of Odyssey's public float. Moreover, much of the float was held by a few investment firms. No reductions in their positions were reported after the NMS transaction. And the total combined size of positions reported by major holders rendered it all but mathematically impossible for Fairfax to have added anything approaching 4.3 million shares to its own Odyssey stash.

Other possibilities than a straight short sale came to mind. Perhaps the transaction was arranged as a naked short sale. This might explain why no build-up in short position was reflected in NYSE reports. Or the shares could have been provided indirectly by Fairfax itself. In the first case, Fairfax's claim to ownership of the shares would be questionable; in the second, it would be double-counting shares to reach the level required for consolidation.

Clearly *some explanation* was required as to how 4.3 million shares of Odyssey stock could appear on Fairfax's ledger without disappearing anywhere else. An August 25, 2006 Morgan Keegan report asked whether "Fairfax's original 2003 'purchase' of 4.3 million ORH shares was synthetically facilitated." If so, it asserted, "this raises the question as to whether such a mechanism passes muster with the Internal Revenue Service."[4]

ICP Capital, in a counterclaim in the Fairfax litigation, alleged the NMS transaction was a naked short sale that didn't give Fairfax ownership of the stock. In its view, Fairfax was dealing in what Patrick Byrne would call "phantom stock." Fairfax, however, has announced that it survived an IRS audit of its 2003 and 2004 tax years and that one of the issues examined was the NMS deal. Although this does not necessarily put paid to the matter, it would not seem to bode well for ICP's counterclaim. If the IRS looked at the transaction and found it not worth challenging (despite the hundreds of millions involved), a court might hesitate to find it fraudulent.

In 2006, Fairfax unwound the transaction. Odyssey had sustained losses as a result of Hurricane Katrina and so consolidation for tax purposes provided no additional benefits. Rather than simply reversing

---

[4]When Fairfax was first questioned about this transaction on a Fairfax conference call, a spokesman said Fairfax "had an IRS ruling before we did this." Fairfax later admitted this was not the case.

the original stock for notes deal, however, Fairfax and NMS treated the two notes differently. Here began phase two of the story, with additional complex benefits to Fairfax.

Yes, I know. A few paragraphs back I was casting aspersions on the NMS deal just because the company's disclosure reads like the work of a committee of French intellectuals, badly translated into English. So Fairfax decides to clean it up and, never satisfied, I have a problem with *that* too? Why can't I leave this company in peace?

But wait. It gets better. Put simply, Fairfax may have cleverly structured the unwinding of the NMS transaction in a way that goosed the price of Odyssey stock shortly before selling 10 million shares to the public—and quite possibly without breaking any laws. If so, its creativity deserves to be appreciated.

In May 2006, without making this fact public, Fairfax paid down $9 million on the note provided for the 1.4 million share purchase. This amount covered 400,000 of the shares. At around the same time, Odyssey stock began a several month run-up, adding over 50 percent to its price. In August 2006, Fairfax provided a clue to the possible connection between these two facts. An SEC filing described a $23 million payment by Fairfax to NMS. Together with the earlier $9 million payment—which the company now got around to mentioning—that retired the note provided for the 1.4 million share purchase. Fairfax stated that the $23 million payment would result in NMS purchasing one million shares of Odyssey stock on the open market or elsewhere. It didn't say whether the purchase would go to cover an open short position. The company was also silent on whether the earlier $9 million pay-down on the note had resulted in NMS buying 400,000 but, if so, that would help explain the buoyant share price.

Someone paying close attention might ask: Doesn't all this come down to NMS buying Odyssey stock on behalf of Fairfax in two stages—first the short sale, then the cover? And wouldn't that inevitably push up the price of Odyssey stock, including the 80 percent of the total owned by Fairfax? If so, the company had that covered. The same filing stated the Odyssey purchases made by NMS would conform to the requirements of an SEC "safe harbor" rule permitting companies to buy back their own stock without triggering accusations of market manipulation. This backdoor way of buying Odyssey stock probably attracted far less attention than had Fairfax announced it was buying 1.4 million shares of Odyssey stock in the months before one of its insurance subs sold 10 million Odyssey shares to the public.[5]

After paying off the first note, Fairfax still owed NMS for the remaining 2.9 million shares. In November 2006, however, NMS exercised an option under the contract to take back those shares in exchange for cancelling the second note, thus capturing considerable appreciation in the price of Odyssey stock.[6]

The final wrinkle, at least as to anything touching the public record, was a shelf registration filed by Odyssey in late 2006 to facilitate the public sale by NMS of the 2.9 million shares. The odd element was that NMS would "use the proceeds received in such sales to buy an equal number of [Odyssey] common shares."[7] Odyssey acknowledged that these purchases might boost the market price of its stock. It did not explain why NMS would sell Odyssey stock and then do an about-face to buy back the same number of shares.

When I read this, I grabbed my head like a stunned monkey. I was tempted to simply throw in the towel and admit defeat. The more I learned about Fairfax, the less I understood, an experience shared with others who tried to sort out this enigmatic company. But it was too intriguing to just let it go. It was like discovering a new art form. Cubist financial disclosure. There was enough there for the company to claim it had hit the marks, but not enough to allow the reader to put it all together into a coherent whole. A situation not easy to create.

★ ★ ★

One of the things that held down Fairfax stock for years was the fear that the company's runoff (slow-motion liquidation) operations would drain away whatever cash it could produce through its more successful investments. Since 2007, however, management has insisted these units

---

[5] The offering was priced 50 percent above where the stock had been in May, when Fairfax made the $9 million payment on the NMS note. There are, of course, many factors that could have affected the price of Odyssey stock during this period, most notably the company's financial results, which were much improved from the same period in 2005, the year of Hurricane Katrina. It should also be noted that Odyssey stock has generally remained above the offering level since then.

[6] Of course, if the shares were borrowed, this would have benefited the source of the shares after they were returned to it.

[7] By this time, a different offshore subsidiary of Bank of America Securities had been inserted into the transaction, but I will to refer to it as NMS for purposes of simplicity.

would not be a cash drain on the parent company ever again, and sell-side analysts have taken this at face value. The financial pivot upon which turns the European side of the company's runoff operations is its Irish subsidiary, nSpire Re. Headquartered in Dublin, nSpire backstops (by reinsuring) billions of dollars in potential liabilities of various Fairfax entities, including its European runoff operations. Among these are some inherited Lloyd's of London "syndicates" with enormous asbestosis liabilities. Claims against such "long-tail" coverage—to use the industry vernacular—can mature decades after a policy is written as policy-holders finally show symptoms of a covered ailment. Thus liabilities are hard to estimate and can be devastating if, as occurred with some Lloyd's syndicates, major risks were not recognized.

From Fairfax's SEC filings you would almost certainly conclude that its runoff operations are under control and will, in the fullness of time, wither away as claims are applied against reserves. Claims paid by European runoff—at least as reported to the SEC—follow an encouraging trend. In 2006, "losses on claims" were a mere $39.7 million, a huge improvement over losses of $247.0 and $187.8 million in 2005 and 2004, respectively. The next year, 2007, looked even better: a loss on claims of a piddling $16.5 million. Management made certain the sell-side picked up on this good news.

But nSpire, which covered most of the losses, files its own reports in Ireland.[8] Only *one* a year—and they look like the product of a yard-sale typewriter—but what's there tells an interesting story. These reports show that over the five years from 2003 to 2007, nSpire paid claims averaging $530.8 million a year, while seeing rapidly declining assets, as shown in the following table.[9]

Year	2007	2006	2005	2004	2003
Total Assets (in U.S. $000)	1,812,247	2,038,718	2,997,491	3,993,885	4,703,206
Claims Paid	241,488	544,612	363,947	839,579	664,220

---

[8]The Irish "Companies House" doesn't necessarily do anything with the filings other than file them. Oddly, it charges *more* for companies that don't want their reports reviewed. nSpire has gone for that option.

[9]By changing its fiscal year-end date, nSpire avoided making its regulatory filing for 2008 year until October 2009. Its reported losses on claims for that year were a relatively modest $150 million, although this may have been affected by the claims holiday provided by the solvent scheme of arrangement described below.

The difference between the numbers in the U.S. and Irish filings over these five years totals $2.65 billion. This is more than nSpire's total current assets. The gap is the result of the company's netting out of the raw figures that appear in the Irish filings the cash received from unwinding finite reinsurance treaties in 2004, 2005, and 2006, and by reducing reserves for future claims in 2007. Whether or not the accounting treatment is valid, the reported figures could give a severely mistaken picture of the company's claims history. You can find some of this information in the small print of SEC reports if you look hard enough, but no one seems to have done that.

Even the larger numbers from the Irish filings may give an overly rosy picture. In 2005, Sphere Drake, the most problematic unit reinsured by nSpire, enjoyed a partial holiday from claims payments. By entering into a "solvent scheme or arrangement"—a U.K. procedure allowing insurance companies to liquidate claims outside bankruptcy—it was given most of a year to gather up known claims, evaluate them, and decide whether to pay them in one lump, thus permanently eliminating the overhang of potential future claims. Meanwhile, it was making payments on none of them. This procedure can be a tremendous boon for property and casualty companies facing substantial long-tail liability. Policyholders who have not yet developed symptoms of a covered illness, of course, will not know to submit a claim and so will be permanently screwed.

Fairfax, however, decided against concluding the scheme, possibly from lack of ready cash. Nevertheless, it arranged a second such claims holiday that began in late 2007. Fairfax has been extremely stingy with information about this proceeding. As of this writing, it has not, so far as I have been able to determine, revealed how much it has received in the way of claims or if it intends to complete the "scheme."

The more difficult question, however, is just how good are nSpire's assets. Contogouris insisted that it had inflated its balance sheet by $1 billion with a phantom dividend from a Hungarian subsidiary and double-pledged other assets. In any event, the bulk of nSpire's assets consists of claims against other Fairfax entities: as of the end of 2007, all but $200 million of its $1.8 billion in total assets. These interests hard to value and their composition can change drastically and abruptly.

In 2007, without explanation, Fairfax radically restructured nSpire's balance sheet. For some time nSpire's biggest asset had been $1.26 billion in the preferred stock of Fairfax Gibraltar, which, in turn, controlled most of Fairfax's U.S. assets. That put it somewhere in the center of the Fairfax organization. Then, suddenly, it wasn't. nSpire "sold" its interest in Fairfax Gibraltar and got in return $1.73 billion in unsecured and mostly interest-free Fairfax debt. The entity on the other side of the deal is not disclosed but a big bump up the balance sheet category for "claims against affiliates" suggests it was another Fairfax entity.

nSpire booked a gain of $465 million on this transaction. This reflected the appreciation of the Euro against the dollar from the point nSpire acquired its Fairfax Gibraltar stock. This seems odd in that Fairfax Gibraltar owns mainly U.S. assets.

Questions, clearly, abound, but the only disclosure about this transaction by Fairfax is a single sentence buried in a long paragraph: "As a result of a restructuring completed in 2007, nSpire no longer holds a direct or indirect equity interest in any Fairfax affiliate." That's it. Nothing that explains the purpose of the restructuring or what it portends for the company.

The swap of Fairfax Gibraltar stock for Fairfax debt suggested a possible attempt by Fairfax to protect its core operations from the potential insolvency of nSpire. There were reasons for such concern. nSpire's cash balance had gone down year after year and there was little indication of liquidity elsewhere on nSpire's balance sheet. At the end of 2007, it had cash of $92.7 million and investments outside the Fairfax corporate maze of $107.6 million, but $105 million in current liabilities. From the face of the report, that left nSpire with something short of $100 million while its annual liabilities for claims had been in the hundreds of millions for many years. This was despite the fact that Sphere Drake's solvent scheme of arrangement presumably took away some of the pressure that year.

The company would undoubtedly say that nSpire is only part of the picture for European runoff and its financial resources are, for complicated reasons, much deeper than this analysis suggests. And perhaps the Sphere Drake solvent scheme will go forward and plug the biggest hole in the Fairfax boat.[10] But this is entirely too much guesswork for a public company to inflict on its investors. Assume for a moment the company's

---

[10] As of the end of 2009, the company had not announced the implementation of the scheme, which, given the amount of time that has passed, suggests it has decided not to do so.

detractors, presently huddled in their foxholes, have it something like right. Assume for argument's sake that the company's offshore operations are a big shell game hiding a huge capital deficiency. What, then, will finally bring this to an end? The bear scenario was that the investment side of Fairfax would be unable to bail fast enough to keep losses from the insurance side from swamping the company. Thus it would eventually just roll over and die.

So how does that theory look these days?

Not good. In a stunning investment feat, Fairfax made, with minimal commitment of capital, $1.5 billion from shorting the U.S. financial sector in 2007 and 2008, mostly by loading up on credit default swaps that bet on the financial deterioration of investment banks, "monoline insurers" and other such pillars of the credit system. Prem Watsa had been out early proclaiming, with a degree of prescience, the coming collapse. In May 2007, he warned of a "hundred-year storm." He reduced Fairfax's equity positions substantially and hedged much of what was left by shorting the S&P 500 Index. But the play on credit default swaps was the *piece de resistance*. After racking up several years of paper losses, these bear bets on the solvency of AIG, Ambec, and other major-losers-to-be paid off handsomely when the credit market seized up in 2008.

While this remained mostly paper profit, there was some doubt about Fairfax's ability to "monetize" it. These doubts proved mistaken. Fairfax cashed in its positions with astute timing. The result was a huge run-up in its stock and a tidal wave of liquidity that washed through the Fairfax structure, with much of it going to nSpire. As had happened at least twice before, Prem Watsa confounded his detractors with his Houdini-like ability to get out of tight situations. The bears thought they had him handcuffed, in a straitjacket, nailed into a coffin, and dropped into the ocean. Then he appeared at their shoulder, dry as a bone.

If opaque disclosure and aggressive litigation were, in fact, tools used by Fairfax to keep critics at bay long enough for its bear gamble on the credit market to pay off, the tactic was a stunning success. The element of time, which the shorts had believed to be on their side, proved their undoing.

Nor would the SEC provide them with any measure of vindication. Its investigation was closed last year without enforcement action. The SEC's lawyers and accountants may have completed a thorough

investigation of the company's various issues and found no wrongdoing,
Or perhaps they never got past their initial concern—the possible misuse
of financial reinsurance—and decided that was no longer a hot topic. If
so, time had once again proved to be the company's friend.

Or, then again, the investigators may have surveyed the complexities of the company's financial arrangements, grabbed their heads like
stunned monkeys and decided to investigate something else.

★ ★ ★

Several of the named defendants in the Fairfax litigation won an early
exit after it became apparent they had little or no connection to Spyro
Contogouris or each other and were clearly not involved in any sort of
conspiracy. Copper River was among them.

The Kasowitz firm had suffered a major setback in its other short-
seller conspiracy case, Biovail, when it used documents subject to a
protective order in one case to support the filing of another. The federal district court judge overseeing the matter was not amused. As the
American Lawyer reported, "An aggressive campaign against hedge fund
short-sellers has turned into a courthouse nightmare for Marc Kasowitz."
When Biovail and its chairman became the subject of both civil and
criminal actions, as described above, the credibility of the company's
claims against short-sellers took an additional beating.

The New Jersey suit also hit some bumps. The judge, unlike her
California counterparts, has displayed a certain understanding of the
financial markets and did not recoil in horror at the notion of short-
sellers airing negative views of public companies. Further, she has been
seen to take the bench lugging heavily annotated, Post-It-festooned
copies of the briefs. That she does her homework has made it less likely
she would be seduced by a glitzy story.

She gave Fairfax every chance to plausibly allege wrongdoing by
Copper River. The complaint in its first iteration alleged that Copper
River had unleashed Spyro Contogouris like an evil imp from a bottle
to wreck havoc on Fairfax. Counsel promised evidence. This proved
difficult because Copper River and Contogouris had been completely
unknown to each other prior to the filing of this suit. On further
reflection, Fairfax's litigators decided it was *the Fitch analyst* Copper River

put up to trashing Fairfax. This theory too fell flat. As it happened, they also didn't know each other. Did they say the Fitch analyst? They meant to say John Gwynn, *the Morgan Keegan analyst*. Copper River put him up to it. That was it! Unfortunately, it turned out no one at Copper River had so much as spoken with Gwynn until after he published his negative views on Fairfax.

Finally, the judge had heard enough. She suggested that counsel for Fairfax had been just a little less than straight with her. Since attorneys are required, as a matter of professional ethics, to have a good faith basis for anything they file with a court, she might have expressed herself more forcefully. She booted the part of the complaint relating to Copper River but, generous to a fault, left the door open a crack in case Fairfax should ever come up with anything against Copper River resembling what lawyers refer to as evidence.

★ ★ ★

The last time I spoke with Tom Hanson, the futility of the situation had caught up with him. He sounded down. "I'm sitting here in Melbourne," he said, "awake in the middle of the night, knowing more about this crazy Canadian insurance company than anyone in the world." He gave a long sigh. "And no one cares."[11]

---

[11] Interest in Fairfax is likely to decline further now that it has largely withdrawn from the U.S. securities markets. In late 2009, it chose to de-list its common stock from the NYSE, while retaining its listing on the Toronto exchange.

Chapter 14

The Collapse of the American Financial Sector in One Easy Lesson

I n a recent Hollywood movie, a comic-book super-villain responds to the question, "What ever happened to the American dream?" by crowing: "It came true."

So it did—or some version of it. But only briefly because we borrowed the price of the Dream and now have to pay it back.

Laying aside the question of what ever made *our* dream seem something more elevated and pure than the dreams of, say, Lithuanians, Laplanders, or Easter Islanders, these days it has clearly lost much of its former luster. It has become an object of distrust as we learn from events to be more careful what we wish for. The Dream now appears as a commodity—sold by business interests and politicians of both parties—a brightly-wrapped box holding yet other commodities, all of questionable value.

And first among these commodities: residential housing—bought on credit.

Home ownership promises independence, security, and a steadily improving family balance sheet, which can, in turn, be tapped to provide other accoutrements of the Dream, from big-screen televisions and other products of industrious Asian nations to expensive services provided by our own countrymen. For those troubled by concerns of social inequality, widespread home ownership also promises to reduce distinctions of wealth as everyone is folded into the arms of the great middle class on tree-lined streets from Bangor to Chula Vista. Housing starts and sales also mean fat times for contractors, realtors and other politically well-wired interests.

The only problem: money. Houses are expensive. Not everyone can easily afford their own hunk of dirt with brick and mortar edifice crowding the property lines. But as the goal of home ownership evolved in the public mind from an aspiration to an entitlement, the means were expected to appear. How could it be otherwise? How could the Dream be deferred in this, the richest country in history?

Congress has, over the years, done many things to encourage home ownership. It has treated as sacrosanct the tax deduction for mortgage interest payments, which is now baked into the cost of residential property. Of course second houses are also part of the Dream, as are recreational vehicles financed through equity credit lines, and so deserve the same tax break. The government also encouraged capital flow into residential real estate though local savings and loan associations, until the changing economy, managerial incompetence and misguided regulations caused many to collapse and become wards of the state.

A more durable means of supporting the housing market came about with the creation of Fannie Mae and Freddie Mac. These Government Sponsored Entities (GSEs) were designed as a sort of private-public partnership, with the dividing line poorly defined. Over time, they developed the failings of both sectors: phony financial reporting, excessive executive compensation, inept regulatory oversight, and a propensity to seek advantage over their competition through expensive lobbying efforts.

Still, they had their virtues. Fannie and Freddie aided real estate lending by smoothing the process, making it more uniform, and—by extending their almost-U.S.-government credit ratings across much of the market—making mortgages more affordable for many. Eventually, they controlled half of the secondary market for mortgage paper.

The problem was that the GSEs were supposed to operate as businesses. The mortgages they bought or guaranteed needed to pay off enough of the time that the GSEs earned real profits—not the pretend profits they booked for many years to justify paying substantial bonuses to their executives. Otherwise they became vehicles for throwing taxpayer money into a big hole.

This became more difficult as the federal government saddled the GSEs with the task of increasing home ownership among lower income groups. The banks that dumped loans into the Fannie and Freddie machinery were similarly mandated by Congress—and pushed by private activist organizations—to lend to people who wouldn't have qualified under previous standards. However well-intentioned, lower underwriting standards result inevitably in greater risk of default. The dumbing-down of standards may also have been pushed by the adoption of an increasingly speculative mentality by GSE managers. Their compensation tied to reported profits, they stood to make out handsomely gambling with other people's money, and did. Fannie and Freddie came to resemble giant hedge funds, loosely regulated sinkholes of systemic risk. As of the end of 2009, it appears that taxpayer losses from Freddie and Fannie will eventually exceed $400 billion.

The housing bubble also depended for its long expansion on the availability of cheap credit. A primary villain here is the Federal Reserve Board, under the once-revered Alan Greenspan. After the collapse of the NASDAQ bubble in 2002, it adopted a hair-of-the-dog approach and kept rates at historic lows for several years. While the Fed does not directly set mortgage rates, its rates are a benchmark for others. The effect of the Fed's loose money policies on adjustable rate mortgages—which were cheap for several years and then climbed steadily higher—may also have contributed to the rising default rates that began in 2007.

That the country was awash in liquidity—much of it sloshing through the housing market—also owed much to the perverse tendency of people in other countries to *save* money. Amazingly enough, it can be done. These savings were largely in dollars obtained by selling to Americans consumer goods more cheaply than they could be produced here. In China, the Middle East oil nations, and other non-Western countries savings as a percentage of GDP were, at least compared to our dwindling rate, enormous. It had to go somewhere. And where better than to finance the consumption habits of Americans, including their appetite for McMansions in the Inland Empire?

The flow (some would say force-feeding) of capital into the American markets not only kept the cost of capital low, but nurtured an industry notable for its loose practices: sub-prime mortgage origination. After the crash, anecdotes of Animal House orgies of wildly irresponsible conduct burst from the ruptured industry like candy from a piñata. No job? No money down? No problem. Some of these companies defrauded mortgage applicants. Some were defrauded *by* mortgage applicants, all the way to the bank. Federal and state regulators looked on and shrugged. Congress, whose members received $370 million in campaign contributions from subprime lenders over a 10-year period, did nothing to halt the decline in lending standards.

But there is a piece missing. Low rates and no questions asked brought in mortgage applicants by the truckload. Fannie and Freddie were willing to hold their institutional noses and eat or guarantee a certain number of less-than-prime mortgages. So were many banks—as the price of avoiding regulatory and public relations headaches. That, however, was not enough to create the worldwide market for subprime mortgages and other dodgy real-estate-related assets that led to the market meltdown. Also critical was a broad linkage between purveyors of these assets and potential buyers, which required processing and packaging those assets so they would appear to fit within the risk tolerances of the buyers.

No easy task, that; but our financial services industry proved up to the challenge and profited enormously for over a decade from doing so. Fortunately, America had arranged its incentives so that our best and brightest—eschewing such socially marginal activities as medicine, engineering, and education—would devote their professional lives to creating wealth from acts of faith. This concentration of talent managed to create a trillion dollar market out of the raw material of subprime mortgages, auto loans and credit-card receivables through the sausage-making process of securitization. The risks inhering in the underlying assets were supposedly segregated out through this financial wizardry and the remaining interests determined through statistical analysis to be as safe as mother's milk. Human judgment and experience were supplanted by computer algorithms in the hands of technicians.

Of course, not every sausage would do. It had to be sausage of certified quality or someone might actually ask to see the contents. This was the pivotal role played by the rating agencies: Moody's, S&P, and Fitch. Paid by the purveyors of these instruments for supposedly objective opinions, their role raises the same potential conflicts of interest as the relationship between public companies and their "independent" auditors. The rating agencies, however, were less sensitive to this issue because not disciplined by the experience of frequent litigation over their mistakes. The models they employed were notable for their failure to fully incorporate the potential for a major and sustained downturn in the housing market, despite the obvious emergence of a real estate bubble.

The appetite for these products proved enormous and increased when regulators allowed banks, both commercial and investment, to amp up their leverage based on, yes, their own risk analysis models. In the early 90s, as an important example, the SEC proved regrettably permissive in allowing the investment banks under its jurisdiction to increase their leverage to 35 times equity, as calculated at month end. The rest of the time it might reach 50 to 1.

Not everyone was blindly sanguine that building leaning towers of leverage on top of speculative and opaque assets would work forever. Here again our financial engineers proved their mettle. They created financial instruments providing the ability to gamble on the likelihood that other financial instruments would tank. Thus was born the now-infamous "credit default swap."

This product started out as a simple device for hedging against risk on portfolios of debt securities. Like the "portfolio insurance" of the 1980s, it purported to limit downside risk without unduly sacrificing upside potential. Unlike portfolio insurance—which was essentially a systemic approach to pulling the eject button on stock positions when they hit a certain loss threshold—it was a genuine insurance product with risk shifted to a third party. It works as long as the entities providing the insurance have the ability to perform.

The quantum of risk assumed by providers of credit default swaps increased drastically over time. This was due to the growing popularity of these instruments with entities that did not hold the referenced bonds (and so had nothing to insure) but wanted to bet on an eventual default or decrease in credit-worthiness of the issuer. Perhaps a company heavily exposed to the subprime market or other aspects of the credit bubble—the bet Fairfax Financial played brilliantly. Or even a company, like AIG, that had itself written so many credit default swaps that a significant economic downturn could cause it to suffer huge losses on those instruments. These plays were subject to little regulatory oversight and flourished without anyone knowing how many swaps were out there and, should things turn ugly, which entities, once everything was netted out, might feel a chill wind on their hindquarters.

The slide began not with a bang but a swelling chorus of whimpers as the housing market stalled in 2007 and the default rate on mortgages, particularly those no sane person would have written in the first place, rose. The process gathered steam month after month. The companies furthest out on the risk continuum—the Countrywides and NovaStars—were the first to falter. What followed resembled a daisy chain of Alpinists plunging into an abyss when one falls and the rest find they were not so well-attached to the mountain as they had hoped.

Institutional investors examined their portfolios and realized they had outsourced their due diligence to rating agencies run by faceless technocrats and didn't understand what they owned. They eyed their counterparties and wondered if they were standing on piles of junk that meant they would be unable to honor their obligations. The accounting standard-setters picked this moment to crack down on the widespread practice of valuing assets based on arithmetic models of projected cash flows. Instead, they pushed companies to look to what people were actually willing to pay for the assets. While this dictate did not expand the categories of assets subject to "mark-to-market" accounting—and many assets held by financial institutions fall outside that standard—it nevertheless caused firms to take painful write-downs based on the disappearance of any active market for entire asset categories. The howls of protest were pitiable.

If the American financial system stumbled in adjusting to the decline in the housing market, it took a pratfall when one of its foundational institutions, investment banking, proved to have adopted a business model unable to adjust to severe dislocations in the credit market.

The first to take the drop was Bear Stearns. In June 2007, two of its sponsored hedge funds with heavy subprime exposure blew up. This initially seemed a containable event. But slowly at first and then very, very quickly, the market's faith eroded in Bear's ability to honor its commitments on its derivative contracts and to the hedge funds that entrusted it with their trading accounts. The tipping point came in March 2008 when the firm went from reasonably cushioned, under established regulatory standards, to insolvent in the span of a few days.

The cause of this sudden seizure admits to more than one explanation, with various causes and effects emphasized depending on viewpoint. It is hard to dispute that Bear's business model proved peculiarly vulnerable to certain types of market disruptions. Bear's operations were funded, almost literally, on a fly-by-night basis—with credit aggressively leveraged from a balance sheet notable for opaque and speculative assets, and from the hypothecation of client positions that could be withdrawn at any time. Not a good design for stability in a storm. A recent biography of the firm by William Cohan, appropriately entitled *House of Cards*, quotes former Bear Stearns honcho Alan Schwartz: "The model became wholesale banks [like Bear] using collateral to finance themselves instead of using deposits. It didn't work when the collateral invading the world [structured products] became non-transparent."

It is also arguable that Bear was kicked over the edge by the unintended consequences of a poorly regulated financial innovation. As the firm's reported losses mounted, a toxic symbiosis seems to have developed between short sales of the company's stock and the price of credit default swaps on its debt. As sales by shorts and discouraged longs pushed down the stock, the swap market paid attention and bid up the cost of insurance on the firm's debt. Meanwhile, Bear clients saw these developments and protected themselves by withdrawing assets. The result was a self-reinforcing spiral that turned into a run on the firm. Bear, from the very nature of its business, was peculiarly vulnerable to this sort of crisis. As an investment bank, its stock in trade was largely trust and confidence, a commodity as to which perception easily becomes reality.

This scenario lends itself easily to charges of "bear raid." To whatever extent a feedback loop developed, however, there seems little reason to doubt it evolved from hundreds of independent actions by anxious traders, with others acting in a narrowly opportunistically way, rather than something characterizable as intelligent design.

In March 2008, Bear Stearns was hustled off by the Treasury Department into a shotgun marriage with J.P. Morgan, at great loss to Bear's shareholders. If the government had been slow off the dime in trying to arrange sources of liquidity for Bear, and then abrupt and heavy-handed in pushing it into a merger, it could at least claim that a potential catastrophe had been averted. Bankruptcy would have been disastrous for bondholders and numerous counterparties and likely caused a major dislocation in the credit markets. By the standards of the day, this is remembered as a regulatory success.

Had Bear Stearns been the only investment bank to fail, the global credit crunch and its devastating effects on the "real" economy would surely not have occurred, at least at the same order of magnitude. But within six months other major financial entities were teetering on the brink and the government was stumbling to the rescue. Or not, depending on the firm at issue. And the effects on the American financial system and the world economy—not forgetting the microcosm of Copper River—would be deep and lasting.

★ ★ ★

In September 2008, the ground opened under the world financial system, destabilizing economies from Iceland to India. Even though things had been wobbly for a year, the suddenness and severity of it took the world by surprise.

The subprime meltdown was, by then, over a year along, with no end in sight to the carnage. Marginal mortgage companies like NovaStar had shut up shop, their investors left empty-handed. The housing market was dominated by foreclosure sales in those areas of the country where speculative excess comes in the water supply. Financial stocks had been flattened across the board. Bear Stearns, pregnant with pending asset write-downs, had been hustled off a month before into the waiting arms of J.P. Morgan, with a substantial dowry provided by the U.S. Treasury.

Similarly, Merrill Lynch was being crammed into Bank of America with much behind-the-scenes encouragement from the regulators.[1] And Fannie Mae and Freddie Mac had been more or less nationalized.

But, all in all, it could have been worse. The credit markets still had a pulse and no major financial institution had been allowed to fail. The government was doling out a daily dose of happy talk. Treasury Secretary Hank Paulson was staying on message: The problem had been contained. There was no need for panic. Nothing to fear but fear itself.

Then, on Sunday, September 14, Lehman Brothers announced it was entering a bankruptcy proceeding and "fear itself" became one kick-ass problem. While it was common knowledge that Lehman would need more capital to survive, the bailout of Bear Stearns had encouraged confidence that the government would do whatever was necessary to prevent its failure. Why this turned out to be a false assumption admits to many possible answers. The Treasury Department and the Bush White House were getting grief in the press and from Congress over the supposed "moral hazard" they had fostered through the Bear Stearns rescue. The concern was that other financial institutions might be tempted to risk wreckage on the rocks of speculation if they could count on government aid in the ensuing salvage operation. Apparently the near-elimination of Bear's public equity, the humiliation of its management, and the loss of its status as an independent entity wouldn't suffice as an object lesson to others tempted to follow its lead.

There has been unkind speculation, also, that Lehman was considered expendable because its failure would not unduly harm Goldman Sachs, the fair-haired boy of investment banking, at least in the eyes of Hank Paulson and the other Goldman alumni running Treasury. This theory gained traction when the government bailed out insurance giant American International Group (AIG)—to which Goldman *did* have significant exposure—the day after Lehman's collapse. Goldman, in its own defense, claims its AIG exposure was fully hedged with credit default

---

[1]There was a certain hook-or-by-crook aspect to this. According to Ken Lewis, former CEO of Bank of America, he learned of mounting losses at Merrill before the consummation of the merger. He considered scuttling the deal but was pressured by Treasury Secretary Paulson and Fed chairman Bernanke to complete the transaction without disclosing the Merrill losses to his shareholders. The result was a weakening of Bank of America's balance sheet and additional borrowings from the government. As the *Wall Street Journal* put it, "In the name of containing 'systemic risk,' our regulators spread it."

swaps and other strategies. A recent government report casts some doubt on this assertion.

Most likely the failure to backstop Lehman was primarily the result of regulatory tunnel vision. Treasury wanted to show it could draw the line somewhere short of full-blown "lemon socialism." The taxpayers shouldn't be on the hook for every Wall Street blowup. So why not make Lehman the sacrificial goat? It wasn't so big or tightly interconnected with other major players that a failure of its U.S. operations would tank the financial system. Best guess, anyway. As for the foreign operations: they were someone else's problem.

If that was the reasoning, however, it failed to recognize how little national borders represent financial barriers these days. U.S. entities did extensive business with Lehman's London OTC desk and other foreign facilities. The potential loss of assets when these foreign offices shut their doors had tremendous implications for U.S. traders. The daisy chains stretched around the world.

Also, such a cavalier view ignores how easily the fear factor can whipsaw sentiment in a market already in a froth of anxiety. If Lehman could fail today, why not JPMorgan or Goldman tomorrow? Both hemorrhaged assets rapidly after Lehman went down. And when a money market fund with a wad of Lehman paper announced, in a stunning historical anomaly, that it would "break the buck" (return less than 100 cents on the dollar to its investors), a run on money market funds ensued that required an immediate federal guarantee across that sector. Also contributing to the atmosphere of panic was the looming shadow of credit default swaps. How much of this paper had Lehman written and—much harder to determine—how much had others written referencing Lehman debt? As it happens, the swap liability tied to Lehman's solvency was not system-threatening in itself, but no one knew that at the time, including Treasury, and it was one more reason for investors and lenders to treat the market as a house on fire and rush the doors.

Whatever the rationale for letting Lehman fail, the results were catastrophic. Credit spreads yawned wildly. Equity markets swooned. Governments were forced to prop up tottering banks. The world looked over the edge and couldn't see bottom.

This chaos may also have changed the outcome of the American presidential election. By mid-September the two candidates, Senators

Obama and McCain, were running neck-and-neck in the polls. Then Lehman failed. McCain sputtered ineffectually about greed on Wall Street while Obama surged in the polls while blaming the situation on the deregulatory policies of the Bush administration. However effective, this charge was misplaced. The Bush administration may have done an indifferent job of enforcing existing regulations but it didn't eliminate any of note. To the contrary, the Sarbanes-Oxley Act, passed during Bush's first term, imposed substantial new disclosure and governance obligations on public companies that many continue to resent to this day.

The record of regulatory mistakes that contributed to the crisis, in fact, implicates both parties. The Fed's loose monetary policies promoted asset bubbles during both the Clinton and the Bush administrations. The decision not to regulate credit default swaps and other derivatives was made at the end of Bill Clinton's second term, with support from both sides of the aisle. Allowing investment banks to substantially increase their leverage—based on computer models no one seems to have understood—was a gift from the Bush SEC, but with its Democratic minority on board. Both parties at one time or another played the game of promoting mortgage credit for the unqualified, although Democratic legislators were the more persistent. In short, it took a concerted bipartisan effort over a period of many years to so completely undermine the American financial system.

Former Treasury Secretary Paulson has been at pains to acquit himself of blame for what may be remembered as the biggest regulatory blunder since tight monetary policy helped bring on the Great Depression. He insists his hands were tied by factors both legal and political. And in fairness, the Lehman crisis presented the administration with enormous problems with little time for reflection. Treasury had been excoriated in some quarters, including the Halls of Congress, for putting up taxpayer money to save Bear Stearns. It would have taken great political courage to step up again with an even bigger rescue package for an even more unpopular investment bank. Unlike Bear and AIG, the bailouts that bookended the administration's decision to write "no extraordinary measures" on Lehman's chart, there was no room to pretend that money going to Lehman would ever come back. The hole Dick Fuld and his colleagues had dug into the subprime wasteland was simply too deep.

That presented serious issues under the legislation empowering Treasury to act as lender of last resort. Finally, no one really knew how bad the result of the administration's inaction would be until after the fact. Paulson was not alone in underestimating the effect of a Lehman bankruptcy on the global financial system.

Nevertheless, history tends to shove such factors into footnotes, and will likely file the Lehman debacle under the label "Paulson's Folly." Hank Paulson, like Herbert Hoover, may be remembered in caricature.

Chapter 15

Ashes, Ashes,
All Fall Down

My East Bay house sits two blocks from the Hayward faultline. According to the *San Francisco Chronicle*, this geological time bomb should spawn a large quake every 136 years or thereabouts. We are now four years overdue. Shortly after my wife and I moved in, the 70-something woman who lives next door inquired if we were ready for "the Big One." She made it sound like the judgment day. She had good advice, having given the prospect much thought over the years. Keep a pair of shoes under your bed, she said, along with a crowbar in case you need to pry open a door or window to get out of your collapsing house.

I should have asked for her thoughts on what to do if the bad decisions of a bunch of investment bankers and government officials rocked the financial landscape. Although here again a crowbar might have its uses.

★   ★   ★

Copper River did much of its options trades through Lehman's London OTC desk. Some Lehman clients were sufficiently smart or plugged in to yank their accounts before the ax fell. That stampede, of course, was exactly the reason it became too late for everyone else. We were not that prescient. While the Bear Stearns bailout was preceded by significant buzz that the firm was toast, the Lehman bankruptcy came with less warning. Our questions to our account rep about the status of the firm were answered with soothing promises that the situation was well in hand. On Tuesday, September 9, Lehman held a conference call to reassure nervous customers. It claimed to be on top of its liquidity needs, although the specifics were lacking.

The next day we learned that our account rep had bailed from the firm. The writing on the wall now in Day-Glo spray paint, we began unwinding our ill-timed swap trades, with the cash due early the next week. A day or two earlier and we would have been out of most of our positions before the bankruptcy filing. As it was, we weren't, and the consequences for Copper River were severe.

Lehman's U.K. operations were not included in the U.S. bankruptcy. They went into a liquidation proceeding overseen by the U.K. Financial Services Authority. This resulted in a freeze of client assets of uncertain duration. The Brit accountants in charge cheerfully estimate it will take years to sort out the thousands of claims against Lehman U.K.'s remaining assets. "Remaining" because approximately $8 billion was swept from Lehman U.K. to Lehman U.S. accounts on the eve of the bankruptcy filing. This may have contributed to Lehman U.K.'s abandonment to liquidation while the bulk of the U.S. operations, by contrast, were sold to Barclay's.

On September 14, the day of the U.S. bankruptcy filing, Lehman U.K. held over $100 million in Copper River assets. While this is no one's idea of small change, it was not in itself enough to endanger the fund, even if it all stayed gone. Indeed, we would still have been up for the year to that date. More was needed. It would take nothing less than the combined efforts of our prime broker, Goldman Sachs, and the Securities and Exchange Commission to bring us to destruction.

The SEC took the first shot.

In July 2008, two months before Lehman went down, the SEC had applied "emergency powers" granted to it by Congress after the September 11 attacks to place temporary restrictions on short sales of 19 financial stocks, most notably Fannie Mae and Freddie Mac. The rule required that short sales now be done on the basis of a "hard borrow," not merely a "reasonable belief" the stock could be located and delivered. The intention was to prevent naked shorting of Fannie, Freddie and the other listed stocks. This being an emergency rule, no analysis was provided of the need for this particular measure beyond bald assertions that naked short selling is, like, bad. *Bloomberg* columnist Jon Weil wrote: "The SEC has presented no facts suggesting that anything like this [attacks by short-sellers] has happened at these 19 companies, or at any other major financial firm." Given that the listed stocks were mostly easy to borrow, it was unclear why anyone would bother to short them naked, even if he could find a prime broker who would allow it.

Whatever its purpose, the emergency rule appears to have had little effect. During the period it was in force, while a few of the stocks on the list spiked briefly, on average they underperformed other financial stocks. You might therefore conclude that these stocks had *not* been the victims of naked short-selling, but that would require resorting to logic. You might also decide that the SEC was playing a hypocritical game of shoot the messenger. As the *Financial Times* phrased it: "Mr. Cox seems to be implicitly blaming the shorts for the unprecedented fall of bank, government-sponsored agency and brokerage stocks over the past year—even though short-sellers were the very group that warned of the dangerous credit cycle and its consequences."

Chairman Cox, however, defended this rulemaking with an opinion piece in the *Wall Street Journal* that found him channeling Bob "the Easter Bunny" O'Brien. He explained that the Commission's action had been taken, in close consultation with the Fed and Treasury (ominous in itself), to prevent investors being "stampeded" out of worthy financial stocks by "short and distort artists" spreading false rumors and "turbocharging" the declines with naked short sales. He did not mention that many of the protected companies were potentially insolvent and had balance sheets stuffed with assets of the now-you-see-them-now-you-don't variety. The miscreants targeted by the SEC regulation, so far as one could tell from the chairman's article, lived in the realm of the hypothetical. The SEC has, in fact, brought exactly one negative rumor case in its seventy-four year history and it did not involve collusion between traders. Moreover, the number of confirmed cases of manipulation by naked shorting precisely matches confirmed sightings of Elvis Presley subsequent to his alleged demise. So a certain leap of faith was required.

But at least the chairman didn't include a chart linking together in a grand conspiracy people and entities largely unknown to each other and with no clear connection to the topic at hand.

The willingness of Chairman Cox to belly up to the Easter Bunny's Kool-Aid stand was doubly perplexing because, from my understanding, his own staff viewed such conspiracy theories as stuff and nonsense. One SEC official has referred to the anti-naked-shorting crowd as "bozos." Moreover, in 2006 the SEC's in-house economists hosted a round-table discussion on the regulation of short sales, with introductory remarks by the chairman himself. Economists are the only group aside from financial reporters who see any reason short-sellers should be allowed to occupy space on the planet—but they love the shorts to death. Sitting in the audience for this event did much for my self-esteem. For several hours, a parade of well-credentialed economists, including the Commission's chief economist, expounded on the market benefits of a vigorous short-seller presence. These benefits come down to greater liquidity and transparency: at that time still considered by the Commission to be good things. The service of short-sellers in combating pump-and-dump schemes came in for particular praise.

The result of this conference was the elimination of the "uptick rule," enacted in 1938 to prevent short sales in a declining market. At least after decimalization made upticks easy to come by, most short-sellers—at least those who take long-term positions rather than jumping in and out of momentum situations—hardly noticed the rule. But it's the thought that counts.

Also in July 2008, the SEC began to make noises about hunting down rumormongers in the market. Only those suspected of benefitting the short side, of course. Subpoenas were sent out to funds known to short financial stocks. The saber-rattling had an effect. Hedge-fund managers were advised by their lawyers to avoid saying anything not effusively positive about any U.S.-listed equity. Reporters complained that no one would offer on-the-record comments critical of any public companies. Like many bad ideas, this one traveled well. In England the Financial Services Authority made similar threats. In Latvia, a university professor spoke out about excessive leverage in the nation's banking system. He was arrested and briefly jailed.

★　★　★

Short-seller Jim Chanos runs a small lobbying group to promote the interests of short-biased funds. When the Commission starts fooling around with emergency rules, no one is safe. So Chanos asked for an audience with Chairman Cox, hoping to give a perspective on short-selling different from that of corporate CEOs who have never met a setback that was not caused by vulgar, conniving, loud-mouthed, un-washed, uncouth, and utterly un-American short-sellers. Copper River received a last minute invitation. The meeting took place on August 22 and went as well as could be hoped. The chairman and members of his staff uttered the appropriate noises about being sensitive to our concerns and promised that future changes to the rules governing short sales would be done through the usual process of notice and comment rather than by emergency rule. This repeated previous assurances from another commissioner and the head of the SEC's Division of Trading and Markets.

It was a sensible, responsible position. Had the Commission held to it, I would today be collecting my chips from what have proved prescient bets by Copper River on a number of flawed companies, rather than chronicling my misadventures in the hedge-fund trade. More to the point, our investors would be reaping an appropriate reward for having invested in a hedge fund that genuinely *hedged* exposure to the sort of bear market then in play. As it is, they found their financial insurance policy cancelled at the whim of the government when most needed.

Between the August 22 meeting and mid-September, credit and eq-uity markets continued to erode. Then Lehman failed and chaos ensued. Financial stocks went into a vertiginous slide. Interbank credit shriveled to nothing. And regulators around the world attempted to quell panic in the investing public and in their own offices.

On September 17, three days after the Lehman bankruptcy petition, the FSA banned short-selling in U.K. financial stocks. The following day, the SEC did the same for U.S. markets. Styled as another emergency rule, this measure was authorized in a night session of the SEC, without public notice or comment, and made effective at market open the following morning. The number of stocks on the no-short list was initially over 700 and eventually hit 1,000 as other companies clamored to be included.

The rationale for this approach was dubious. Financial stocks were falling, not as a result of manipulative selling, but because *no one wanted to own them*. This, in turn, was the result of concerns about the accuracy of the companies' asset valuations, their continued access to the capital markets and their future business prospects in a stalled economic environment. Yes, money managers can play a game of "telephone" that stokes worries about a stock. And the interplay between short-selling and trading in credit default swaps may, in some instances, have fueled declines. But these factors, at most, exacerbated existing concerns; they didn't create problems where none existed before.

Nor does it appear that the SEC's rule provided any market-calming benefits. Rather, it became a study in unintended consequences. Volatility spiked. Liquidity dried up, "chased out of the market" by the SEC's short-sale regulations, as one securities industry magazine reported. Quotes were seen as less reliable, artificially supported, as they were, by the SEC's antishorting rule. The many trading strategies that rely on shorting to hedge risk against long exposure were suddenly no longer viable, eliminating many potential buyers from the market. The convertible arbitrage market, which depends on short sales to hedge away the risk of owning converts and plays an important role in raising capital for public companies, simply evaporated, with many convert-arb funds sustaining killing losses. And a host of money managers decided to stand on the sidelines until the situation returned to something that might be called normal. These destructive consequences of the SEC's rule were undoubtedly unintended but the agency's failure to foresee them showed a remarkable lack of understanding of the degree to which shortselling is a basic component of a broad spectrum of market activity. It was, in short, an amateurish blunder.

Informed comment on the measure was relentlessly negative. Among my favorites is this Motley Fool post:

> This story ultimately won't have a happy ending. The SEC is abetting the Treasury and the Fed in artificially inflating share prices, creating a void beneath their value. Since nature abhors a vacuum, it's quite likely that once the ban is lifted and trading resumes, these protected stocks will collapse once again. It won't happen, you say? Fannie Mae and Freddie Mac were among the 19 stocks "protected" by a temporary shorting ban in July, and we know how *that* tale turned out. Also on the list were Lehman Brothers and Merrill Lynch, both of which are disappearing, and Morgan Stanley, which is negotiating a merger with Wachovia.

Picking up on the clearly manipulative intent of the rule, *New York Times* columnist Floyd Norris wrote: "it [i]s not the job of the exchange or the commission to set share prices. It would be nice to hear that someone still thinks that basic principle applies."

Had the SEC limited itself to simply posting a no-shorting sign in front of a bunch of financial stocks, the effect on Copper River would have been slight. The fund was not a player in the U.S. investment banks that were at the heart of the government's concern. Only two of our shorts, the Canadian insurer Fairfax Financial Services and the U.S. business development company American Capital Strategies, made the list. The irony with Fairfax, of course, was that it was being protected from any negative effects of short-selling on its stock while making out like a bandit from, in effect, shorting the U.S. financial system with its portfolio of credit default swaps.

The SEC's exercise in regulation by ambush included other measures, however, that would prove highly damaging to us and many other funds. First, the SEC threatened to make hedge funds and other money managers publicly disclosure any large short-positions that they did not dispose of immediately. There would then be on-going reporting requirements more onerous than those applied to long positions. This would have been an open invitation for issuer retaliation and copy-cat trading on a real time basis. In the August meeting, Chairman Cox had assured us the agency understood these concerns and therefore had decided that short reporting was not under immediate consideration. So this, too, had gone by the boards. Although the reporting provision was later modified to require only non-public disclosure to the Commission, the threat was taken seriously and surely drove some amount of short-covering.

More critically, the Commission's midnight rule-making eliminated the ability of options market makers to engage in naked shorting for hedging purposes. The SEC's justification for this action, as explained a month later in a release that elevated this "emergency rule" to an "interim temporary final rule," was, first, it looked like the options market maker exception was used a lot and, second, anything that contributed to delivery failures, even if permitted under Commission regulations, raised "concerns" about potential abusive naked shorting. Here the Commission cited letters from Patrick Byrne and NCANS, brainchild of pseudonymous stock tout Bob "the Easter Bunny" O'Brien. There were also piles of form letters whose ultimate origin can be surmised.

The natural reaction is to slap one's forehead and ask: commissioners, what were you thinking? After four years of screwing around with Regulation SHO with no visible sense of urgency, you rewrite it in the middle of the night to remedy a problem previously apparent only to a motley collection of crooks and cranks. You are unable to identify a single instance of "abusive" naked short-selling, the evil to which you purport to respond, but you know it exists because Patrick Byrne, the man responsible for the single most misguided and embarrassing SEC investigation in recent memory, has told you so and has ginned up an Astroturf movement to make it appear this is more than his personal opinion! Moreover, you decide this is a matter of such importance that you are entitled to break out the emergency powers granted by Congress in the wake of the September 11 terrorist attack!

In reality, it may be that this aspect of the SEC's emergency rule was less an instance of bureaucratic gullibility than a device to support the stock market at a politically critical moment. In mid-September, all of the indices were drifting lower. Financial stocks were losing market cap at an alarming rate. There was enormous political pressure to do something, anything, to staunch the bleeding. As Hank Paulson and Ben Bernanke prepared their rescue plan, the scuttlebutt from inside the SEC was that Chairman Cox was simply taking dictation from Treasury on how his agency should support the administration's efforts.

The emergency rule, released in tandem with the Paulson Plan, may have seemed the Commission's best shot at jamming the market when all eyes were on the Bush administration to show results. The SEC could not, of course, make investors rush back into the market or prevent them from selling stock from long positions.[1] What it could do was induce buys-to-cover of heavily shorted stocks, thereby driving up their prices. It could, in other words, try to create traction in a slipping market by throwing short-sellers under the wheels. The anti-shorting initiatives were well-designed for this purpose. The 35 days the SEC granted market makers to cover their naked shorts included only two options expiration dates (for September and October), with the first occurring the following day. Predictably, the result was a scramble by market makers for shares to cover their (legal) naked short positions. Jim Cramer caught the implication and advised his viewers to snap up everything on the Reg. SHO list. The proposed requirement to publicly disclose short positions may also have stampeded shorts to cover before that measure kicked in. A recent study by academics at three universities estimates that the Commission's short-sale ban caused price inflation of $4.9 billion in the covered stocks. It criticizes this action, concluding "the creation of a bias toward long sellers is inconsistent with fair markets."

In *Reminiscences of a Stock Operator*, Jesse Livermore recounted a tactic used by 1920s brokerage firms to fleece their customers:

> In the old days whenever a bucket shop found itself loaded with too many bulls on a certain stock it was common practice to get some broker to wash down the price of that particular stock far enough to wipe out the customers that were long it.

The same practice, known as "the bucket shop drive," was followed in reverse if the establishment had too many bears. When used on the short side, this tactic is simply a "short squeeze" by another name: an artificially-induced episode of short covering used to trigger a spike in

---

[1] A satirical letter to the SEC, commenting on proposals to amend short-selling regulations, urged the latter approach. The letter noted empirical research that confirmed "a rising market makes people happy;" thus "the SEC must intervene to stanch the loss of wealth that flows from a declining market." It concluded: "Rather than tinkering with ad hoc half-measures, the SEC should be proposing the only practical, efficient and final solution to market volatility: a ban on stock selling altogether."

stock price. Short squeezes, when made with manipulative intent, have been held by the SEC and various federal courts to be a form of securities fraud.

The SEC, recall, was established in 1934 to prevent such shenanigans and thereby restore investor confidence that the market was not the wild and woolly playground of stock manipulators. It would be ironic if the SEC contrived the "mother of all short squeezes" for the purpose of broadly inflating U.S. stock prices to coincide with an administration economic initiative. Chairman Cox noted in a December 2008 speech: "rules that might be rigorously applied to private-sector competitors will not necessarily be applied in the same way to the sovereign who makes the rules." If this seems a stretch, the *Financial Times* reported that in November 2008, when "the regulators" were considering how to prevent Citigroup from tanking, they discussed buying its stock in the open market specifically for the purpose of detonating a short squeeze. The article didn't mention whether "the regulators" also considered setting up boiler rooms to tout Citigroup stock to Florida retirees.[2]

Several months later, Chris Cox would describe the SEC's emergency short-sale restrictions as the worst mistake of his tenure as chairman. He claimed that he was forced into it by Hank Paulson and Ben Bernanke, who were desperate to do something to stop the market slide. I understand that Paulson disputes this account.

The British regulations also left a bad taste. According to the *Financial Times*:

> As every investor knows, rigging the market is a criminal offense—unless it is the authorities pulling the strings. Some watchdogs, however, seem to be wishing they had not meddled. The UK's Financial Services Authority did its best to bury an announcement late on [January 4, 2009] that September's ban on shorting UK deposit-takers would not continue. . . . The interventions, intended to stabilize bank shares at a time of real stress, were demonstrably ineffective. In the UK, the stocks placed on the protected list fell three times more than the broader market in the fourth quarter.

---

[2]In his irresistibly-titled book *Don't Blame the Shorts: Why Short Sellers Are Always Blamed for Market Crashes and How History Is Repeating Itself* (McGraw Hill 1990), author Robert Sloan points out that the NYSE used a similar tactic to goose stocks after the 1929 market crash. He also provides a cogent analysis of the benefits short-selling provides to the capital markets.

On September 18, the day the rule went into effect, the average one-day increase for stocks on the Reg. SHO list was approximately 17 percent. The increase for those on the list that Copper River was short was almost twice that. Most of our positions were in "optionable" stocks, which would, of course, be affected more by a rule change targeted at options market makers than would stocks for which no options were available. Copper River's losses for the single day of September 18, 2008, were by far the biggest in our history.

As might be expected, however, the effects of the "emergency" rule were short-lived. The indices soon resumed their downward progress as the financial news remained dour. Stocks on the Reg. SHO list that had received a boost from the SEC's action quickly gave back their gains. Take, for example, American Capital Strategies (see Figure 15.1).

Overstock, self-proclaimed prime victim of short-seller conspiracies, popped from $17 on September 17 to over $21 two trading days later, only to slip back to $17 after another week and then slowly wilt to less than $7 two months later. The SEC's beat-down on short-sellers appears to have had less effect than Overstock's October announcement of yet another unprofitable quarter and the restatement of five years of financial results to correct revenue recognition errors.

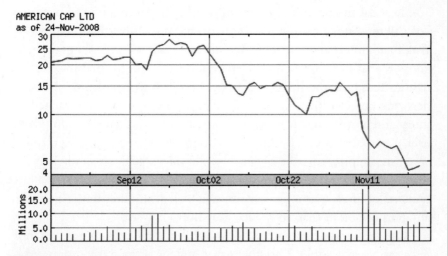

Figure 15.1 American Capital Strategies Chart

SOURCE: Reproduced with permission of Yahoo! Inc. © 2010 Yahoo! Inc. YAHOO! and the YAHOO! logo are registered trademarks of Yahoo! Inc.

Stocks in the Copper River short portfolio declined substantially after their regulation-fueled leap. Many crashed roughly to earth within a few weeks. Had we been able to hang on to our positions, we would have quickly reversed all losses resulting from the SEC's "emergency rule" and the market's transient enthusiasm for the Paulson Plan and racked up substantial gains.

Unfortunately, this was not to be.

★   ★   ★

Copper River had used Goldman Sachs as its prime broker for over 20 years. It paid Goldman many millions for its services, enjoyed a relationship of mutual trust with its account reps, and regarded the firm as its friend.

We would now come to see it as our executioner.

The losses experienced on September 18 deepen substantially the following day: not coincidentally the options expiration date for September. The continuing run-up in many Reg. SHO stocks presumably reflects short-covering by options market makers, responding to the surprise withdrawal of their exemption. The prospect of quick congressional approval of the Paulson Plan also helps to buoy the market.

That day, we receive our first collateral calls. Although in compliance with all regulatory margin requirements, Copper River has transgressed Goldman's internal guidelines. Account agreements typically grant brokers wide latitude to respond to margin defaults or, for that matter, situations that raise the subjective anxiety level of their risk-management departments. Goldman now insists that, from the point we breached its internal requirements, it is vested with absolute discretion to do whatever it chooses to our positions, short and long, including liquidation at whatever prices it can obtain, even if all defaults are remedied. In short, Goldman now owns us. Late in the week, Goldman also prohibits transfers of funds out of our accounts, as well as all other transactions for any purpose other than to reduce our short exposure.

Our losses on September 18 and 19 are gut-wrenching, but not necessarily irreversible. The stocks that hurt us are not rising on fundaments but, we believe, because of a government-created short squeeze.

Not a situation likely to persist. Our leverage, while significant, cannot be compared to the amount carried by investment banks, for example Goldman. So even at our lowest point, we have a substantial asset cushion, limiting any potential risk to our prime broker.

Marc and our very capable traders Carol Ju and Andre Ameer work madly to reduce our deficiencies before the weekend. They do well, but it is a delicate process. Every purchase to reduce a short position threatens to push the stock higher and increase our deficiency, in turn requiring more purchases, and so on, in an accelerating cycle. The more illiquid the stock, the more rapid the process. Thus we face the prospect of digging our own grave with Goldman standing behind us yelling "Faster, faster!"

The $100 million in Copper River assets locked up by the Lehman insolvency is now sorely missed. It could have filled holes and slowed the bleeding. Finding other sources of cash in our portfolio, with the markets in turmoil, is on the far side of difficult. Marc's attempt to sell an illiquid long position fails when a prospective buyer, traveling abroad, proves unreachable. The firm has a close relationship with another hedge fund whose short positions we manage. Marc negotiates with them to take certain of our short positions and, based on an e-mail exchange, tells Goldman we have a deal. Welcome news to Goldman. Until the deal falls through. The other firm has not, we learn, given final approval and, in any event, no borrows can be found to enable it to take on the positions.

Goldman is upset. Getting its hopes up prematurely was a bad move. Bad moves are not allowed when you have a knife at your throat.

As the week ends, the firm's survival hinges on two things. First, the market headwind must abate. The boost to heavily shorted stocks provided by the SEC's emergency rules and the general bullish effect of the proposed Treasury bailout cannot end soon enough if we are to begin reversing our losses. Second, Goldman management must calm down and allow us a reasonable time to remedy any remaining deficiencies.

We get one out of two.

On Monday, September 22, we lose close to $247 million. Although the Dow drops 379 for the day, our shorts defy the downward trend as

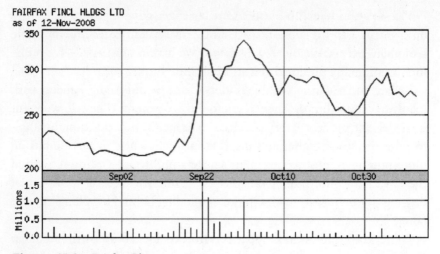

Figure 15.2 Fairfax Chart

Goldman forces us to cover in volume. It tells us to cover 25 percent of our six largest short positions, half by noon and the rest by market close. As it might have predicted, the effects on these six stocks are enormous. Fairfax, for example, jumps $60 that day to close at $326 (see Figure 15.2).

Not all of this stock's gain comes from Goldman forcing us to inflate its share price. Benefiting from the squeeze and its presence on the SEC's no-short list, the company is quick on the draw with good news releases. Well before time for its quarterly earnings release, it announces big profits from the sale of credit default swaps, as well as a 1.2 million share stock buy-back. These several factors feed off each other in further juicing the stock.

Turning the screws tighter, Goldman hits us with default notices. These state it has "the right to buy in or close-out, in [its] sole and absolute discretion, any of your open short positions." In other words it can, if it chooses, fire-sale our positions without articulated standards of manner of sale or the ultimate margins it intends to reach. That day it also increases our "haircuts" (discounts to asset values) on many positions. This, of course, widens the gap we have to close. Goldman claims this reflects the reaction of its computer model to changes in our portfolio: changes, that is, demanded by Goldman.

Among the half-dozen people in the Larkspur office, Russell is the most visibly affected by the snowballing crisis. Barely sleeping at night, he looks haggard and bleary. In a hallway conversation, he blurts, "I feel like such a failure." This disturbs me as much as anything that has happened yet. First, because none of this is in any way his fault. But beyond that, I'd always thought of Russell as completely on top of his life. He is smart, unselfconsciously personable, and free of the emotional baggage that burdens many high achievers. With a few more years experience, he will be a good bet to effectively manage piles of other people's money. But now, as I have been slow to realize, his future chances are fading before his eyes. With financial firms shedding jobs by the thousands and hedge funds falling like autumn leaves, the market for people with his skills—however strong—is vanishing. If the firm goes down, his gig as Marc's designated successor will be hard to replace. Probably impossible, at least any time soon. I don't know where that will leave him and his young family and, I'm sure, neither does he.

On Tuesday, September 23, our relationship with Goldman moves from purgatory to the inner circle of hell.

Our losses for the day are severe, again largely because forced liquidation of our positions is moving prices against us. Far from letting up, Goldman now begins trading our portfolio directly. It first announces it will take over *all* trading but, when it can't get decent results, grudgingly allows our traders to work in tandem with theirs. With grim humor, Marc tells a Goldman exec that, after they destroy us, they should hire Carol, our head trader.

Managing director Richard Sussman is now our primary contact at Goldman. But today he is out of the office and we must deal with his superior. While Sussman seemed reluctantly resigned to the losses inflicted on our fund, higher management is arrogantly indifferent. Tempers fray in every conversation.

The situation deteriorates further when Marc asks whether Goldman is front-running the trades it is forcing on us. We have suspected, without knowing, that Goldman's proprietary trading desk has been buying illiquid stocks we are short—thus pushing up prices—in the expectation their prices will rise further when we are required to make buys-to-cover, including, perhaps, from Goldman's prop desk. Front-running is illegal and *should be* prevented by "Chinese walls" at Goldman, but this would explain bump-ups in some of our names that precede our volume buys. It would also explain the aggression with which Goldman is savaging our positions.

So would another theory that Russell proposes. He wonders if Goldman failed to borrow shares it shorted for our accounts, perhaps relying on the trusty options market-maker exemption, and, with the tightening up of the SEC's short-sale rules, is now making *us* cover these naked positions at rapidly escalating prices.

Normally, reducing a short position returns shares to the pool of available borrows. But this does not seem to happen from the short covering forced by Goldman. If Goldman shorted naked, covering those sales would not free up borrowed shares for new loans because, by definition, none were borrowed in the first place. Also, we have noticed that Goldman has sometimes been able to provide locates not available elsewhere. Could it be it never actually had locates and shorted naked? If so, everything it charged us on those transactions would be pure profit to Goldman.

It would also mean that Patrick Byrne's prime broker suit may turn out to have merit, offering empirical support for the popular blind-pig theorem.

But all of this is speculation based on a few data points. Goldman will say that it is doing what it needs to do to protect itself from what it now recognizes to be a highly volatile portfolio. That the volatility is attributable, in part, to a regulatory drive-by shooting, the effects of which are certainly transitory, and, in part, to Goldman's own response to that sad episode, it will say is irrelevant. The risk exists—that is apparent from the magnitude of our losses—and it is the job of Goldman management to shift as much of it as possible onto us, no matter the consequences to a long-term client.

We attempt to limit our losses by selling positions through private transactions. On September 23, hedge fund Acme Capital Management[3] is in our office doing due diligence on positions it may take from us. It is also considering investing in Copper River directly. The hope is this new money will get us past our immediate liquidity crisis. Then Acme will join in the party when our short positions rebound. But this falls through when Acme is unable to pin down Goldman—its prime broker

---

[3] A pseudonym.

as well as ours—on how far it intends to go in reducing our positions. Acme is naturally wary of investing in a fund that may be put out of business at the whim of an unpredictable prime broker.

The brutality of Goldman's campaign is beyond anything previously experienced by our people. It's like watching a road accident unfold in slow motion. An Acme analyst who witnesses the scene in our office stalks into the men's room and vomits. Either he's come undone over the bloodshed here or panicked that his firm, which also has concentrated, margined positions in illiquid stocks, could be next up on the Goldman scaffold. Or both.

Dissuaded from taking a direct stake in Copper River, Acme bargain hunts in our battered portfolio. It's a one-time Black Friday on our short positions. But Goldman scuttles this too. While the Acme team is rooting through our research files, as I'm told later by Marc, someone on the Goldman prop desk calls Acme's chief financial officer, another Goldman alum, and warns him against dealing with us. We have, he says, "no more than two days left to live." If so, this would suggest Goldman's Chinese walls have not kept its prop desk from following the drama at Copper River.

Acme complains to Goldman that its treatment of us is outrageous. All the same, this incident chills its interest in taking any of our positions. The team in our office vanishes. This will turn out to be unfortunate for Acme because the short positions it was considering acquiring will later rocket in value. Goldman has done no one any favors.

The experience with Acme stuns us. Goldman now seems to be acting out of sheer malice. Has it decided it would rather see us weak or dead than in a position to sue it over its conduct? It has to be considering the possibility of litigation.

The next day, September 24, the market moves strongly in our favor, meaning down lots. The effect of the SEC's emergency regulation may have faded as short-covering by market makers trails off. This is as expected. We assumed our initial losses were the result of a temporary and artificial situation and would reverse out if we could hold onto our positions long enough.

Despite additional reductions, we're up dramatically for the day.

Our relationship with Goldman improves temporarily. Sussman is back in the office and seems apologetic. He explains that Goldman was responding to "an 8-alarm fire," and implies it may have made mistakes. Further, he assures us "the book is okay"—meaning no further reductions to our short positions are required. At least until his supervisor gets off break. Or the SEC logs another night session. He promises to send us an "antidefault letter." As we understand it, this means we are out of the penalty box and can regain control of our trading.

We begin looking for other brokers to take our accounts, hoping they will not make the same killing demands as Goldman. Initial indications are good, but it will be a complicated process. And, most worrying, it will require some measure of cooperation from Goldman.

Thursday, September 25, is like a paper airplane; it goes very much up, then very much down, and ends with a thud. In the morning, Sussman reaffirms that our "book is okay." He says the antidefault letter is on his desk and coming soon. None of our funds are now "on call" (out of compliance with collateral requirements), nor will they be again. Nevertheless, Sussman tells us Goldman has arranged block trades to further reduce two of our short positions. After those trades are completed, he promises, our situation will be acceptable.

Our traders have seen no sign off these blocks coming on the market and wonder if they may be from the Goldman prop desk. If so, we hope it will be the last time it will use us as a captive buyer at prices it has had much to do with inflating.

But even this limited détente proves too good to last. In mid-morning, a Goldman manager, citing "a lack of trust on both sides," says Goldman is taking over our book. No other explanation is offered. You would think that after *20 years* of straight dealing we would have a few chips to cash in. As for us trusting Goldman, he's right we don't—but how does that enter in? Has he decided to trash us some more simply for having hurt Goldman's institutional feelings? After I beat you, darling, I feel you don't love me; therefore, I must beat you again. He admits that he is "overruling his own team." Sussman later confirms this, telling us stiffly, "This was not a decision that was communicated to me."

Then, for several hours, the line goes dead.

Goldman dodges our calls and ignores our messages. God knows what these guys may be up to when out of our sight. When we finally get through, they tell us they have traded some of our positions and want to know what additional trades we've made. Even though we reduced positions Goldman wanted reduced, they initially refuse to take our trades. Apparently they have decided that rationality is overrated. When we receive a trade report for the day, we learn Goldman traded more of our positions than it said and did it badly. Some trades were executed at surprisingly high prices.

Late in the day, the temperature cools slightly. Sussman admits we do a better job of trading our names than they do. No dispute there. And his supervisor agrees we can trade in parallel with their people so long as we keep them well-informed.

Friday, September 26, takes us one step forward, two steps back. Previous assurances now worthless, Goldman again demands we reduce our larger short positions. How far is far enough, we are left to guess. Communications become confused and we are uncertain what our traders are permitted to do. One of our contacts at Goldman says he is unable to speak with us without authorization from his superiors. Everything is being dictated by upper management, but the motivation and ultimate goal are unclear. Is Goldman skinnying down on leverage in preparation for becoming a commercial bank, or out of fear for its own stability, or maybe because it is being told to do so by Treasury? Richard Fuld, former head of Lehman, claims that, back in April, Paulson told him Treasury wants to "kill the bad hedge funds and heavily regulate the rest." Does being on the short side automatically make us "bad"? And, if so, is Goldman carrying out the bidding of its former chairman? Or maybe it's gotten personal. Has Marc pissed off the Goldman manager by getting in his face, and this is the result?

Despair breeds paranoia and anything seems possible.

We have accounts at another firm that will accept some of the positions Goldman wants to shed. But Goldman management refuses to let us transfer *any* accounts unless *all* are transferred. It claims it is difficult to transfer funds piecemeal.

Getting out from under Goldman's thumb was our last best hope. It now seems a remote prospect.

The following week brings more of the same. It is now death by a thousand cuts. We continue to obey Goldman's demands for additional reductions, without knowing how much will be considered enough. Due to the uneven way our reductions have been done, some funds are too short and others too long. We ask to be allowed to rebalance. Even though that would improve our margin situation, Goldman refuses. Its compliance desk insists we trade only to wind down positions. Again, the blindfold slips and we glimpse before us the path to the hedge-fund cemetery.

The market continues to move in our favor, as stocks previously pumped up by the SEC's emergency regulations now leak out their gains, but our positions are so depleted that the benefits are minor.

We finally receive the promised antidefault letter. It provides no comfort, simply stating that Goldman has chosen, for the moment and at its God-like discretion, not to do *everything* to us it could under our account agreements. Our general counsel asks several times to speak with the Goldman legal department in hopes of amending the letter to prevent future wildings of our accounts. He gets no response. Finally Sussman tells us no changes to the antidefault letter will be permitted. "The letter is the letter." He says if we sign it we can freely trade our accounts again. We comply. Once again, we comply.

On Monday, October 6, we regain full control of our portfolio. By this time, however, no reprieve is possible. It's gone too far. Across all Copper River funds, we have lost 55 percent for the year. This is on top of shedding the 25 percent we were up before the SEC's midnight adventures in regulation. Had we kept our positions through the several-day market spike that began on September 18, all Copper River funds would, by the end of October, have posted huge profits for the year to-date. Our investors would have been amply rewarded for their patience. As it is, they become collateral damage to the combined follies of regulators and a financial services firm.

★ ★ ★

Other short funds experienced significant losses in late 2008, but we were among the hardest hit. This was partly due to the fund's investment model. While its use of leverage was not great compared to other hedge funds, its "commitment" to its investment decisions meant concentrated positions. Lots of chips on a few numbers. Many of the companies it saw as "frauds, fads, or failures" were shallowly traded and heavily shorted. This made it hard to get out the door quickly when things went wrong. Copper River can perhaps be accused of having failed to protect itself against the worst-case scenario—whether analogized as the perfect wave or a flock of black swans—but it might also be remembered that the worst turned out to be very bad indeed and came from more directions than might have been anticipated.

Given our losses, extensive redemptions were all but certain. For several weeks Marc attempted to marshal enough support to continue on a scaled-back basis. The prospect of laying-off a dozen people, all of whom he regarded as friends, was traumatic. Some may have stored up enough over the years to retire. Others—the younger employees, particularly those with families—would face real hardships. I was somewhere in between. Marc truly seemed to feel worse about his partners and employees than his own losses, which, given his personal investment in the fund, must have been huge.

He complained very little. For someone with a history of going on for hours about government attorneys who "aren't doing their jobs" he expressed little resentment. Mostly he seemed bewildered, like someone who, thinking himself to be in prime health, is abruptly diagnosed with terminal cancer.

Prospects emerged and collapsed. Russell tried to get something going on his own but didn't have the name to pull it off. He and Marc and a friend who manages a small short fund considered combining forces. But this too fell through.

After about a month Marc admitted "We have nothing" and resigned himself to letting it go.

He now visited the office irregularly, spending more time with his family. When he did come in he was mostly quiet. No stomping around with his cell phone at his ear saying, "This is beyond bad! Just listen! This is totally dastardly!"

★ ★ ★

Carol Remond at Reuters was the first to write the firm's obituary. She got most of it right. Lehman. The SEC's stealth attack on short-sellers and its consequences. But she had only a vague idea of the destruction wrought by Goldman, our oldest business relationship. She noted:

> Copper River made a name for itself as an aggressive short-selling fund that didn't shy away from controversy. Former manager David Rocker,

who retired in 2006, was often very vocal against companies whose stock the fund deemed overvalued.

The same could be said of Marc. In his willingness to get squarely in the face of what he saw as corporate dishonesty—and hopefully make a buck in the process—he was a rare breed. Who else would show up at a shareholder meeting in a striped referee shirt and toss a red flag at management hype? Or worry about how much a contract between a Cyprus software company and a Bulgarian government ministry is actually worth? Or contact every listed office of a subprime mortgage company to see how many actually exist?

No one. Not anymore. It's too dangerous. And no one cares anyway. If it doesn't move stocks up, it has no place in a market dedicated to forever blowing bubbles.

Epilogue

Picking up the Pieces

Beside the Richmond Bridge, the San Francisco Bay shines in the afternoon light with the metallic brightness of an abalone shell. It is early March 2008. I am making my last commute home from the Copper River office, which is closing for good this weekend.

In the back seat, among piles of office junk, Paddy hangs his head out the window, ears flapping in the breeze. He is a wonderful animal, a Wheaton Terrier with a great attitude. Nothing worries him. He cares only that someone rubs his belly regularly and fills his food dish.

I am unable to imitate his easy acceptance of circumstances.

My mind is occupied with thoughts of retribution. Someone should pay for the outrages that torpedoed a hedge fund of 20 years vintage and a solid history of making the capital markets less safe for scam artists. Someone, that is, other than *me* and Russell, Monty, Marc, and everyone who had money with Copper River.

The candidates are so numerous the choice is difficult. Who deserves to be penalized more: Chris Cox or Dick Fuld; Goldman Sachs or the CEOs of a half-dozen crappy companies?

But, then, why choose?

Just load them all on the bus.

The punishment I settle upon, after much thought, seems both humane and constructive. The whole lot should be sentenced to live together in a re-education camp dedicated to earthy-wholesome-and-sensitive values. A sort of back-to-the-land commune someplace they can't speculate in property values and they must produce whatever they consume—cabbages and zucchini and organic honey. Nothing that can be easily misrepresented, franchised or used for leverage. An experience that will rehabilitate, as well as justifiably humiliate. I believe this would be politically popular.

I realize I am thinking too narrowly. The net should be thrown wide, to catch not only those who screwed the pooch in ways harmful to Copper River, but all those whose collective pooch-screwing constituted a veritable Kama Sutra of financial bestiality so extravagant it body-slammed the global economy. That wouldn't let any of the above worthies off the hook, but would provide them with much company.

And quite a crowd it would be. A rogue's gallery of crooked executives, conniving investment bankers, squirrelly technocrats, and pear-shaped regulators who dithered as the economy collapsed into a like configuration. The list goes on. Internet stock touts who urged mom-and-pop investors to purchase doomed stocks with credit cards. Young people who applied skills acquired in the fast-food industry to the mass-marketing of mortgages. And the solid citizens who sucked up these mortgages by claiming they had real jobs when, in fact, they were too busy pyramiding real estate 24/7 to pursue honest employment. Not to mention the elected officials blind to every abuse and excess in the financial services industry so long as it could be milked for campaign contributions. The same officials who now go into paroxysms of moral indignation over the unbridled greed of the very companies and executives they once patronized and that patronized them. The problem, as these officials now see it, did not derive from the mixture of economic myopia, political opportunism, and moral arrogance behind their willingness to let the American Dream be poured into a bottle labeled "cheap credit." No, it happened because *others* sold that commodity too aggressively or drank too deeply from the bottle.

Hey, they say, who knew?

We can all feel a righteous disdain for greed, defined as the financial ambitions of those who make more money than we do. What could be more contemptible? But to say that the inhabitants of the financial world are greedy is like saying monks are devout. They have chosen a life in which success is measured in dollars. They are *supposed* to be greedy. Making money through financial alchemy is their version of the American Dream, built on facilitating and sometimes exploiting the more modest dreams of others. It is to be expected they will weasel, scheme, and otherwise test the system with little consideration of extraneous social values. They will develop new and better products for making money from money, in the tradition of junk bonds, portfolio insurance, no-doc mortgages, and credit default swaps. That is their job. As it is the job of our financial referees to monitor them, keep their noses pointed in the right direction, and punish those whose dollar chasing activities lead them astray. However, the referees now seem critically overmatched. The financial system meltdown exposed a *much* greater array of regulatory failures than the wave of accounting frauds of a half-decade before, touching, indeed, every level of American government. Not that anyone took responsibility. Our leaders performed a general duck-and-cover reminiscent of a 1950s nuclear attack drill. The velocity of money hit a new high as the buck stopped nowhere.

It would be comforting to think the mistakes these events exposed were of recent vintage, newly sprung and therefore quickly reversible. In conversations with other former SEC attorneys, I hear a general nostalgia for a supposed golden era before things started to fall apart. Alumni of other agencies probably have similar conversations. However, we each date the slide into muddle-headedness as beginning with our own departure from government. Like the ward full of mental patients each believing himself to be Napoleon, we can't all be right.

In reality, the collapse was a long time gestating and owed its severity to the interaction of many financial innovations: some, in themselves, reasonable and beneficial, others the indefensible product of financial or political opportunism. These developments had become so complex and rapidly mutating that, when the system they supported suddenly collapsed, the powers-that-be were caught wholly by surprise and reacted with the frenetic inefficiency of the proverbial one-legged man in an ass-kicking contest. It was not pretty to watch, nor did it bode well for our financial guardians' ability to prevent future problems.

Sad to say, it is not realistic to hope we can greatly improve the effectiveness of our regulatory agencies. Talent runs out of the government like water through a colander, pulled out by the bigger dollars available outside, or pushed out by administrative folly. In addition, our financial regulators often have little industry background to inform their efforts. Mostly lawyers, they struggle to apply legal categories to arrangements whose purpose and effects they don't understand. The SEC's failure to catch Bernie Madoff until he confessed was not a fluke. So poorly do government agencies understand the entities they regulate, they can sometimes be confounded by even thinly disguised frauds.

Not that the private sector is perpetually astute when it comes to seeing the risks that lurk in the market's inventions and refinements. Business executives, financial mavens and their professional attendants reveal their limitations in times of crisis as much as do government bureaucrats. Then former lords of finance stare up bewildered at the great and complex edifice they helped create. They understand what happens when they push certain buttons and pull certain levers, but when these controls stop working and the machine starts to sputter and smoke, they scratch their heads, give the thing a few kicks, and look for someone else to fix it. Probably the government.

It then becomes apparent how much people controlling billions of dollars act on a deep and profound *faith* that the system works as is should. That numbers in financial statements mean something. That the value placed on companies by the market reflects a consensus of informed opinion. That financial experts know whereof they speak. That the regulators have at least the most important things under control.

When events conspire to discredit some form of faith-based investment—whether in CMOs, junk bonds or Internet stocks—the fall can be quick and brutal. Much of the recent credit crisis, the most significant economic dislocation since the Great Depression, was produced by uncertainty. If you looked under the hood of the mathematical models used to value complex derivatives, would you find a hamster on a treadmill? What dark secrets lay buried in a counterparty's balance sheet? The government is not, and realistically can't be, in the business of valuing economic assets. It was for this reason that the original thrust of the Bush Administration's Troubled Asset Relief Program—proposing to rescue failing financial institutions by purchasing their toxic assets—went nowhere. There were no magic numbers that Treasury could use to set prices. The government can only enforce rules requiring transparency in the marketplace. Assets will then be valued by the best judges of their worth: people willing to risk their own money to own them. The market as arbiter of economic value is, indeed, a bedrock principal of our system of financial reporting, however often honored in the breach.

The goal, therefore, is, as before, to make the financial machinery more open and understandable. Discourage blind faith, guesswork, and mob behavior and promote informed decision-making. Many reforms have been proposed and a few implemented. The best require better disclosure of the substance behind complex transactions and greater internalization of risk by those who create and profit from it. More market-based valuations. Fewer off-balance-sheet entities and offshore black boxes. No shadow markets. Elimination of the informational blind spots that encourage excessive risk taking.

But regulatory fixes go only so far. When the government imposes rules that come down to telling economic actors to "tell the world what you're really up to" some will regard this as more a challenge than a directive. Something to finesse when the stakes are high. And experience teaches that they will often succeed in getting around the new rules and the government sloggers who enforce them—until they become altogether too good at it and bring on the next crisis. A cycle of creative destruction that creates less than it destroys.

The trick, it would seem, is to encourage people with the necessary financial expertise and potential motivation to dig up the negative information that others are so well incentivized to conceal. But who are these strange beings and how do we know we can rely on what they tell us? Will they be truthful whistleblowers or mere disreputable troublemakers, come to mislead us? They may be short-sellers—spreading rumors as lethal as the joke in the Monty Python skit so hilarious it killed whoever heard it—dispatching red-blooded American companies without ever raising their voices above a whisper.

That is the perpetual fear. But is it grounded in reality or mere prejudice and rumor?

Short-sellers and the few journalists who listen to them have exposed many bad companies. A few are described above but there have been many more. This has gone beyond spotting the occasional rotten corporate apple to touch on broad issues. For example, contrarians were sounding the alarm about bad lending practices, residential and commercial, long before anyone chose to listen.

But what about the companies that claim they have been the victims of bear raids and similar nefarious conduct? Some may be sincere in their complaints, but, more commonly, companies that claim to have been bullied by short-seller cabals are later revealed as themselves the bullies—and worse.

Yet none of this seems to matter. However often companies that attack their critics turn out to be crooked, the initial presumption of credibility never seems to diminish. The SEC has been willing—indeed eager—to jump on weakly supported allegations of short-seller manipulations. I've devoted Chapter 11 of this book to the Gradient fiasco. David Einhon in his book *Fooling Some of the People All of the Time* recounts the SEC Enforcement scrutiny he received after going public with criticisms of the business development company Allied Capital. I've heard from other hedge-fund managers that they became objects of suspicion after publicly "talking" their short positions.

Bear conspiracies make a good story. Simple to understand, with clear villains and victims. And, anyway, who likes nay-sayers? Who can sympathize with those who don't share the American dream of endlessly ascending stock indexes? Don't we all suspect that's where the blame ultimately lies for every market decline? Risky commercial practices, inept regulation, and incompetence in the financial community may, in some way, have contributed to our reversals. That can be conceded. But was the root cause really any those things? Couldn't it have been, at bottom, a simple failure of belief? A turning away from the dream, from faith in the financial gods, to indulge in the apostasy of doubt and analysis? Banish those who would infect us with these failings, destroy their evil works, and all will be well once again.

And indeed efforts to tar skeptics as the villains of the financial world and so exclude them from polite conversation is going well despite repeated failures of proof. Fewer contrarians are willing to show their stripes in public. What percentage is there in orating on soapboxes to the onrushing crowd? If it stops to listen at all, it will only be for long enough to jeer and throw rocks before continuing on its way.

The short-sellers whose adventures provided the early chapters of this book are mostly gone, or have at least gone quiet. The independent research shops once lauded by the SEC as an antidote to sell-side bias, such as Gradient and "The Eyeshade Report," have been knocked around or eliminated by the companies they criticize while the SEC watched in silence. The mainstream financial press, for its part, displays dwindling interest in investigative pieces. The sort of work Jesse Eisinger and others did on Lernout & Hauspie is no longer likely to appear in the pages of the *Wall Street Journal*. Mostly this is dictated by economics. Assigning teams of reporters to long-term speculative projects is hard to justify in an era of budgetary starvation. *Fortune*, the *New York Post* and other publications have shed financial reporters as part of general staff cutbacks.

It might be thought the vacuum is being filled by "new media" gadflies. Renegade reporters and amateur sleuths posting their views on blogs and other internet sites. Some, like Gary Weiss, have tried to profit from their work by selling advertising space based on eyeball count, or, like reformed crook Sam Antar, by promoting themselves as experts for hire. But they struggle to attract much attention beyond a niche audience. And what does it say about our system that some of the most effective work on potential corporate misconduct is being conducted by an ex-felon with a dead parrot? Can it really be that the only ones willing to speak up are those with nothing to lose? And how healthy is that for a system whose most fundamental principal is full and accurate disclosure?

Not that I expect anyone will answer these questions. They are simply not on the agenda. I might as well put them to my canine companion as he gulps the Bay breeze from the car's rear window.

At least he won't hold it against me for asking.

About the Author

Richard Sauer has been, among other things, an Assistant Director with the Enforcement Division of U.S. Securities and Exchange Commission, a partner in an international law firm, and an analyst with a Northern California hedge fund. In his dozen years as an SEC attorney and administrator, he was responsible for many prominent financial fraud cases. His articles on legal and financial topics have appeared in numerous publications including in the *New York Times*, the *Wall Street Journal*, and *Barron's*. He is also a published novelist and holds a doctorate in law (S.J.D.) from Harvard Law School. He lives in Berkeley, California, with his wife, Eileen Killory.

Index